SUPERPOWER POLITICS

SUPERPOWER POLITICS

CHANGE IN THE UNITED STATES AND THE SOVIET UNION

**Michael Pugh and
Phil Williams   Editors**

Manchester University Press

Manchester and New York

Distributed exclusively in the USA and Canada by St. Martin's Press

Published by Manchester University Press
Oxford Road, Manchester M13 9PL, UK
and Room 400, 175 Fifth Avenue,
New York, NY 10010, USA

Distributed exclusively in the USA and Canada
by St. Martin's Press, Inc.,
175 Fifth Avenue, New York, NY 10010, USA

British Library cataloguing in publication data
Superpower politics: change in the United States and the
    Soviet Union.
1. United States. Government. Policies. 2. Soviet Union.
Government. Policies
I. Pugh, Michael C. (Michael Charles), *1944*– II.
Williams, Phil, *1948*–
353'.072

Library of Congress cataloging in publication data
Superpower politics: change in the United States and the Soviet Union
    edited by Michael C. Pugh and Phil Williams.
    p. cm.
    "Some of the chapters are revised versions of papers delivered at
a residential course organised by the Defence Studies Unit of the
Politics Department, University of Southampton" – Pref.
Includes bibliographical references.
ISBN 0-7190-3283-0. – ISBN 0-7190-3284-9 (pbk.)
    1. United States – Foreign relations – Soviet Union. 2. Soviet
Union – Foreign relations – United States. 3. United States – Foreign
relations – 1989– 4. Soviet Union – Foreign relations – 1985–
I. Pugh, Michael C. (Michael Charles), 1944–   . II. Williams,
Phil, 1948–   .
E183.8.S65S92 1990
327.73047 – dc20   89-49212

ISBN 0 7190 3283 0 *hardback*
      0 7190 3284 9 *paperback*

Typeset in Great Britain
by Williams Graphics, Llanddulas, North Wales

Printed in Great Britain
by Biddles Ltd, Guildford and King's Lynn

Contents

Preface

This book on the changing condition of the superpowers in their quest for domestic and international stability is designed with undergraduates and the general reader in mind. We have provided, therefore, a brief list of further reading at the end of the book. But we believe, also, that specialists will find value in the analytical approach of the authors and the incorporation of much original research in their chapters.

Some of the chapters are revised versions of papers delivered at a residential course organised by the Defence Studies Unit of the Politics Department, University of Southampton, and our thanks go to Rosemary Morris, Defence Studies Administrator; to the Commander Education South-East District, Col. A. Ian MacKay, B.Sc., MA; and to Maj. Doug Murgatroyd, MA, Dip.Ed., RAEC, for making the course possible. We are also much indebted to Margaret Pugh for copytyping and indexing, and to Juanita Bullough, Jane Carpenter and Richard Purslow of Manchester University Press for their help and advice. In the final chapter, the extract from *The Limits of Power: America's Role in the World*, copyright © 1967, by Eugene J. McCarthy, is reprinted by kind permission of Henry Holt and Company, Inc.

The views expressed in each chapter are those of the author(s) responsible and do not in any way represent those of the MoD or any other institution. By the same token, the contributors had complete freedom to interpret change in the superpowers in whatever way they saw fit, and we are gratified that a variety of standpoints and interpretations could be presented in the following pages.

Michael C. Pugh and Phil Williams
Southampton, September 1989

Contributors

Robert McGeehan is Department Head of International Relations, US International University — Europe (London), and member of the US–UK Educational Commission (the Fulbright Commission), formerly Lecturer in International Relations at Oxford University and member of St Antony's College.

M. L. Merritt is completing a D.Phil. on Soviet political thought at St Antony's College, Oxford. She worked in the Press and Cultural Section of the United States Embassy in Moscow in 1985–6 and has travelled and interviewed extensively throughout the Soviet Union.

Clark Miller is studying at the University of Illinois, Urbana, where he is a participant in the Arms Control and Disarmament Program. He was a research intern on the International Security project at the Royal Institute of International Affairs, London, during the summer of 1989.

J. R. Oldfield is Lecturer in History, University of Southampton, formerly Visiting Professor, University of South Carolina. He has written several articles on American social history and is the author of *Alexander Crummell and the Creation of an African/American Church in Liberia*, Lewiston, NY, Edwin Mellen Press, 1990.

John E. Owens is Senior Lecturer in United States and British Politics, Polytechnic of Central London. He has written various articles on American politics and economic policy and has contributed to the *British Journal of Political Science* and *Political Studies*. He is co-author of *After Full Employment*, Hutchinson, 1986.

R. C. Plummer is a retired Army Brigadier and former Military Attaché at the British Embassy, Moscow. Previously he was head of a General Staff branch concerned with the study of the Soviet armed forces. He has contributed articles to *Royal Engineers Journal, Army Quarterly*, and *Bulletin of the Council for Arms Control*.

Michael C. Pugh is Lecturer in International Relations, University of Southampton. He has contributed articles to the *International and Comparative Law Quarterly, International Relations, Arms Control* and *The World Today*, and is the author of *The ANZUS Crisis, Nuclear Visiting and Deterrence*, Cambridge University Press, 1989.

Steve Smith is Senior Lecturer and Director of the Centre for International Public Choice Studies, University of East Anglia. He has also taught at the State University of New York. He has written extensively on foreign policy analysis, arms control and defence policy. His latest book (with Martin Hollis) is *Explaining and Understanding International Relations*, Oxford University Press, 1990.

Bill Tupman is Lecturer in Soviet and Chinese Politics, University of Exeter and also Director of the Centre for Police and Criminal Justice Studies. His previous publications have mostly been on the role of violence in politics. He is currently working on a comparison of reform in the USSR and the People's Republic of China.

Rachel Walker is Lecturer in Communist Politics, University of Southampton. She completed a Ph.D. on ideology in the USSR and has contributed articles to the *British Journal of Political Science* and *Détente*. She has two forthcoming books: *Soviet Marxism—Leninism and the Question of Ideology*, Cambridge University Press, and *The Politics of Perestroika*, Manchester University Press.

Phil Williams was Senior Lecturer in International Relations, University of Southampton and Honorary Research Fellow, RIIA. He became Professor in International Security, University of Pittsburgh in 1990. His numerous publications include: *The Senate and US Troops in Europe*, Macmillan, 1985 and, with Mike Bowker, *Superpower Détente: a Reappraisal*, Sage and RIIA, 1988.

Abbreviations

ABM	anti-ballistic missile
ADIU	Armament and Disarmament Information Unit (University of Sussex)
AFDC	Aid to Families with Dependent Children
ALCM	air-launched cruise missile
ANZUS	Treaty between Australia, New Zealand and United States
ASAT	anti-satellite
ASEAN	Association of South East Asian Nations
AWST	*Aviation Week and Space Technology*
BMD	ballistic missile defence
BSTS	boost surveillance and tracking system
CBO	Congressional Budget Office
CFE	Conventional Forces in Europe
CGS	Chief of General Staff
CIA	Central Intelligence Agency
C-in-C	Commander-in-Chief
Comecon/CMEA	Council for Mutual Economic Assistance
CPD	Committee on the Present Danger
CPSU	Communist Party of the Soviet Union
CSB	closely-spaced basing (dense pack)
CSBM	confidence and security building measure
CSCE	Conference on Security and Co-operation in Europe
DoD	Department of Defense
EC	European Community
EPA	Environmental Protection Agency
ERIS	exo-atmosphere re-entry interceptor system

ERTA	Economic Recovery Tax Act
FY	fiscal year
GAO	General Accounting Office
GATT	General Agreement on Tariffs and Trade
GBI	ground-based interceptor
GDR	German Democratic Republic
GSTS	ground-based surveillance and tracking system
ICB	International Crisis Behavior Project
ICBM	inter-continental ballistic missile
IISS	International Institute for Strategic Studies
IMF	International Monetary Fund
INF	intermediate-range nuclear forces
GDP	gross domestic product
GNP	gross national product
KGB	Committee for State Security
MIRV	multiple independently-targetable re-entry vehicle
MPS	multiple protective structures
NATO	North Atlantic Treaty Organisation
NCO	non-commissioned officer
NEP	New Economic Policy
NSC	National Security Council
OECD	Organisation for Economic Co-operation and Development
OMB	Office of Management and Budget
R & D	research and development
RIIA	Royal Institute of International Affairs
RSFSR	Russian Soviet Federation of Socialist Republics
RUSI	Royal United Services Institute
SACEUR	Supreme Allied Commander (Europe)
SALT	Strategic Arms Limitation Treaty
SBI	space-based interceptor
SDI(O)	Strategic Defense Initiative (Organization)
SEATO	South East Asia Treaty Organisation
SICBM	small inter-continental ballistic missile
SIPRI	Stockholm International Peace Research Institute
SLBM	submarine-launched ballistic missile

SLCM	sea-launched cruise missile
SNF	short-range nuclear force
SRAM	short-range attack missile
SSI	Supplementary Security Income
SSTS	space surveillance and tracking system
START	Strategic Arms Reduction Talks
TRA	Tax Reform Act
UN	United Nations
USAF	United States Air Force
WEU	Western European Union

Note

Throughout the book: 'billion' is used in the sense of thousand million (10^9), and 'trillion' is used in the sense of million million (10^{12}).

1 *Michael C. Pugh and Phil Williams*

Introduction – the debate on decline

As the end of the twentieth century approaches we are in the midst of exciting changes which are eroding the foundations of post-1945 international politics. The bipolar international system, which has dominated both the behaviour of states and theorising about international relations, has increasingly lost credibility. Of crucial importance in the shift has been change in the two principal actors, the United States and the Soviet Union.

This introduction focuses on the debate about the relative decline of the superpowers. In Chapter 2, Robert McGeehan surveys the behaviour of the superpowers in their relations with one another. This is followed by chapters on the domestic, defence and foreign policies of each state. These complementary aspects are best considered as issues of *relative* power and *systemic* change. Michael Pugh's concluding chapter takes up the theme of systemic (structural) shifts in the international system and gauges the prospects for international stability in the light of change in superpower circumstances.

In order to examine the issue of superpower decline we need to consider the meaning of power and superpower. 'Realist' views of international relations (which is not to say that they accord with 'reality') isolate power as the chief arbiter in international relations. Power comprises both measurable commodities, such as material resources, population and military assets, and less tangible attributes such as domestic social cohesion and international status. In the 'realist' world, accurate perceptions of power should play a vital part in decision making. However, as non-realist theories point out, there is an important distinction between power as capabilities and power as influence. In other words, power cannot always be translated into an ability to achieve goals. History is full of examples of the weak mocking the strong, and the possession of certain capabilities does not guarantee an ability to secure foreign policy objectives. Conversely, it may be possible to operate successfully from a position of weakness. The US State Department is only too aware that although Mikhail Gorbachev presides over an empire in decay, on the international circuit he has been extraordinarily successful in promoting his security concepts.

Hierarchies of power in the post-1945 global system have typically placed the US and USSR at the top as 'superpowers', with China as a potential superpower some way behind. The term 'superpower' was employed as early as 1944 by W. T. R. Fox in his book: *The Super-Powers: the United States, Britain and the Soviet Union – their responsibility for peace*. As his subtitle tells us, terminology is time-bound. The wartime phrases 'United Nations' and 'Allied Nations' came to have very different meanings after the Second World War. 'Superpower' was not generally used until the 1950s. Martin Wight's study, *Power Politics*, which began life as a pamphlet in 1946 but under-went revision in the 1950s and 1970s, avoided the term. Perhaps Wight understood it to be a populist and transient notion. He preferred 'dominant power', defined as one which could be destroyed only by a coalition of others.[1] Nuclear weapons invalidated that equation, however, for during the 1960s it was understood, notably by US Defense Secretary Robert McNamara, that each superpower could assure the 'destruction' of the other without summoning a coalition. Indeed the term came to be synonymous with the two states which are capable of destroying each other single-handedly but which cannot be destroyed by any other single power (though this still leaves room for argument about what constitutes 'destruction').

The United States emerged from the Second World War as a major creditor with its territory unscathed, a booming economy, a nuclear monopoly, and State Department plans for economic management of the globe. Whether the emotive term 'empire' can be stretched to describe the US network of non-territorial 'dependencies' is open to dispute. But the United States has frequently installed military forces, irrespective of the legitimacy of the regime being supported, especially in the Caribbean and Central America, and its sway has not been notably less successful than that achieved by occupation.[2]

American post-war pre-eminence was unlikely to last, of course. And whereas in 1945 the United States accounted for over 50 per cent of the world's wealth in industrial production, by the 1980s it had fallen to about 20 per cent. Relative decline was also marked by the advent of Soviet parity in strategic military power by the mid-1970s. Nevertheless, much commentary on the US position in the hierarchy of states is loose and sensational, and the decline thesis is sometimes misinterpreted. Paul Kennedy, in his *The Rise and Fall of the Great Powers*, and other serious analysts of decline do not consider that the United States is in absolute decline or about to be overtaken by other states.

Kennedy, though, does argue that the United States will have to come to terms with 'imperial overstretch', in that its global interests and obligations are larger than the country's power to defend them. This problem, he contends, is exacerbated by the size of the US commitment to Western Europe, by the budgetary problems which the United States faces, and the fact that it has also become the world's largest debtor nation. Furthermore, in Kennedy's view, the United States is suffering not only from relative industrial decline but also from agricultural decline. At the same time he recognises that the hegemonical position of the United States in the 1950s was abnormal and that part of what is happening is a natural and inevitable process of readjustment.

Of the many objections to the decline thesis three are worthy of mention, although none is entirely convincing. First, economic indicators suggest that the decline thesis is grossly exaggerated. The US economy remained about twice the size of its nearest competitor, was also an open economy, and functioned as a lender of the last resort to the rest of the world. Although its performance slipped between 1950 and the early 1970s, growth rates, per capita income, monetary reserves, and share of world trade and investment, showed a recovery after the mid-1970s, and the US improved its position relative to some countries.[3]

Nevertheless, the *character* of the US economic performance, as opposed to the *level* of activity, made it less self-reliant. True, the budget deficit represented only 3.2 per cent of GNP in 1988, but it had to be financed by borrowing from abroad at high interest rates. Similarly, the trade deficit had to be serviced by borrowing from Japan and Middle East oil-producing countries. Japan, the immediate competitor of the United States, now accounts for about 20 per cent of the world's GDP and finances half the US budget deficit. Conversion of Japan's trade surpluses into assets proceeded at such a pace that in 1989 they comfortably passed the value of US assets, and the Economic Planning Agency in Tokyo hailed this as indicative that Japan had become the richest nation in the world. The United States also remained vulnerable to a major financial crisis. Most of the international debt is held in dollars and owed to American banks. Future defaults could cause a banking crisis, and so the US institutions remain locked into involuntary writing-off and rescheduling of what were, in essence, 'bad debts'.

A second objection to the decline thesis is that it does not allow for successful policy outcomes as a measure of power. According to Bruce Russett, the United States continued to get what it wanted in terms of: its own security, a *cordon sanitaire* around the Soviet Union, the promotion of decolonisation and democracy, the export of Coca-Cola culture, nuclear predominance over Third World states, and stability amongst advanced capitalist countries.[4] However, this assumes that such outcomes are the consequence of US inputs alone. In any event, one could produce without much difficulty a long list of outcomes contrary to perceived US interests, from the Lebanon to Nicaragua, or of reactive compromises, from the emergency financial package to Mexico in 1986 to postponement of a decision on a follow-on-Lance system in Europe.

A third contention, raised principally by Samuel P. Huntington, is that the problems of the 1980s, notably the trade and budget deficits, were solely consequences of the Reagan Administration's policies. What was created can be reversed as quickly (though not without affecting the standard of living). The United States, then, was not in decline. Even if it was, it could reverse the decline relatively easily because American society had comparative advantages in openness, competitiveness, upward mobility and immigration. In addition, argues Huntington, far from becoming a self-fulfilling prophecy, the false alarm about decline should be welcomed, because it will galvanise US energies to ensure that it does not happen.[5]

On the other hand, this is part of the problem. The United States has found it difficult to come to terms with the limits of its power. Yet these limits have long been evident. Even at the height of hegemony the United States had to accept that it could not achieve a military victory in Korea, that it could not mobilise many Third World countries into an anti-communist coalition, and that it could not safely pursue the liberation of Eastern Europe. Subsequent events, such as the defeat in Vietnam and the Soviet attainment of nuclear parity, underlined the limits of American power. Nixon and Kissinger attempted to compensate with skilful diplomacy – co-opting the Soviet Union into a *détente* relationship, co-opting China into a pattern of triangular diplomacy, and co-opting its allies into greater burden-sharing.

For a variety of reasons the co-option strategy failed. The Carter Administration sought an alternative approach and attempted to change the diplomatic agenda to one involving North–South and world-order issues on which the United States could still provide the lead.

With Carter's failure and his defeat in the 1980 election the Reagan Administration pursued a policy designed to transcend the limits of American power. Although this was far from a complete success, Reagan nevertheless restored America's self-image. Yet several academics suggest that an ethos of social cohesion and responsibility could not be encouraged easily by a government whose role was to reduce its own socio-economic responsibilities. Trenchant critics remarked that the Reaganite exuberance and image of strength was akin to a drug, blinding the US to declining educational standards, the breakdown of authority in several urban areas, and burgeoning rates of crime and drug abuse. To expect private initiative to resolve public problems was 'to engage in a form of social pathology'.[6]

On balance Huntington is correct to note that the United States remained strong in all departments of measurable power. The US has no single challenger, though if the European Community could act in a unified way it would be more of a challenge than Japan which is highly dependent on food and raw material imports. It is also true, as John Oldfield indicates in Chapter 3, that the political consensus was successfully maintained by Reagan's successor.

But Bush inherited predicaments in the economy, as John Owens argues in Chapter 4, and in defence and security, as Steve Smith shows in Chapter 5. These would not be put right with the facility which Huntington implies. In the international arena there can be little doubt that the limits of American power and limits to the willingness of other states to accept US policy were brutally exposed in the 1980s. As a Reagan supporter commented during the dispute with New Zealand over nuclear deterrence, supposedly an issue on which the entire Western security system stood or fell: 'If the US can no longer successfully maintain a longstanding alliance [ANZUS] with the region's only stable democracies, the question will arise: What can the US do?'[7] In general, tighter constraints on the US international position have proceeded irrespective of the government in office. It has been cogently argued, indeed, that Ronald Reagan's ascendancy was a function of the politics of decline.[8] The Bush policy review, examined in the chapter by Phil Williams and Clark Miller, suggests a greater awareness in Washington of the limits of power.

It is apparent, however, that the Soviet Union's predicaments are far more serious than those confronting the United States. The Soviet Union emerged socially disrupted and economically devastated from the Second World War, but with large, if exhausted, forces controlling territory in Eastern Europe. Justification for describing the Soviet Union as a superpower is nevertheless more problematic. Soviet leaders and analysts rarely used the appellation, though they were determined that the Soviet Union should catch up with, and be treated as an equal by, its chief rival. By 1969 the Red Navy had sufficient nuclear-armed submarines to guarantee a devastating second-strike capability in retaliation for an American first strike. Continued Soviet numerical military strength is not in serious contention: in excess of 10,000 nuclear warheads, and conventional forces which are deemed in the West to be generally superior in number to those marshalled by NATO. But Paul Dibb has given persuasive reasons why the USSR should be considered an 'incomplete superpower', for it lacks economic, technological or ideological clout, and is incapable of global dominance.[9] It was in recognition of this reality that, as Bill Tupman's chapter points out, Gorbachev introduced *glasnost* and political transformation as essential preconditions for making *perestroika* work.

The main controversy in the West about the USSR's decline is about its extent. Western commentators have been predicting the imminent collapse of the Soviet economy since the Bolshevik revolution. But in the late 1980s Gorbachev himself acknowledged that the survival of the system was at stake. As Martha Merritt explains in Chapter 8, the Soviet economy stagnated under a system designed for the 1930s. Growth rates fell steadily between 1970 and 1985, and there was a woeful lack of investment in industrial capital stock.

Yet if CIA estimates are to be believed, the Soviet economy is still the second or third largest in the world (see Table 1.1). Soviet GNP quadrupled in the thirty years after 1958. From 40 per cent of the US GNP in 1955, it rose to 53 per cent by 1986, in which year industrial output, agriculture and GNP expanded by 3 per cent or more. But the Soviet authorities do not publish figures for GNP, perhaps because they do not know what they are, and the World Bank does not commit itself. US intelligence estimates are disputed in the world of commerce, partly because they are suspected of being based on an inflated rouble–dollar conversion rate. Extrapolating from comparisons with Yugoslavia, Poland and Hungary, sceptics suggest that Soviet GNP is less than half that claimed by the CIA and therefore smaller than

Table 1.1 *GNP and per capita GNP: 1988*

	GNP ($US billion)	Per capita GNP ($US)	Purchasing power per capita ($US)
USA	4,863	19,780	19,000
USSR (1987 est.)	2,375	8,330	n/a
Japan	2,576	21,040	13,800
FGR	1,131	18,530	13,500
France	898	16,080	13,400
Italy	765	13,320	—
UK	730	12,800	12,500
Canada	437	16,760	—
China	356	330	—
Brazil	329	2,280	—
India	271	330	—
Australia	204	12,390	—
South Korea	150	3,530	—
Hong Kong	52	9,230	—

Sources: World Bank Atlas, Washington DC, World Bank, 1989, except for USSR estimate, in CIA, *Handbook of Economic Statistics,* Washington DC, Directorate of Intelligence, 1988, p. 31; OECD figures for purchasing power parity, at 1987 prices.

Japan's and probably that of France. Purchasing power per head would be on a par with South Korea's.[10] We *can* say with some confidence that Soviet economic stagnation was leaving the Soviet Union further behind the West.

However, the USSR cannot be dismissed as 'Zaïre with rockets' — as its problems with industrial pollution testify. In human and material resources, and in military strength, the Soviet Union will be more than just a middling European power, even as its hegemony over Eastern Europe diminishes. Paradoxically, in its bid to cease being a closed society, the Soviet Union has had to cut its losses and retreat from its global ambitions. As Rachel Walker shows in Chapter 9 the Soviet leadership has had to completely revise its concept of international relations in recognition of the limits of Soviet power. And in turn, as Robin Plummer discusses in his chapter, this has had a sobering impact on the Soviet defence establishment.

But for both superpowers the use of force and military intervention has been far less effective in settling problems than one would have imagined from their military capabilities. Even so-called 'soft targets' such as Grenada required considerable military commitment. Indeed the term 'superpower' may well have outlived its usefulness. Under demographic and budgetary pressures both superpowers will be obliged to seek a new force equilibrium, one which will have to reflect a retreat from power projection in furtherance of bipolar confrontation. There will be problems of adjustment, obviously, but also new opportunities for reducing tension between the blocs. A fuller discussion of these problems and opportunities is provided in the final chapter.

Notes

1 Martin Wight, edited by Hedley Bull and Carsten Holbraad, *Power Politics*, Harmondsworth, Penguin and RIIA, 1979, pp. 45, 52; see also Robert W. Cox and Harold K. Jacobson, *et al., The Anatomy of Influence*, New Haven, Conn., Yale University Press, 1974, pp. 437–43; Ian Clark, *The Hierarchy of States. Reform and Resistance in the International Order*, Cambridge, Cambridge University Press, 1989.

2 Walter Russell Mead, *Mortal Splendor. The American Empire in Transition*, Boston, Houghton Mifflin, 1987, pp. 11–18.

3 Michael C. Webb and Stephen D. Krasner, 'Hegemonic stability theory: an empirical assessment', *Review of International Studies*, XV, 1989, pp. 183–98.

4 Bruce Russett, 'The mysterious case of vanishing hegemony: or is Mark Twain really dead?', *International Organization*, XXXIX, 1985, pp. 207–31.

5 Samuel P. Huntington, 'The US – decline or renewal?', *Foreign Affairs*, LXVII, Winter 1988/9, pp. 76–96.

6 Richard J. Krickus, *The Superpowers in Crisis: Implications of Domestic Discord*, McLean, Va., Pergamon – Brassey's, 1987, p. 222; Mead, *Mortal Splendor*, p. 208. See also, J. D. Lees and Michael Turner, eds, *Reagan's First Four Years: a New Beginning?*, Manchester, Manchester University Press, 1989.

7 Owen Harries, 'Crisis in the Pacific, *Commentary*, LXXIX, June 1985, p. 53.

8 Joel Krieger, *Reagan, Thatcher and the Politics of Decline*, Cambridge, Polity Press, 1986, pp. 189–90.

9 Paul Dibb, *The Soviet Union. The Incomplete Superpower*, 2nd edn, Basingstoke, Macmillan and IISS, 1988, p. 280.

10 Correspondence from J. K. Wright, international consultant economist.

Sparring partners – the record of superpower relations

Superpower politics has been the most salient aspect of international relations since 1945. The United States and the Soviet Union have indeed been 'sparring partners' in their efforts to skirmish for advantage over each other, but unlike boxers who spar as companions for practice or exercise, the superpower contest has always been serious and at times highly dangerous. To understand the long rivalry of the cold war, the subsequent moves towards *détente* and the related factors which have conditioned current changes in world affairs, it is necessary to recall the unusual circumstances produced by the Second World War. Most important amongst these was the fundamental change in the global balance of power.

The term 'superpower', first coined by an American scholar writing in 1943 about prospects for peace in the post-war world,[1] itself reflects both the pre-eminence of the USA and the USSR and the virtual absence of other great powers after 1945. The modern state system has long been associated with the concept of the balance of power, a vague but widely acknowledged international process, whereby whenever any one state attempted to achieve dominance over the others, the latter would co-operate to preserve their independence by preventing (by war if necessary) the one state from becoming overly powerful.

Historically, this process checked the hegemonical ambitions of Spain, France and Germany; but it always depended upon there being a number of 'powers', that is, strong states, available to counter the would-be arrogator. The most striking fact of post-war international politics was the impossibility of continuing the historical balancing process, due to the debilitation or disappearance of the former great powers. Defeated Germany and Japan surrendered unconditionally, Italy was impotent and even the victors France and Britain were badly weakened and soon began to lose their imperial possessions. Only the USSR and USA remained pre-eminent.

This bipolar situation, which is presently showing signs of systemic change, has been the paramount feature of international politics for almost half a century. Post-1945 bipolarity meant that there were only two sparring partners sufficiently comparable to compete: the military power of the United States and of the Soviet Union in comparison with that of any other states was so overwhelming that they dominated the global strategic balance.

Cold war confrontation in Europe

The rationale for Soviet–American collaboration during the Second World War was their common interest in the defeat of the Third Reich. Once this was achieved, the basis for further concurrence diminished. Had the superpowers been able to co-operate after 1945, or if they had at least been sufficiently non-hostile to coexist without each sensing that the other was a threat to its own security, the extended confrontation of the cold war would have been mitigated if not largely avoided. But the combination of power-political rivalries and ideological incompatibilities, compounded by a considerable degree of misperception and national anxiety, resulted in the United States and the Soviet Union confronting each other as adversaries. This adversarial relationship assumed global proportions only later on; its most intense focus from the late 1940s until the early 1960s was in Europe, and it was in the German arena that the sparring partners fought hardest for advantage.

Germany's total defeat resulted in the country's division into zones of military occupation by the victor powers in the short run, and the partition of the nation into two separate states thereafter. Such was the strategic importance of Germany that neither superpower could have allowed the other to gain control of a unified German state without facing the prospect of losing the cold war, since the balance would increasingly have favoured the side which harnessed German power potential. By 1949, the Western zones became the Federal Republic of Germany, and the Soviet zone the German Democratic Republic; in 1955, these states became members of the rival alliances, respectively the North Atlantic Treaty Organisation (NATO) and the Warsaw Pact.

The East–West division of Europe was hence solidified by the late 1940s, and Western European security was underwritten by the American abandonment of isolationism. The United States embraced a policy of virtually permanent involvement in European affairs, symbolised politically by the Truman Doctrine, economically by the European Recovery Program (the Marshall Plan), and militarily by NATO and the assignment of American divisions to Europe in peacetime.[2] The strategy adopted by the United States and its NATO allies was containment, to ensure that Soviet power would not extend beyond the limits it had reached.

Containment rested upon deterrence, a concurrent strategic concept which in its crudest form prevents attack by guaranteeing that the penalty for aggression would be much greater than any conceivable benefit. In contrast to most historical bipolar confrontations, the cold war rivalry of the superpowers did not produce war. This was, above all, because of their nuclear capabilities and the resulting condition of mutual assured destruction should deterrence fail. This 'balance of terror' precluded not only direct attack by conventionally superior Soviet forces, but also other varieties of coercion or intimidation which from the Western perspective would surely have materialised if Moscow had been free to explore avenues of psycho-political blackmail.

The record of superpower relations during the cold war will continue to be a subject of controversy as documentary and other evidence continues to become available; what will be lost as time passes is the sense of the reality of the East–West struggle felt by the statesmen and other national decision-makers responsible for security during a time of upheaval and confusion. Only recently, for example, have Soviet spokesmen begun to admit that their post-war policies were such that the West had a legitimate fear of military attack;[3] for most of the cold war period, each side adopted a posture of self-rectitude and proclaimed the other a threat.

The Soviet position, elaborated both by its own spokesmen and later by the 'revisionist' school of Western scholars, emphasised the enormous Russian losses suffered during the Second World War, the vulnerability of Soviet territory to attack and the security requirement of 'friendly' (i.e. communist) states along its borders in order to provide defensive depth (not least against the future possibility of German revanchism). The Soviet argument further stressed the Russians' fear of American aggression, underlined specifically by the temporary US monopoly of the atomic bomb and, more generally, their apprehension that American policies were directed towards the establishment of democratic–capitalist states on the periphery of the Soviet Union and the consequent expulsion of Russian influence from Eastern Europe.[4]

In brief, according to these arguments, Soviet perception of hostile Western anti-communism justified extensive defensive measures to protect the Soviet sphere of security. These 'defensive' measures, however, were so sweeping that Americans and West Europeans were persuaded that Soviet ambitions went beyond legitimate defence needs.

While the origins of the superpower conflict may be traced as far back as the beginnings of Western relations with the new Soviet state in 1917,[5] the more immediate sources of apprehension about Moscow's post-war intentions were both numerous and well-founded. After the defeat of Nazi Germany, Soviet control was militarily imposed on the countries of Eastern Europe. The Red Army, the largest military force in the world, was not demobilised. Communist régimes were established in Poland, Hungary, Romania, Bulgaria and Czechoslovakia. Earlier Western hopes for free elections and the establishment of democratic systems were ended as Soviet control was consolidated and police-state conditions were applied. Moscow rejected participation in the American Marshall Plan for European recovery and imposed a blockade on Allied-controlled West Berlin in 1948. Soviet territorial acquisitions of some 200,000 square miles included areas taken from Finland, Poland, Germany, Czechoslovakia and Romania. In 1940, the Soviet Union had already annexed the independent Baltic republics of Estonia, Latvia and Lithuania, and after the war refused to consider their claims for independence.

These Soviet power-political moves in themselves would surely have produced conditions of superpower animosity, especially when compounded by the complications of the German question, but in addition there was the particular nature of the Soviet state. The Soviet Union was in no familiar sense a traditional great power, but a totalitarian system with an all-consuming communist ideology, committed not to the international status quo or territorial security, but to a creed of Marxism–Leninism itself dedicated to the globalisation of communism. Moreover, the Soviet Union was ruled by Joseph Stalin, a ruthless dictator with whom normal relationships were effectively out of the question. Later denounced by his successors in the Kremlin, Stalin during the cold war personified evil for Western leaders whose domestic political constituencies required much more than traditional balance-of-power arguments to convince them that substantial sacrifices had to be made to meet a new threat so soon after the triumph over the Nazi menace.

Changing superpower politics and nuclear crisis

Until the outbreak of the Korean War in 1950, Western observers saw the cold war as a confrontation of hostility, tension and potential for escalation, marked by political competition, psychological warfare, ideological disputes, propaganda battles and ongoing efforts towards gaining advantage by all means other than the direct use of force. The North Korean attack, assumed to have been either ordered by or acquiesced in by Moscow, seemed to signal that international communism had shifted to military means to achieve political objectives. Comparisons were drawn with the European situation; the imbalance of conventional forces to the disadvantage of Western security prompted the United States to demand the immediate rearmament of Germany in the interests of NATO's policy of containment through deterrence.

This American demand was premature both for Germans and for the European NATO allies, but it led during the next few years to the building of Western defences which brought long-term security to Europe (although to some it led to an unnecessary militarisation of the cold war and the further deepening of the East–West divide).[6] In any case, once it was clear that neither superpower could either gain control of all Germany or without undue risk be able to dislodge the other from positions secured in the early post-war years, the cold war became a prolonged time of rigidity and hostility. The other side of the coin, however, was that such a relationship brought a stability perhaps only recently appreciated as the kaleidoscopic changes of Mikhail Gorbachev's *glasnost* and *perestroika* have opened anew the uncertainties of political and military change in Eastern Europe. For the rest of the 1950s, superpower politics settled into patterns of competitive behaviour which, while pugnacious, eschewed the risks of direct confrontation – the 1956 Soviet invasion of Hungary without any Western countermove being the most obvious case in point.

In retrospect, the cold war was probably much less dangerous than was assumed at the time. The balance of power in Europe, a curiously contrasting one of American atomic and strategic superiority and Soviet conventional and regional preponderance, was never tested in a crisis situation of political–military confrontation. Such a crisis occurred, far from the central front, only in October 1962 when the Soviet Union deployed nuclear-armed missiles in Cuba and the United States demanded their removal. The missile crisis, the only direct nuclear confrontation between the superpowers, was peacefully resolved when Moscow agreed to withdraw its weapons in return for an American pledge not to invade or otherwise attack Cuba. This settlement, involving the prestige of the superpowers and hence making it especially difficult for either to yield, was reached only after tense confrontation worsened by communications problems and moments when it was feared the situation was becoming uncontrollable.

The importance of the missile crisis for this chapter is not so much its military lesson, which was one of demonstrating that the regional superiority of the United States in air and sea power meant that the Soviet Union was unable to support its distant gamble, but its political and psychological impact on superpower behaviour. Soviet and American leaders had been alerted to the acute danger of escalation partly because communications facilities for crisis management were inadequate. The proximate result was, in 1963, the first 'arms control' agreement relating to strategic stability, the establishment of a direct telecommunications link between Moscow and Washington, the Hot Line. This was quickly followed by the Limited Test Ban Treaty governing the testing of nuclear weapons. These measures signalled the beginning of superpower *détente*: the relaxation of previously existing tensions whose potential for escalation might in extreme circumstances have led to a nuclear holocaust.

Détente I and superpower relations

The sparring partners had always recognised, albeit tacitly, the rules of the game which their power positions forced upon them, especially the necessity to control any situation which could bring war. In a direct sense, then, the Cuban missile crisis was a 'mistake' whose terrifying possibilities led directly to conscious efforts to improve superpower relations.

Détente was an imprecise concept, and its ambiguity was initially beneficial as Moscow and Washington began to explore the ways in which they might normalise their relationship. During the 1960s, the Soviet Union continued to seek geopolitical equality through acquiring weapons which would symbolise strategic parity. The United States continued to perceive communism as a source of aggression and conflict, emanating if not from Moscow then from Beijing or Hanoi. American doubts about the normalisation of relations with the Soviet Union were dramatically compounded by such developments as the

Soviet-instigated Warsaw Pact invasion of Czechoslovakia in 1968. They were further exacerbated by Moscow's support for North Vietnam and Soviet efforts to gain influence in the Middle East and Africa. Yet despite hesitations about whether relations with an ideologically hostile state seeking power-political advantage on a global basis could ever be normalised, the United States turned its attention to what would become the centre-piece of East–West relations in the next decade, enhanced security through arms control.

The cold war confrontation in Europe had already been eased by the beginning of the 1970s through the success of the *Ostpolitik* of the Federal Republic of Germany, whereby the Bonn Government recognised the political and territorial realities of the post-war settlement and on this basis decided to build closer relations with the states of Eastern Europe, including the German Democratic Republic as well as the Soviet Union. Once treaties had been concluded accepting the status quo with the Soviet Union and the other states against which West Germany might have pressed territorial claims (which claims would have been a permanent source of instability), the main precondition for increased superpower understandings was met. Now that the Federal Republic recognised the East German state, Soviet propaganda could no longer invoke the excuse of incipient West German revanchism as a reason to delimit European *détente*. There followed a broadening of the relaxation of cold war restrictions as progress towards normalisation was registered in matters of security, economics and human rights.

The high point of *Détente* I was the SALT agreement of 1972, when the superpowers reached an arms control accord covering limitations on strategic nuclear weapons and the non-deployment of defensive systems against ballistic missiles (the ABM Treaty). Other concurrent measures, such as the accord covering the 'Basic Principles of Relations', went rhetorically beyond what might have been politically realistic; it was agreed, for example, that neither superpower would try to 'obtain unilateral advantage at the expense of the other, directly or indirectly'. Such exaggerated hopes should perhaps have given some indication that expectations were being generated which were bound to be frustrated as it was realised that there were limits to *détente*.

Yet the main objective of Moscow, formal recognition of strategic parity between the superpowers, was obtained at minimal cost. This was because of the prevailing view in Washington, pessimistically epitomised by the Nixon–Kissinger belief that American power was in decline, that the best that could be hoped for from arms control was a deceleration of the Soviet Union's growing military power. *Détente* I also embraced numerous developments in addition to security matters, especially the extension of credit to Eastern European countries and the opening of previously closed avenues of trade and commerce. It was, however, in the field of human rights that Western aspirations and Soviet realities most sharply clashed.

The 1975 Helsinki Final Act of the Conference on Security and Co-operation in Europe, signed by the United States, Canada and thirty-three European states, was both the greatest achievement of the decade and the beginning of the decline of *Détente* I. While it was fully realised that in the nuclear age there was no alternative to peaceful co-existence, the superpowers did not share an understanding of the meaning of *détente*. For the Soviet Union, it meant normalisation of East–West state-to-state relations, but not an end to the ideological contest or to the struggle for advantage in the Third World arena. The result was a contrasting picture: mollification of relationships in Europe, but increasing conflict in other areas. Expansionist Soviet involvement in Angola, Ethiopia, Yemen, Cambodia and elsewhere meant, contrary to American hopes, that there was neither a 'spirit of arms control' which might spill over into other areas nor a 'code of *détente*' which would apply to non-European competition.

Even though further strategic weapons limitations were agreed in mid-1979 in the SALT II accord, by the end of that year super-power relations had dramatically deteriorated. The Soviet invasion of Afghanistan in December definitively ended the first experiment in normalisation, and at least temporarily the baby of arms control had to be thrown away with the soiled bath-water of discredited *détente*.

Cold War II and return to containment

Even before the end of the Carter presidency, American complaints about Soviet human rights abuses, other violations of the Helsinki Final Act and international adventurism had reflected the soured atmosphere of superpower relations. But these factors were minor compared to the preoccupation of the incoming Reagan Administration with the perceived imbalance of military power and the putative advantages and opportunities this gave to the bellicose Soviet leadership. Ronald Reagan's first term in the White House was characterised above all by an emphasis on rebuilding American military strength while deterring further Soviet adventurism.

The short-term gap, it was believed, could be bridged by invigorating Washington's policy of deterrence through manifestation of resolve and determination. Pending the materialisation of the planned massive weapons buildup, the President invoked his skills as a communicator and in so doing revived the rhetoric of the cold war. Branding the Soviet Union an 'evil empire', he contrasted the Western record of restraint with Moscow's policy of weapons acquisition far beyond any reasonable defensive needs. The Soviet bid for superiority was typified by the relentless deployment of intermediate-range SS-20 missiles, and compounded by hypocritical Soviet protests against NATO's plans to redress the Euro-strategic imbalance by bringing in its own INF systems if arms control efforts should fail.

Successive changes in the Soviet leadership in the early 1980s aggravated the difficulties of bringing superpower relations back onto a track of co-operation, and Western resolve to resist Soviet blackmail was strengthened when Moscow attempted to intimidate the European allies by stating that any country which accepted new American missiles would be added to the Soviet nuclear target plan.

Nor were the sparring partners limited to trading blows in Europe alone. Events elsewhere, such as the use of United States military forces to restore democracy to Grenada and the later bombing of Libya in response to that country's support for terrorism, indirectly checked Soviet ambitions. More importantly, such Reagan Administration policies, while condemned by many, restored American self-confidence and the nation's image as a superpower willing to use force if necessary to defend its vital interests. Once the self-esteem of the United States had been restored, the President took advantage of the more evenly balanced power position as a starting-point for a less hostile superpower relationship.

Even at the worst point of Cold War II, the polemical battle had not been accompanied by confrontational or irresponsibly dangerous behaviour on the part of either Moscow or Washington. The United States did not provoke the Soviet Union by selling sophisticated weapons to the People's Republic of China or by trying to destabilise Moscow's Warsaw Pact allies. Nor did the Soviet Union invade Poland, undertake new and offensive Third World gambles, or compound its error in Afghanistan by going beyond a holding action.

Striking a balance: *Détente* **II**

With the adoption of new policies in Moscow following Mikhail
Gorbachev's assumption of power, and the desire of Ronald Reagan
to project the image of a 'man of peace', the superpower relationship
could again be normalised. Arms control negotiations were resumed
in 1985, and later in the year there was held in Geneva the first summit
meeting since the collapse of *détente* in 1979. From the American
perspective, the imbalance of military power inherited from the false
détente of the 1970s had been redressed, and this meant that the
superpower strategic relationship would again be stable and reliable.
A popular but temporary protest against nuclear weapons (vigorously
supported by Soviet propaganda) receded in Western countries, and
general acceptance of the condition of mutual assured destruction over-
came the complaints of its critics. Just as Richard Nixon had earlier
possessed the domestic anti-communist credentials for the American
opening to the People's Republic of China, Ronald Reagan's credentials
for a more intimate relationship with the state so recently branded an
'evil empire' were beyond censure (even though the change in the Soviet
leadership was a precondition for the American shift).

By 1987, arms control efforts produced the first-ever nuclear
weapons disarmament treaty, when superpower agreement was reached
on the complete elimination of all ground-based INF. Arms control
negotiations continue on a very broad range of subjects, and it has been
agreed that in 1990 the Soviet leader will visit the United States for
meetings with the American President.

George Bush is a cautious and prudent person, one who in many
ways is the ideal Western answer to the atmospherically dynamic
onslaught of 'Gorbacharm'. Upon assuming office, he announced a
sweeping 'strategic review' of American policies, in order to take stock
of the state of the superpower relationship and, discreetly, distance
himself from the policy trends of his predecessor which he felt were
developing too precipitately. President Bush has assembled a foreign
policy team more experienced than any in the post-war era; such talents
will be needed if Western security is to be preserved at a time when
the temptation to move quickly could be disastrous. The fading of the
Soviet threat, the great staple of both cold war periods, raises hopes
but also creates problems: the challenge is to use this to advantage in
such manner that should *Détente* II not prove to be sustainable, the
loss to NATO security can be minimised.[7]

Conclusions

This overview of the relations between the superpower sparring partners may be briefly concluded in the light of the detailed chapters which follow. The most obvious observation is a fundamental one: the interests of the superpowers are better served by exploring mutually advantageous accommodations than by the perpetuation of an adversarial posture. Yet while the cold war as a phenomenon of post-war contemporary history may have ended, the competition which is the essence of international politics has not.

Power is by its nature relative, and the superpowers in relation to other states and groupings have become less powerful than in the recent past. Both the Soviet Union and the United States, although in the case of the latter much less so, have sensed the vulnerability which is associated with national overextension, when military spending and global activities stretch beyond their economic foundations. While American world-wide responsibilities grew out of economic preponderance and the involvements of the cold war, the efforts of the Soviet Union to achieve superpower status resulted from deliberate policies of trying to offset a position as an objectively backward country by assuming a global role. Economic factors notwithstanding, it remains doubtful that any other strategic rival will in the near future be able to compete with either the United States or the Soviet Union. The sparring partners are thus, in a sense, politically doomed to remain in the ring together even as unprecedented changes push the heritage of the cold war into the increasingly remote past.

Notes

1 William T. R. Fox, *The Super-Powers*, New York, Harcourt, Brace, 1944.

2 An excellent analysis is provided by A. W. DePorte, *Europe between the Super-Powers*, New Haven, Conn. and London, Yale University Press, 1986 (2nd edn).

3 During a debate on West German television in September 1989, the Soviet Deputy Foreign Affairs Minister, Viktor Karpov, admitted that the Soviet military posture was offensive, a carry-over from the early post-war period. *Atlantic News*, No. 2149, 15 September 1989.

4 Arthur Schlesinger, Jr, 'Origins of the Cold War', *Foreign Affairs*, October 1967, pp. 22–52.

5 D. F. Fleming, *The Cold War and Its Origins*, Garden City, NY, Double-day, 1961.

6 This was later argued by the 'father' of the policy of containment, George F. Kennan.

7 For a detailed discussion, see Phil Williams, 'US—Soviet relations: beyond the Cold War?', *Foreign Affairs*, Spring 1989, pp. 273—88.

3 *J.R. Oldfield*

From Reagan to Bush – political change in the United States

The election of George Bush in 1988 was no ordinary affair. Not since the Roosevelt–Truman era had either political party won three consecutive presidential elections. Much of the credit for the Republicans' success at the polls must go to Ronald Reagan, who left an indelible mark on the presidency. Certainly, there was no doubting Reagan's popularity. He left office with an approval rating of 63 per cent, back to his pre-Irangate score. Given the opportunity, an estimated 41 per cent of Americans would have voted him in for a third term. It might have seemed that George Bush would be unable to match the public standing achieved by his predecessor. However, not only has President Bush gained considerable public respect, but in addition, as this chapter will show, the transition to a new administration has been remarkably smooth.

To understand the Reagan phenomenon it is necessary to understand the character of America's recent history. The 1960s opened on a note of optimism and high idealism inseparable from the personality of John F. Kennedy. Kennedy's assassination in November 1963 stunned and desolated Americans. Although there followed a period of social and technological advance, it was punctuated by a series of political trauma: the riots and assassinations of 1967–8, Vietnam, Watergate and Nixon's resignation in 1974. In 1976, voters turned to Jimmy Carter, an outsider whose clean-cut image seemed to present a refreshing contrast to the corruption of the Nixon Administration. But if Americans had wanted someone to nurse them through the next four years, they got instead a severe critic of American society who made no secret of his conviction that things were going to get worse before they got better. Ultimately, Carter's 'defeatism' and his efforts to turn governing into a dialogue with the American people were seen as signs of weakness. The two factors which did most to damage him politically were his alleged 'softness' in foreign affairs and his inability to deal adequately with the twin domestic problems of inflation and unemployment. In the domestic sphere, between 1973 and 1983 the median real income of a typical young family headed by a person aged 25 to 34 fell by 11.5 per cent. In the 1970s, for the first time in American history, the economic value of a college degree declined.[1]

Reagan and the image of strength

The failures of the Carter Administration were a vital factor in the election of 1980. But this should in no way detract from Reagan's skills as a communicator or the attractiveness of his message. Reagan offered Americans what they wanted: an image of strength and reliability coupled with a determination to get on with the job and leave them alone. The amiability and positive outlook of the man were reassuring. Reagan's humble origins, his optimism and plain common sense struck a responsive chord in a country wearied by the uncertainties of the Carter years.[2] Above all, Reagan promised to make America strong again. In the wake of the Iranian hostage crisis, Reagan charged Carter with an almost criminal neglect of American power, a drift into an acceptance of weakness; and he proposed as the first imperative a return to the old orthodoxy of confrontation and containment of the Soviet threat. Reagan's panacea for America's ills was simple (perhaps too simple): lower taxes, lower domestic spending, a bigger defence machine, and a tougher foreign policy.

In focusing his campaign on the restoration of American strength Reagan was capitalising on a swing to the right in American politics and, in particular, the emergence of the New Right, a broad coalition of conservative men and women, many of them 'born again' Christians, who shared an apocalyptic vision of the dangers facing American society. In generating support, direct mailing was the life-blood of the New Right's system of operations. Richard A. Viguerie, who can lay some claim to have created the New Right, used the latest information technology to tap the immense resources of groups like the National Rifle Association and the National Right to Life Committee. By 1980 what passed as the New Right (quite literally a coalition built inside Viguerie's computers) numbered some 4½ million Republican voters with the organisational ability to sponsor right-wing candidates and have a say in the selection of a suitable presidential candidate.[3]

The New Right's agenda was relatively short and easy to understand. Through the Heritage Foundation, a research institution founded in 1975 by the Colorado brewer Joseph Coors and his Washington political operative, Paul Weyrich, New Righters argued a solid if highly partisan case for a strong defence policy and a stance on social issues that included opposition to abortion and gay rights. On defence, at least, the New Right also drew vital support from the Committee on the Present Danger (1975), a group of prominent American foreign policy experts that included George Shultz, Richard Perle, Eugene Rostow and Paul Nitze. Fiercely anti-Soviet, although in the case of Shultz not stridently or inflexibly so, the CPD was to provide the first Reagan Administration with ideologically committed, high-ranking personnel (Shultz became Reagan's Secretary of State, Perle his Assistant Secretary for International Security Policy, Rostow Director of the Arms Control and Disarmament Agency, and Nitze the key strategic arms control negotiator).[4]

Quite deliberately in the 1980 presidential campaign Reagan stressed both his sympathy with right-wing ideologues and his credentials as a 'born again' Christian. His subsequent victory was to mark the start of a new era. Where Jimmy Carter had been synonymous with defeat and depression Reagan became a success symbol. Under his presidency the United States appeared to grow militarily and economically stronger, and accordingly recovered its sense of national pride. Despite Irangate, despite the stock-market crash of 1987, there is no doubting Reagan's achievements. The new President arrived promising to cut taxes, increase military spending and reverse America's economic decline. Indeed, Reagan cut the top tax rate to 27 per cent and granted the Pentagon $2 trillion. By the time he left office unemployment was at its lowest rate since the early 1970s at 5.3 per cent; inflation, meanwhile, remained under 5 per cent. In foreign policy Reagan's record was no less impressive. Despite the rhetoric of the first term, military action was only taken when retaliation was highly unlikely, for instance in Grenada and Libya, and where the threat to American lives guaranteed bipartisan support. Reagan's big foreign policy success, however, was the *rapprochement* with Moscow. It was seen as a vindication of the President's belief that a strong national defence would ultimately force the Soviets to the negotiating table. Solid as these achievements were, they only explain so much about the Reagan phenomenon. His main success was in changing the national mood. Reagan made Americans feel good about themselves and about their country. The ceremonials for the Los Angeles Olympic Games in 1984 and the rededication ceremony for the Statue of Liberty in 1986 were exuberant celebrations of national well-being.

The flaws in Reaganism

There is still something almost mysterious about Reagan's communion with the American people. They seemed to respond to the strength and clarity of his character. But his highly personal style had mixed results. On the one hand, Reagan provided a much-needed symbol of strength and national pride; on the other hand, he lured Americans into a false sense of security. While defence spending boomed under Reagan, basic research in civilian technology stagnated, thwarting attempts to compete effectively with Japan. Deregulation and Wall Street's obsession with take-overs created instability and, to some extent, affected business confidence. While the wealthy benefited, the poorest 20 per cent saw their incomes fall slightly in real terms. A 7 per cent cut in human resources programmes between 1981 and 1984 fell heavily on ethnic minorities and expanded an already large underclass. Crime and the drugs menace in America's cities escalated alarmingly. Above all, Reagan failed to moderate growth in government spending. When he left office in 1989 the national debt stood at a staggering $2.6 trillion. The annual budget deficit alone was $200 billion.[5] The outcomes of the economic programme known as 'Reaganomics' are discussed in greater depth in the next chapter. Suffice it to note here that for all the Reagan Administration's success in controlling inflation and unemployment, it turned the United States into a debtor nation.

There was also a negative side to Reagan's foreign policy successes. His administration reinforced a tendency to consider external matters only in so far as they affected American lives. The result was an obsession with the issue of American hostages held in the Middle East that culminated in the humiliating Irangate crisis in 1987. Reagan, moreover, betrayed a wariness about consulting troublesome or unreliable partners, a frustration with international agencies like the United Nations and a determination to go it alone.[6] Not surprisingly, the President's unilateralist actions in Grenada, Nicaragua and Libya, caused disquiet among America's European allies, though the use of force against Grenada and Libya was popular at home. The November 1985 Geneva summit with Gorbachev, hailed as a triumph for the Administration, did little to disguise the fact that Gorbachev had outmanoeuvred a seemingly befuddled Reagan, or that it was Moscow, and not Washington, which was producing arms control initiatives.

Most damaging of all in the long term, however, was the growing realisation that Reagan was not in control of his own staff or the details and implementation of policy. The problem became a crisis during the 1987 Irangate scandal, when for the first time Americans became aware of a high-level operation involving an arms-for-hostages deal with the Iranians and illegal aid to the Nicaraguan Contras. As the crisis deepened it was revealed that Reagan's officials, including his national security advisers, Robert McFarlane and John Poindexter, and their trusted aide, Lt. Col. Oliver North, had been given virtually a free rein to pursue these initiatives. In its report on the Irangate affair the Tower Review Board (appointed by Reagan and chaired by former Republican senator, John Tower) drew particular attention to the wide-ranging freedom enjoyed by the President's staff and reserved special criticism for Reagan's detached approach to government:

The president's management style is to put the principal responsibility for policy review and implementation on the shoulders of his advisors. Nevertheless, with such a complex, high-risk operation and so much at stake, the president should have ensured that the NSC [National Security Council] system did not fail him. He did not force his policy to undergo the most critical review of which the NSC participants and the process were capable. At no time did he insist upon accountability and performance review. Had the president chosen to drive the NSC system, the outcome could well have been different. As it was, the most powerful features of the NSC system − providing comprehensive analysis, alternatives and follow up − were not utilized. The board found a strong consensus among NSC participants that the president's priority in the Iran initiative was the release of US hostages. But setting priorities is not enough when it comes to sensitive and risky initiatives that directly affect US national security. He must ensure that content and tactics of an initiative match his priorities and objectives. He must insist upon accountability. For it is the president who must take responsibility for the NSC system and deal with the consequences.[7]

Subsequently, Reagan changed his methods and brought in a skilful manager, Howard Baker, as his Chief of Staff. The crisis passed. Nevertheless, the President's image had been badly dented and the whole débâcle undoubtedly helped to make managerial competence a central issue in the 1988 presidential campaign.

The rise of George Bush

At first glance, the man given the task of building on Reagan's achievements seems rather bland and ineffectual. In marked contrast to Ronald Reagan, Bush's background has all the marks of East Coast wealth and privilege. His father, Prescott Bush, was a Wall Street banker and a powerful Republican senator who opposed Joseph McCarthy and supported civil rights. After five years at the prestigious Phillips Andover Academy George Bush enlisted in the Navy Air Corps. His war record was exemplary. He flew fifty-eight missions and on at least four occasions survived when his aircraft were badly damaged. The war was followed by four years at Yale. Bush resisted the temptation to follow his father into banking and chose instead to seek his fortune in the oilfields of Texas. Richly successful, Bush stayed on. His love affair with Texas, and his yearning to be a Texan, is an essential feature of his character. He also preferred the advice of like-minded 'achievers', whilst distrusting intellectuals and ideologues.[8]

He had shown an interest in politics after the war, but his career would take a somewhat unusual course. A moderately successful Republican Congressman for Texas, Bush's fortunes suffered a set-back in 1970 when he lost a Senate race to Lloyd Bentsen, who, ironically, was to be Michael Dukakis's running mate in 1988. Sub-sequently, at Richard Nixon's prompting, Bush side-stepped to take over the chairmanship of the Republican National Committee (1972). Seemingly unaware of the political conspiracy directed against the Democrats, he soon found himself leading the defence of Nixon and the Republican Party through the worst days of the Watergate crisis. Subsequently, in 1975 Bush became America's envoy to China, and was later made Director of the CIA to restore that institution's somewhat tarnished image. In 1980 he stood down as a presidential candidate in time to position himself as Ronald Reagan's running mate.[9] In many ways this was a tough portfolio, but Bush emerged as a cool professional, often charming, yet also persistent and competitive. Bush's public persona may appear moderate, but it is important to remember that he is no stranger to ruthless political infighting.

Bush's political career is significant for two other reasons. Where Ronald Reagan could at least draw on his experience as Governor of California, Bush was frequently cast in the role of a 'one-man clean-up squad for the Republicans', valued more for his loyalty than a brilliant grasp of policy details.[10] In an interview with *Time* magazine shortly after his election he admitted: 'Yes. I've started going into the numbers *finally*, and they're enormous. I've been sitting down with Budget Director-designate Richard Darman, going over the realities of the budget that we face.'[11] Although such honesty might strike some observers as alarming, in fact Bush was anxious to demonstrate more active management than his predecessor. In addition, he did not embrace all the policies which he inherited, and has called for a whole series of policy reviews.

In the second place, Bush served some very powerful political masters and to all intents and purposes appeared to be content to do their bidding. In the future his greatest task will be to stamp both his authority and his personality on the presidency. To do this he must come to terms with the demands of television, the key medium for influencing public opinion. Whereas Reagan might be described as the first complete TV president, Bush finds the medium alien. He struggles to project a positive, easy manner, though he generally succeeded in combating the 'wimp' tag which dogged him throughout the 1988 presidential campaign. His ability to deal authoritatively with the budget deficit and challenges to the United States abroad, is likely to prove critical in reassuring Americans that the positive features of the Reagan legacy have not been squandered.

A deliberative president

While a definitive judgement on Bush will have to wait further developments, certain signs became clear during the first six months in office. First, Bush was careful to project an image of expertise and professionalism. In selecting his cabinet he stressed qualifications and experience. Bush was also at pains to portray himself as a more caring and more accessible president. Whilst 'on the stump', he pledged to create tax-free savings programmes to help people pay for education, home purchases, or starting a business; to distribute $50 million among the states for innovative programmes in education; to provide low-income families with a tax credit that could be used to subsidise day-care for children; and to create 30 million jobs within eight years. In his maiden address to Congress Bush reiterated most of these promises and went further by aligning himself with environmentalists on issues relating to offshore drilling in California, acid rain and toxic dumping.[12]

The nagging problem, of course, is the huge budget deficit and

Bush's pledge not to raise taxes. Most commentators agree that it will only be possible to meet the Gramm–Rudman–Hollings target of a $100 billion deficit by fiscal year 1990 by raising taxes. Bush faced an almost impossible dilemma; how to honour his no-new-taxes vow while at the same time protecting the defence budget and financing new programmes in education and child care. Bush may well find himself having to make a U-turn on taxation. At the outset he chose to protect his social programmes, though at a relatively low level of funding, by freezing the defence budget and introducing what are disingenuously described as 'revenue raisers' (for example, the sale of unassigned radio frequencies).[13] Critics dismissed Bush's budget proposals as unworkable. A more charitable view might be that he took the first constructive steps in dealing with the budget deficit, and in the process challenged Congress to use its discretionary power over a $136 billion pool of popular programmes like the Amtrak railroad network and environmental protection.

Bush's decision to push ahead with social programmes reflected his understanding of the political climate and his determination to review the Reagan policies. There was simply less support among Americans for draconian cuts in domestic spending, and more concern with the environment and issues like education, crime and moral standards. Alert to a subtle shift in popular opinion on the environment, Bush proposed major steps to reduce acid rain, emissions of toxic chemicals, and smog caused by exhaust fumes. At the same time, he has aligned himself with the supporters of Pat Robertson, a 'born again' Christian and staunch conservative who made a strong showing in the 1988 Republican primaries. Bush assuaged Robertson hardliners by supporting amendments to the Constitution to ban abortion and forbid desecration of the American flag. In doing so, his political credibility (and his popularity) soared. Bush watched his approval rating rise to 70 per cent, higher than Reagan ever achieved.[14]

Bush's successes in the domestic sphere vindicated his calm, deliberate approach to policy-making. In foreign affairs, too, he began to show his mettle. Fears that Bush was in danger of losing the propaganda war with Moscow, and with it the support of some of his European allies, proved groundless. At the May 1989 NATO summit in Brussels he neatly headed off a possible confrontation with the West Germans over the modernisation of short-range nuclear systems by putting conventional arms reductions at the top of the agenda.[15] It remains to be seen how Bush responds to the reality of a world in which Japan, the newly industrialising countries, and a more economically integrated Western Europe affect America's economic power. One other underlying issue looms large, and that is the scale of America's commitments around the world. The publication in 1988 of Paul Kennedy's *The Rise and Fall of the Great Powers* appeared to agitate many American readers. But whether there will be strong domestic pressure on Bush to reduce military forces overseas is not certain. However, he may have to pay heed to a quasi-isolationist mood in the United States if it is fuelled by growing alarm over the budget deficit and the seeming ingratitude of many of America's allies.

A smooth transition

The apparent ease with which George Bush came to terms with his new responsibilities demands closer attention. Undoubtedly, part of his success derived from his decision to retain many of Reagan's closest advisers. In stressing expertise and professionalism Bush also relied on continuity. James Baker, Bush's powerful Secretary of State, was Reagan's first Chief of Staff and then Treasury Secretary; Richard Darman, the new Budget Director, was Staff Secretary to Reagan and a key aide and confidant to James Baker; Nicholas Brady, Bush's Treasury Secretary, succeeded Baker as Treasury Secretary under Reagan; Craig Fuller, Bush's Chief of Staff, was an intern in Reagan's California Governor's office and cabinet co-ordinator in Reagan's first term in the White House. By the same token Bush was careful to distance himself from ideologues, and he did not have to consider retaining Perle, Weinberger (Reagan's first Defense Secretary), or John Lehman (Reagan's first Navy Secretary), ideologues who had left office by the end of 1988. The shake-up in the Reagan Administration in 1987, a shake-up that in part was intended to put the emphasis on managerial competence, undoubtedly made the transition to Bush easier, but so too did the hesitancy of the New Right. Confounded by what many saw as Reagan's about-face on issues like abortion and gay rights, and demoralised by a series of scandals within two of the largest fundamentalist congregations, New Righters found themselves increasingly at odds with moderates who saw George Bush as a more reassuring and attractive figure than, for example, Pat Robertson.

Essentially a team player, Bush was at pains to appoint a cabinet of experienced and trusted members of staff to help him shape his agenda. The choice of Dan Quayle, a senator from Indiana, as his running mate was another indication of the importance Bush attached to loyalty, an attribute he learned to respect during eight years in Reagan's cabinet. Quayle, nevertheless, appeared to lack political clout. Throughout the 1988 campaign he was kept virtually out of sight, consigned almost exclusively to small, solidly Republican Southern and Midwestern towns. For some within the party he may have been an embarrassment, noted more for gaffes than political acumen. The vice-presidency will be an important learning process for Dan Quayle and he may yet emerge as a formidable politician. But there are no strong indications that the American public would be enthusiastic about the prospect of a Quayle presidency.

In general, Bush profited through his association with Ronald Reagan. For better or worse, Bush continued to be identified with Reagan and Reagan's peculiar success story. He had sound foundations to build on and a ground swell of public support. In the late 1970s there was a marked shift to the right in American politics. There is little sign of this dominant conservatism being undermined. In the 1986 mid-term elections, and again in 1988, the Democrats made gains, but there was no mass migration of voters away from the Republican Party and no revival of liberalism. Indeed, conservatism has been particularly evident among the young. 'Baby Boomers', the 76 million Americans born between 1946 and 1964, voted heavily for Reagan in 1980 and again in 1984. During the 1984 campaign Reagan's best receptions came on college campuses. Bush, too, capitalised on the self-contemplative mood among young Americans, many of whom associate the Democrats with the failures of the Carter years.

The Democrats

The weakness of the Democrats remains another political asset to George Bush. The Democrats have now lost five out of the last six presidential elections and face a crisis of confidence not unlike that faced by the Republicans during the 1940s. The reasons for this decline are not difficult to find. Chief among them is the race issue. During the 1960s the party nailed its flag to the mast of civil rights. Johnson's Civil Rights Act of 1964, together with the Voting Rights Act of 1965, caused the greatest upheaval in American race relations since the Civil War. Hailed as a legislative triumph, Johnson's reforms nevertheless lost the Democrats vital support among Southern whites. The emergence of a strong Republican Party in the South was the direct result.[16]

But it was not only Southern whites who drifted away. The Democrats' support of affirmative action, preferential treatment for blacks in filling jobs and meeting quotas in higher education, and their vigorous enforcement of court-ordered school busing led to a growing perception that they were 'soft' on race. As the political tide turned and more and more middle-class whites began to question the wisdom of an open-ended commitment to the social advance of blacks, so the fortunes of the Democrats waned. No Democratic presidential candidate since Lyndon Johnson has captured a majority of white voters, while union voters, Catholics and, significantly, Jews have deserted the party in increasing numbers.[17]

The Democrats were seen as being 'soft' on two other important issues, namely, crime and national defence. Admirable as it may have been, the party's opposition to measures like the death penalty was unpopular among many voters, black and white. One in sixteen urban Americans has been a victim of crime, often of a violent nature. Dukakis's handling of the death penalty issue in televised debate with Bush during the 1988 campaign showed little sensitivity to the plight of these victims and tended to confirm an impression that Democrats were over-concerned with the rights of criminals. For many, the party's attitude towards national security was even less reassuring. Haunted by the Vietnam experience, Democrats did little to dispel the image that they are weak on defence. Dukakis's support for a nuclear freeze, and his attempt to stop the Massachusetts National Guard from going on a training mission in Central America, severely damaged his credibility as a realistic choice for president, as did his refusal to admit that Reagan's defence spending may have played a part, however, small, in bringing the Soviets to the negotiating table. Not surprisingly, a strident George Bush had little difficulty in exposing Dukakis's position on defence as being dangerously naive.[18]

The vulnerability of the Democrats' position was exposed in 1984 when Walter Mondale ran a race tailored to meet the demands of special interests (unions, women and blacks). Mondale's crushing defeat caused the Democrats to revise their outlook. Eager to avoid a repeat of 1984, Michael Dukakis concentrated his campaign on his competence as a manager and in doing so distanced himself from the party's most charismatic and progressive figure, Jesse Jackson. Jackson's strong showing in the 1988 Democratic primaries demonstrated not only the strength of the black vote within the party, but his ability to attract white voters as well. Jackson won three times as many white votes in

1988 as he had in 1984. But Jackson's very success was his undoing. As the race narrowed down to two candidates, one of them black, many whites deserted Jackson for Dukakis. Subsequently, to add insult to injury, Jackson was not invited to campaign for Dukakis in the contest with George Bush, nor were his ideas and policies incorporated into the Democratic platform.

Lacking appeal and vitality, and seemingly unwilling to harness the energies released by Jackson, Dukakis ran a poor race against George Bush. For the Democrats, the result was a depressing slump in the polls that was only halted when, belatedly, Dukakis went back to reiterating liberal policies. Another defeat left the Democrats in dire need of an overhaul of outdated policies and in search of a way to convince some of the party's best political leaders that it would be worth running for president. Bill Bradley and Mario Cuomo, to name but two, both refused to run in 1988, leaving the field open to a rather stolid candidate who was simply not up to the task of fighting a sometimes tough and underhand campaign. The Democrats will need a far more charismatic figure at their head if they are to have any chance of making a better showing in 1992.

And yet the Democrats' poor results at the national level were countered by successes at the state level where party labels are less important. Much to the Republicans' dismay, the 1988 election marked the first time since 1960 that the party winning the presidential race lost ground in Congress. Sizeable Democratic majorities in both the Senate and the House of Representatives hinted at the possibility of a difficult time ahead for the new President. Bush got off to an awkward start when the Senate Armed Services Committee, led by Sam Nunn, refused to confirm John Tower's appointment as Defense Secretary. But this victory began to rebound when leading congressional Democrats were caught up in allegations of improprieties. The dramatic resignation of Speaker Jim Wright in May 1989, accused among other things of improperly accepting $145,000 and the use of a condominium from a Texas oil magnate, brought consternation in Democratic ranks and enabled the Republicans to recover. With the possibility of more investigations on the way, Democrats were suddenly cowed and on the defensive. George Bush, meanwhile, managed to emerge unscathed from the Irangate affair, which for a time seemed about to engulf him, and went on to make a series of firm and well-timed policy announcements.

Conclusion – caution and pragmatism

The transition from Reagan to Bush was remarkably smooth. Aided by a strong staff and Democratic weaknesses, Bush was able to ease himself into the presidential office at his own pace. What at first looked like drift and indecision was really only a matter of the new President taking his time. By mid-1989 a distinctive style was emerging. Where Reagan was often too easily managed by his advisers, Bush was quick to insist on extensive consultations, be it with industrialists, environmentalists, or congressional leaders. Above all, the new President succeeded in letting Americans know that he was active and engaged. Bush also began to show skill in dealing with the media. His impromptu question-and-answer sessions came as a welcome change after the stage-managed Reagan press conferences, and his warmth and gregariousness began to shine through. Perhaps just as important, by mid-1989 there was a modest improvement in the public's general perception of Dan Quayle.

Nevertheless, Bush's early successes should not blind us to the obstacles facing his administration. The budget deficit may yet prove an impossible burden to carry, particularly once Democrats in Congress have regained their confidence; and any prospect of an increase in unemployment and inflation are sure to dent confidence in the President's residual commitment to Reagan's economic policies. Having given his support to a proposed constitutional amendment to ban abortion, Bush will also find his administration under increasing pressure from the Republican right wing. In foreign affairs, Bush's greatest task will be to give resonance and meaning to the *rapprochement* with Moscow and set about dealing with Gorbachev's arms control pronouncements, while at the same time recognising the limits to America's power. The new President will bring to all of these problems a determined and a professional outlook. But his resolve is yet to be tested, and there must be a question mark over his ability in the event of a major crisis to fill the vacuum left by Reagan.

Looking back, we can now see that the Reagan years were a necessary stage in America's national recovery. After the gloom and despondency of the 1970s Reagan gave Americans a sense of pride in themselves that they had not possessed since the halcyon days of John F. Kennedy. But even before he departed office there were signs that his political competence was waning. Seemingly unable or unwilling to capitalise on his immense popularity, Reagan faltered badly during the Irangate affair, and so for a time did his public image. Imperceptibly, the national mood shifted once again. More confident in their ability to control their own destiny, towards the late 1980s Americans began to re-evaluate the accumulated problems confronting their society. In George Bush they may have found what they wanted: a professional manager. Already the new broom is having an effect. Bush's America will be a more caring America but like the new President himself it will also be an essentially cautious, moderate and pragmatic America.

Notes

1 Sidney Ratner, James H. Soltow and Richard Sylla, *The Evolution of the American Economy: Growth, Welfare and Decision Making*, New York, Basic Books, 1979, pp. 524–8; Manuel Castells, *The Economic Crisis and American Society*, Oxford, Basil Blackwell, 1980, ch. 2.

2 By far the most perceptive analysis of the Reagan phenomenon is Gary Wills's *Reagan's America*, New York, Doubleday, 1987. See also Robert Dallek, *Ronald Reagan: the Politics of Symbolism*, Cambridge, Mass., Harvard University Press, 1984.

3 Richard A. Viguerie, *The New Right: We're Ready to Lead*, Falls Church, Va., Viguerie, 1981; Phyllis Schlafly, *The Power of the Positive Woman*, New York, Harcourt Brace Jovanovich, 1982.

4 Allan Crawford, *Thunder on the Right: the 'New Right' and the Politics of Resentment*, New York, Pantheon, 1980, pp. 10–11, 37; Dallek, *Ronald Reagan*, pp. 135–42.

5 *Newsweek*, 7 March 1988, pp. 18–43; *Sunday Times*, 15 January 1989.

6 Stanley Hoffmann has identified the Reagan Administration's tendency towards unilateralism in 'Semidetached politics', *New York Review of Books*, XXXI, 8 November 1984, pp. 34–6.

7 Cited in *Washington Post*, 27 February 1987, p. A21.

8 Gary Wills, 'The ultimate loyalist', *Time*, 22 August 1988, pp. 10–13.

9 Ibid. See also *The Times*, 6 and 10 November 1984; *Sunday Times*, 18 October 1987.

10 *Time*, 22 August 1988, p. 14.

11 *Time*, 30 January 1989, p. 15 (my italics).

12 *Time*, 21 November 1988, p. 17 and 20 February 1989, pp. 28–30.

13 *Independent*, 11 August 1989.

14 *Guardian*, 28 June 1989.

15 McGeorge Bundy, 'The emperor's clothes', *New York Review of Books*, XXXVI, 20 July 1989, pp. 3–7.

16 For Southern politics see Earl Black and Merle Black, *Politics and Society in the South*, Cambridge, Mass., Harvard University Press, 1987.

17 Joseph A. Califano, Jr., 'Tough talk for Democrats', *New York Times Magazine*, 8 January 1989, pp. 28–9, 38, 43.

18 Ibid.

The legacy of Reaganomics

One of the most distinctive aspects of US domestic policy since Reagan was first elected in November 1980 has come to be known as 'Reaganomics'. In a climate of widely perceived relative American decline, Reagan embarked on an economic experiment which was probably as significant as the New Deal of the 1930s. Rejecting traditional Keynesian ideas and promising price stability, Reagan proposed massive tax cuts, reduction in the growth of federal spending, deregulation of industry, and strict control over the money supply. These remedies, Reagan argued, would allow the nation to recover from the economic malaise of the 1970s. They would provide greater incentives for people to work, save and invest productively, and unleash the energies of 'free enterprise America'. Four years later, Reagan was re-elected by a huge margin, having presided over his country's strongest and longest economic recovery since 1950. More than 17 million new jobs were created between 1982 and 1988 and the US achieved its lowest unemployment rate since 1974.

This chapter outlines the circumstances of Reagan's election, examines the nature and impact of his economic policies, and considers the consequences for the Bush Administration.

The circumstances of Reagan's election

In 1980 the American economy was actually contracting after years of sluggish growth.[1] The so-called 'misery index' (the inflation rate plus the unemployment rate) was at a near-record post-war level: inflation was over 10 per cent and unemployment over 7 per cent. Hardly surprisingly, economic issues dominated the 1980 presidential election campaign and contributed to Reagan's resounding victory over incumbent Democratic President Jimmy Carter. At a time when real per capita income was declining, Reagan asked the American electorate: 'Are you better off than you were four years ago?' The answer of at least 26 per cent of those entitled to vote in 1980 was emphatically negative, and it was clear that they blamed Carter.[2]

Apart from the immediate economic circumstances of the election, it is clear in retrospect that Reagan benefited from propitious political conditions bound up with the decline of a Keynesian consensus. The consensus, based on Keynesian assumptions that economic equilibrium could be achieved at any level of employment, and that fiscal and monetary powers could be used to regulate overall economic demand, was established in the 1960s. Responding to the stimulative effects of Kennedy–Johnson tax reductions, and against the background of American hegemony in international trade and finance, superior technology, and stable commodity prices, the American economy experienced its longest recorded period of peacetime expansion. A pervasive and effusive optimism developed which was based on an almost naïve, technocratic faith in the ability of government, manned by the 'best and the brightest', to remedy permanently more or less all economic, social and political problems.

This optimism, and the development of what we can call America's full-employment welfare state, soon gave way to increasing pessimism and uncertainty. By the early 1970s, three political problems had become evident, preparing the ground for a shift away from Keynesianism.

First was the decreasing ability of government to satisfy heightened popular expectations. Stimulated by policy makers' optimism that most problems were susceptible to governmental solutions, new political groupings – blacks and other racial minorities, women, the poor, the young and the elderly, environmentalists and consumers – became increasingly active. The upshot was an increase in political demands which, as Americans subsequently discovered, 'big government' could not satisfy.

Second, as a consequence of this expansion of political activity, the size, cost and functions of the federal government increased. Public spending – particularly on income maintenance programmes, job creation and training, housing and community development, natural resources, industry, education, health and social services – rose substantially between 1960 and 1980, from 7 to 15 per cent of GNP. Such spending continued to rise, moreover, while the economy began to stagflate. The number of government agencies and the regulatory and redistributive functions of the federal government also expanded considerably.

Third, the New Deal electoral coalition – based on the Democratic Party, the labour unions, some farmers, the big city political machines of the North and East, and some portions of big business – weakened significantly by the late 1960s. Business support, which had been courted so assiduously by Kennedy and Johnson, had begun to wane. Business (and to a lesser extent labour), complained increasingly about social regulatory policies (e.g. environmental and consumer protection, health, safety and civil rights legislation) introduced in response to the demands of the new social movements. Following real wage growth in the late 1960s and early 1970s, labour unions also found their heightened income expectations increasingly subject to restrictive wage and price controls, particularly during the Nixon–Carter years. As early as 1968, mounting public concern about 'big government' was an important theme in George Wallace's third party movement and in Richard Nixon's appeal to the 'silent majority' of mainstream non-activists.

Each of these problems became more pressing during the 1970s in the context of a declining economy unable to deliver high employment and low inflation, and unresponsive to traditional Keynesian demand management solutions.

Reagan's economic programme

During his election campaign, Reagan exploited the declining legitimacy of the full-employment welfare state and promised to end what he called 'big government's stifling of initiative'. In his Inaugural Address in January 1981, he declared: 'It will be my intention to curb the size and influence of the federal establishment ... It is not my intention to do away with government. It is rather to make it work – work with us – not over us; to stand by our side, not ride our back. Government can and must provide opportunity, not smother it.'

Rejecting both Keynesianism and the traditionally conservative routes of tight credit and balanced budgets, the Reagan Administration launched its economic programme with two politically convenient (and partly contradictory) theories that had hitherto been on the periphery of conservative thinking. Both theories espoused the free market and descended from the ideas of the Chicago economist, Milton

Friedman.[3] One was a new form of monetarism which emphasised the importance of rational expectations; the other was supply-side economics.

Indeed it should be noted that, as in the New Deal of the 1930s, there was never any coherent body of economic thought called 'Reaganomics'. The ideas which influenced the new Administration, even in the early 1980s, derived from a number of different (often conflicting) doctrines, with proponents of each stressing diverse objectives and exerting only partial influence on the overall direction of policy. What united them, however, was a celebration of free market principles and a commitment to reduce government 'interference' in their operation.

Drawing on Friedman's ideas, monetarists within the Administration interpreted the staglation of the 1970s as the direct result of misguided Keynesian attempts to manipulate aggregate demand through periodic changes in monetary and fiscal policy. According to the rational expectations theory − the particular brand of monetarism which they endorsed − inflationary expectations of workers and business people would be quickly reduced once government or the monetary authorities gave advance notice of their intention not to expand the money supply for bailing out companies or providing jobs. In this way, so it was argued, inflation could be reduced without a severe effect on unemployment.[4]

When Reagan took office in 1981, the Federal Reserve Board under Chairman Paul Volcker (a Carter appointee) was already pursuing a restrictive monetary policy. Reagan immediately endorsed this, but demanded that the growth rates of money and credit be steadily reduced to half those of 1980 by 1986.[5]

When combined with even more restrictive growth rates in other major economies, real interest rates in the United States rose to their highest levels since the Second World War. The high interest rate policy was not relaxed and, in worsening international conditions, the economy moved into sharp recession in 1981.

The onset of the 1981−2 recession (and lower world commodity prices) caused inflation to fall dramatically − from 12.4 per cent in 1980 to 1.9 per cent in 1986. However, the social and economic costs of contraction were enormous. Between July 1981 and January 1983, unemployment rose to 10.8 per cent of the work-force (the highest since the 1930s); workers were denied billions of dollars as a consequence of shorter hours or lower wages; and production worth about

$650 billion was permanently lost.[6] Borrowing costs were forced up, thus discouraging business investment. The dollar became so over-valued, as mobile international capital flowed in and US exports grew more expensive, that American industry – particularly motor vehicles and steel – was subjected to even more intense foreign competition.

Largely due to the abandonment of the monetarist experiment in October 1982 and the largest real monetary expansion since the Second World War, the economy recovered in 1983–4, though interest rates remained high. Yet inflation did not rise significantly, and by the time Reagan left office it was no higher than 4 per cent – low by inter-national standards.

The second theory underpinning Reagan's early economic pro-gramme was supply-side economics. 'Supply-siders' made four important and (in the context of 1970s stagflation) increasingly plausible arguments.[7] First, they said that rising tax rates discouraged and distorted work effort and market patterns of saving and investment. Second, cuts in marginal tax rates (i.e. rates actually paid after allowances) would lead to increased investment and employment, although they might lead to a budget deficit. This would be more effective in producing jobs than government spending, since in the long run increased output would raise tax receipts. Third, it was argued that the whole paraphernalia of government regulation, particularly social regulation, was a disincentive to production and employment since it increased firms' costs. Fourth, basic welfare benefits and income maintenance programmes were disincentives to work effort. Implemen-tation of these policies between 1981 and 1988 is discussed in the next three sections.

Federal spending

The first Reagan Administration proposed to reduce and reorder federal spending and taxation so as to balance the national budget by 1984.[8] Reagan's new spending priorities involved reducing social programmes, business subsidies and aid to state and local governments, whilst drastically increasing military expenditure from 5.5 to 8 per cent of GNP. In his first budget of Fiscal Year (FY) 1982, the Director of the Office of Management and Budget (OMB), David Stockman, proposed $7.2 billion more for the military and $41.4 billion less for the civilian sector. Under the Omnibus Budget Reconciliation Act of July 1981, Reagan received more or less all he wanted. Virtually all military requests were granted and cuts of $35 billion for FY 1982 fell primarily on federal grants-in-aid to state and local government for education, employment, training, health, income-assistance and social services. Cuts totalling $130.6 billion were projected for FYs 1982–4. Even Reagan's opponents conceded the magnitude of his victory and the shift in budgetary policy it signified. The Democrat Chairman of the House Budget Committee, James Jones (Oklahoma), called it 'clearly the most monumental and historic turnaround in fiscal policy that has ever occurred'.[9]

Although as a candidate, Reagan had made no mention of substantial spending cuts in his 1980 electioneering, the scale of the Republican victory in congressional elections in the South and West persuaded many Democrats to support his initial programme. The packaging of the Administration's spending proposals into one bill, the speed and skill of Reagan's budget team, and the President's appeals for popular support over the head of Congress all contributed to a stunning congressional victory.

It was, however, Reagan's greatest budgetary success in eight years as President. Subsequently Congress agreed to much more modest spending reductions, though Reagan continued to propose substantial new cuts and changes to the structure of domestic programmes. Even by late 1981, Congress denied Reagan further domestic cuts and tried to curtail increases in military expenditure. With an ever-increasing budget deficit hanging over negotiations (see Fig. 4.1), the remaining seven years of Reagan's presidency were characterised by bitter confrontations with Congress. His administration consistently proposed lower levels of spending on domestic programmes than were actually enacted.

In the political stalemate, Reagan blamed the deficit on Congress, especially the Democrat-controlled House of Representatives, which he said refused to cut back 'unnecessary' programmes. Democrats countered by accusing Reagan of inducing the deficit through 'excessive' tax cuts and 'wasteful' military spending at the expense of the elderly, the farmers and the disadvantaged. Democrats, however, were extremely reluctant to propose tax increases or oppose military increases lest they be labelled the 'tax and spend' or 'weak on defense' party. Indeed party divisions were so intense that they were typically resolved by Congress approving huge, last-minute appropriation bills. When agreement could not be reached, the federal government ran out of money. Then, employees were laid off until a continuing budget resolution could be passed.

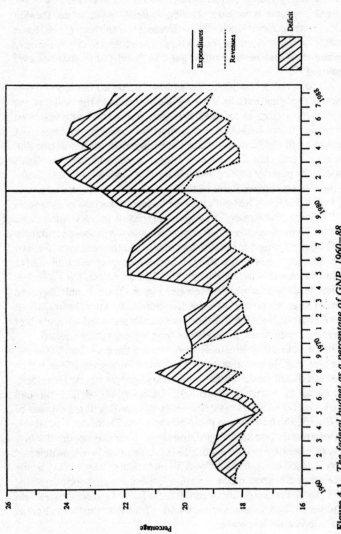

Figure 4.1 *The federal budget as a percentage of GNP, 1960–88.*
Source: *The Economic Report of the President, 1989,* Washington DC, USGPO, 1989, Table B-76.

One important result was that the overall level of federal spending as a percentage of GNP remained more or less the same in 1988 as in 1981, though it rose between 1982 and 1986. This was somewhat disappointing to Reagan, as he could only stabilise spending after allowing it to increase. As William Niskanen, a former member of Reagan's Council of Economic Advisers, complained ruefully: 'The most conservative President since the 1920s, a Republican Senate, and the energies of a remarkable budget director [Stockman] were not sufficient to change this pattern.'[10]

Yet while Reagan failed to reduce real spending, he achieved considerable success in reordering budget priorities. The military slice of the cake, especially procurement, grew, but not to the 8 per cent of GNP promised. Congress finally reined in military expenditure after FY 1983, and for the first time in many years actually reduced the budgetary authority for defence in FY 1986. This did not, however, prevent Reagan from endorsing a massive $30 billion increase in the Defense Department's FY 1987 budget, a proposal which had virtually no support elsewhere in the Administration or Congress.

While the military grew fat, civilian spending dropped (see Fig. 4.2). Moreover, despite Reagan's promise that the 'truly needy' would be protected, welfare or 'safety net' programmes were cut.[11] Additional unemployment insurance benefits, linked to national rates, were eliminated. Eligibility requirements and benefits for basic welfare such as Aid to Families with Dependent Children (AFDC), Medicaid and food stamps, were further restricted. Subsidies for school lunches and rents to low-income families were reduced. Again, as Figure 4.2 shows, Reagan was only able to reduce these programmes marginally, not eliminate them altogether. In fact most 'safety net' programmes constituted uncontrollable entitlements which required legislation to amend them. So in the 1981–2 recession these expenditures rose sharply. Reagan's attempt in 1982 to transfer fiscal responsibility for welfare from the federal government to the states was also aborted. When Congress passed the Gramm–Rudman–Hollings Deficit Reduction Act in 1985, it specifically exempted most 'safety net' programmes from the automatic cuts required by the legislation.

With the notable exception of programmes for the elderly,[12] where spending actually increased, other domestic social programmes – notably education, employment training, housing credit, and health – were cut or eliminated. As a result, something like two-thirds of the budget cuts implemented between 1980 and 1988 occurred in social

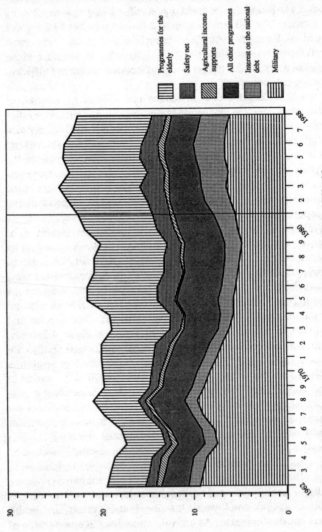

Figure 4.2 *Federal government expenditures as a percentage of GNP, 1962–88.*
Source: *The Budget of the United States, Fiscal Year 1989,* Washington DC, USGPO, 1989, Tables 3.1, 3.3.

Programmes for the
elderly

Safety net

Agricultural income
supports

All other programmes

Interest on the national
debt

Military

spending. The remaining third came from reductions in subsidies for business (but not agriculture), environmental protection, community and regional development, transportation and highways, energy, and especially grants to state and local government (see Fig. 4.3).

Taxation

The Administration also sponsored important changes in taxation policy. These were guided by rather speculative economic and political calculations to say the least. The Administration's 'supply-siders' believed that by cutting taxes and increasing investment incentives they would achieve rapid economic growth which would lead to an increase in revenues and a balanced budget. They also gambled that by cutting taxes first — and subsequently by refusing to raise them — the Administration could pressure Congress into reducing spending, thus averting a revenue gap.

By far the most important tax changes were embodied in the Economic Recovery Tax Act of 1981 (ERTA). In one blow Congress lopped $162 billion off taxes at Reagan's request — the largest tax cut in American history. Most importantly, personal taxation was cut by 23 per cent with the highest marginal rate being reduced from 70 to 50 per cent and capital gains tax cut from 28 to 20 per cent. Personal tax brackets were also index-linked to ensure the permanence of the reductions so that any subsequent tax increase had to be explicitly legislated by Congress while revenue collectors were deprived of 'bracket creep' whereby, without a legislative adjustment, a person's tax bill rises with inflation. Major reductions in business taxation were also enacted, primarily by allowing greater accelerated depreciation of buildings, vehicles, plant and machinery.

The overall effect of ERTA was to redistribute wealth and income towards business and the well-off. Indeed, the new accelerated cost recovery system for business was so generous that it was effectively a subsidy rather than a tax. The value of allowable deductions and credits actually exceeded the tax liability of the income generated by the investment equipment.[13] Thus, as federal spending continued to rise unchecked in 1982, Congress repealed further investment incentives planned for 1985–6. There was also a massive relative transfer of income because of the universal nature of the 1981 cuts in personal taxation whereby the tax liabilities of all income groups were reduced by the same percentage. By 1984, the bottom 40 per cent of families

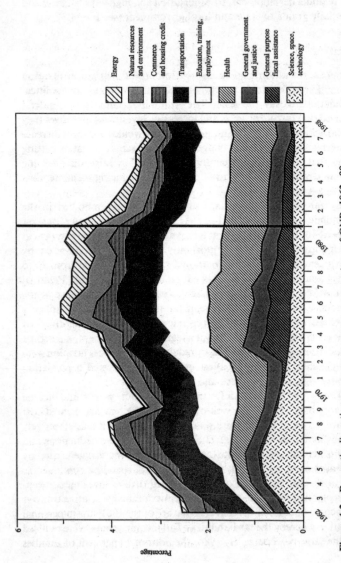

Figure 4.3 *Domestic discretionary programmes as a percentage of GNP, 1962–88.*
Source: *The Budget of the United States, Fiscal Year 1989*, Washington DC, USGPO, 1989, Table 3.3.

Energy

Natural resources and environment

Commerce and housing credit

Transportation

Education, training, employment

Health

General government and justice

General purpose fiscal assistance

Science, space, technology

were paying a proportionately larger share of their income in taxes – particularly the poorest families on whom most of the increased burden fell – while the top 60 per cent were paying proportionately less.[14]

In the wake of fierce criticism on grounds of unfairness, Reagan adopted a more populist taxation strategy which was subsequently reflected in the Tax Reform Act of 1986 (TRA). Seeking to reverse many of the disparities in ERTA, the TRA eliminated many tax allowances, loopholes and shelters for business while completely removing some 4.3 million low-income families out of taxation altogether. In many respects, of course, the changes were dictated by the rising deficit and by the new political situation in Congress. Following the 1986 congressional elections, the Democrats controlled the Senate and formed a more cohesive majority in the House.

Yet, after ERTA and TRA, the changes to levels of taxation revenue were minimal. After eight years in office the tax burden under Reagan (i.e. federal revenues as a percentage of GNP) remained more or less at the same level, at 19 per cent, as in the 1960s and 1970s. The 1981 cuts had reduced this to 18 per cent by 1983. But after 1984 the tax share of GNP increased, partly as a result of rises in indirect personal taxation (e.g. social security and excise taxes).

Although Reagan reordered budgetary priorities, his strategy of 'starving' the budget through tax cuts was only partially successful, primarily because he insisted on such large increases in military spending and found himself unable to control domestic spending.[15] The net result was a sharply rising budget deficit – up from $60 billion in Carter's last year to $210 billion in FY 1986, before falling to $155 billion in 1988. A large slice of the budget (and GNP) was spent on financing the deficit as government borrowing more than doubled and the high-interest policy of the Federal Reserve Board made borrowing expensive (see Fig. 4.2).

Deregulation

A third distinctive feature of Reagan's economic policies was his endorsement of deregulation. As with budgetary policy, however, his attempts in particular areas to dismantle government regulation were much less successful than he claimed.

Since many changes in regulatory policy could be implemented without new legislation (which majority Democrats in the House were sure to oppose), Reagan pursued a vigorous programme of 'administrative deregulation'. Within a month of assuming office, he moved to bring the fifty-five independent regulatory agencies under the supervision and control of the Office of Information and Regulatory Affairs within the OMB. Under an Executive Order of February 1981, all major regulatory agency proposals were to be subjected to cost–benefit analysis. The primary target was the mass of social regulations implemented in the 1970s.

Under pressure from the OMB, expenditure and personnel in the regulatory agencies were severely reduced. Between 1980 and 1982, for example, the Environmental Protection Agency's budget for its air and water quality, hazardous waste, and toxic substance programmes (which represented most of the EPA's regulatory activities) was reduced by almost two-thirds; and between 1981 and 1984, the number of full-time employees in these four major programmes fell by 30 per cent. Regulatory enforcement standards were also relaxed and legal actions against previous violators of regulations were dismissed. Officials were appointed to these agencies who were sympathetic to industry's demands for regulatory 'relief'. Subsequently, a number of these administrative actions and policies were successfully challenged in the courts, while others were overturned in Congress – fuelled by scandal at the Environmental Protection Agency and by concern over the directing role of the Office of Information and Regulatory Affairs.

In regulatory policy, as in the battles over spending and taxation, Reagan obtained less than he wanted. The regulatory movement was only slowed, not reversed, despite a decline in the promulgation of new regulations.[16] Yet, presidential control over regulatory policies reached unprecedented levels.

In one economic policy area, moreover, there was a decisive shift towards greater regulation for the first time since the Second World War. Despite Reagan's frequent espousal of free trade and competition, the share of US manufacturing protected by non-tariff trade barriers increased sharply from 20 to 30 per cent. Trade protection was applied particularly to cars and motor cycles, steel, semiconductors, lumber and textiles.

The nature of the Reagan programme

The main aim of Reagan's policies was higher economic growth. This aim was to be achieved through increased private investment and lower inflation, rather than through increased federal government intervention. Yet, while he repudiated the policies and political arrangements of Keynesian welfarism and celebrated the 'free' market, Reagan (like Thatcher in the UK) did not anticipate a weak role for the state or complete reliance on the 'free' market in matters of economic policy. In the Reagan view, the state (particularly the federal government) was required to assume responsibility for price stability by restraining monetary growth. It must also take responsibility for shifting economic and social priorities in the market, by redistributing income towards private capital and by deregulating industry. Through this 'strong state' strategy legitimated by free-market ideology and populist conservative rhetoric, the Administration claimed that all Americans would benefit from the increased income and employment opportunities derived from renewed economic growth.

The package of programmes called 'Reaganomics', however, contained a number of inconsistencies which led subsequently to policy changes. The most obvious inconsistency, particularly in the early years, derived from tension between monetarist and supply-side policies. Monetarists like Milton Friedman and Beryl Sprinkel believed that the key to high employment and economic growth was price stability through restrictive monetary growth. But 'supply-siders' like Paul Craig Roberts did not accept that government can or should maintain strict control over the money supply. Nor was it the view of traditional fiscal conservatives like Stockman and Martin Feldstein, who applauded domestic spending cuts and tax changes but voiced growing concern over the rising budget deficit and the absence of controls over military spending.[17] An important consequence of the conflict between monetarists and 'supply-siders' in 1981–2 was that the expansionary impact of the tax cuts (and the increases in military and social spending) was dampened by the deflationary effect of the Fed's tight monetary policy which was designed to reduce inflation but in the process made business credit scarce and expensive. Indeed, in these early years the dollar became so grossly overvalued that American industry faced foreign competitors enjoying significant price advantages in the short term, and extra margins in the longer term with which to penetrate US markets, increase investment in research and development, and pose future challenges to US economic and technological leadership.

A second inconsistency concerned the budget deficit. In 1981, monetarists and 'supply-siders' argued from rather different theoretical bases that a large budget deficit would result from the proposed tax cuts. Monetarists believed, however, that if adequate tax and social spending cuts were achieved, the budget could be balanced by 1984. In contrast, 'supply-siders' expected the deficit to rise in the short term but were not overly concerned because they expected higher economic growth to produce additional tax revenues which would offset at least part of the deficit while increased savings rates would help finance it. After just nine months, the 'supply-siders' began losing the argument as the budget deficit continued to grow and interest rates remained high. Contrary to their expectations of high domestic savings, the deficit was financed by Japanese, European and Middle Eastern money.

With growing opposition from Congress, the Federal Reserve, Wall Street, and elements within the Administration (notably Stockman), the supply-side tax cuts were delayed and compromised as spending continued to rise. Moreover, the Administration did not have the votes to challenge the Democrats in the House after the budget victories of 1981. So from late 1982 onwards, the Administration pursued a *mélange* of sometimes contradictory policies. They included considerable relaxation of monetary policy; intervention in the exchange markets to push the dollar down; and greater emphasis on reducing the budget deficit through spending cuts (including cuts in military procurement) and tax increases. Eventually, Congress approved the Gramm–Rudman–Hollings Deficit Reduction Act in 1985. Despite its failures, some of which are discussed below, it served the purpose of focusing the collective minds of the Administration and Congress on the deficit and, in a rather loose way, defined the parameters of subsequent budgetary policy.

Explaining America's economic 'recovery'

Regardless of the deep-seated tensions within these policies, the Reagan Administrations did what the Thatcher Governments in Britain have not done – create millions of new jobs. By the time Reagan left office, the seasonally adjusted level of registered unemployment in the United States had fallen from over 12 million or 10.8 per cent of the civilian population in December 1982 to 6.7 million or 5.4 per cent in January 1989. Following the recession of 1981–2, the US economy experienced the longest sustained economic recovery since the Great Depression of the 1930s and by early 1989 had exceeded any post-war recovery by three years. The mean compound growth rate between 1981 and 1988 was 2.9 per cent – just above the level of the 1970s. Hourly earnings and corporate profits also increased after 1982 without setting off hyperinflation. Inflation was just 4.8 per cent in the second half of 1988.

Reagan's explanation for the recovery was typically populist: 'Hard work and risk-taking has given birth to an American Renaissance. Born in the safe harbor of freedom, economic growth gathered force, and rolled out in a rising tide that has reached distant shores.' A more objective verdict would conclude that the economy recovered as a result of the boost in demand; Reagan's America effectively spent its way out of recession. The over-marketed supply-side policies were a sort of 'back-door' Keynesianism. Against his best intentions, Reagan, like Kennedy and Johnson, had boosted economic demand primarily through tax cuts, large budget deficits and more relaxed monetary policy. These were standard Keynesian macro-economic tools. Indeed, who but the boldest Keynesians would accumulate a $200 billion budget deficit as a cure for 11 per cent unemployment? This much seems clear. Less certain, however, are whether Reagan's solutions were socially just and whether they halted America's long-term economic decline. Doubts are fuelled considerably in the light of the consequences of Reaganomics.

The consequences of Reaganomics

Undoubtedly, Reagan's economic policies incurred extremely high social costs, further encouraging the emergence of a dual or 'split-level' economy in the United States. During his presidency, poverty and inequality increased substantially. Even in 1988, after six years of economic growth, about 32 million Americans, or 14 per cent of the population, were living in poverty, thus reverting to the levels of the early 1960s (before President Johnson's Great Society legislation). Reagan's spending and tax policies, together with higher unemployment and greater inequality, discriminated explicitly against the less well-off, especially the working poor, in favour of the already well-off – a point openly conceded by Stockman.[18] According to most measures, the middle class did little better than maintain its position despite the 23 per cent cut in taxes. Salaries of chief executives, however, increased by some 40 per cent between 1980 and 1984, further concentrating wealth amongst the top 2 per cent of better-off families. At the other end of the social scale, and as a result of cuts in unemployment insurance coverage and increases in structural unemployment, over 70 per cent of the unemployed (5.7 million people) were not receiving unemployment benefits by September 1984 (although in cases of near destitution, and depending on state regulations, they remained eligible for food stamps, Medicaid, AFDC and other benefits). The impact of Reaganomics was especially severe on minorities and households with women as heads.[19]

Geographical and sectoral disparities within the economy also sharpened significantly. The reordered tax and spending priorities, exchange rate increases, and the encouragement given to the increased automation, centralisation and rationalisation of American business, affected states and industrial sectors differentially. Those regions which did well economically in the 1980s were in the so-called 'Sunbelt' of the West, the South-West and South-East, as well as New England where newer (especially high-tech) industries were located. At least some of the growth in these areas was directly attributable to net changes in regional and state flows of federal outlays resulting from Reagan's tax and spending policies.[20] In fiscal year 1982, for example, the Sunbelt states received almost two-thirds of the total net flow of federal money. Of this California and Texas accrued half. Amongst the seven states which shared half of all new prime military contracts in 1982, only one had unemployment levels above the national average. Areas which did less well were the Midwest and North-West where staple industries were older, and the South Central states, particularly Texas and Louisiana, which suffered badly from the sharp drop in oil and gas prices after 1986. Even after six years of economic recovery and a national unemployment rate just above 5 per cent in mid-1989, wide regional disparities persisted.[21]

Reaganomics also caused severe fiscal problems. By any standard, the budget deficits were monumental – an increase from $79 billion in 1981 (2.6 per cent of GNP) to $208 billion in 1983 (6.3 per cent of GNP) before falling to $155 billion (3.2 per cent of GNP) in 1988. Apart from their sheer size, they seem to have become a permanent feature of the US political economy. According to the most reliable estimates, from the Congressional Budget Office, there will remain a budget deficit as large as $121 billion in 1993, notwithstanding the Gramm–Rudman–Hollings Act and various accounting tricks endorsed by the Administration and Congress. Structural deficits of this magnitude so alter the country's fiscal system, by increasing the likelihood that economic recoveries will not generate sufficient revenue quickly enough to eliminate past deficits, that there must be grave doubts as to whether President Bush will be able to spend his way out of future recessions, particularly since personal income taxes are indexed for inflation.

Large budget deficits also mean that for every year in the foreseeable future, the federal government has to borrow at higher and higher costs from foreign investors and domestic savers. Between 1981 and 1988, the cost of servicing the cumulative debt for 1986–8 of almost $800 billion increased from 2.3 per cent of GNP to 3.1 per cent. This scale of government borrowing not only costs taxpayers dearly, it also soaks up their savings which then cannot be invested to generate future economic growth. Since the 1960s, net savings in the United States (private savings minus government borrowing) have fallen sharply from a mean of 7.5 per cent of GNP in the 1960s, to 6.9 per cent in the 1970s, and to 2.8 per cent in the 1980s.[22] Indeed, as Reagan declared in 1981: 'You and I as individuals can, by borrowing, live beyond our means, but only for a limited period of time. Why should we think that collectively, as a nation, we are not bound by that same limitation?' The cost of ignoring his own advice, it seems, will be lower growth in either private consumption or government services.

Large deficits and high interest rates also sucked in considerable foreign investment, notably from the Japanese and Europeans. Larger and larger parts of US industry were becoming owned by non-Americans. By 1986, the accumulation of foreign liabilities made the United States the world's largest debtor country. In 1980, America's net nominal investment position had been a $95 billion surplus; by 1987, the US was $379 billion in deficit. While foreign investment clearly helped meet the strong demand for investment funds in the US, and thus created job opportunities and stimulated economic growth, the shift to debtor status also increased interest payments on foreign investment flowing abroad. Probably more than any other indicator, this signifies the relative decline of American economic hegemony and the demise of a period when the US invested more around the world than it borrowed.

The huge increase in foreign investment under Reagan also caused the dollar to become overvalued. Reagan's unilateralist approach to international economic relations increased the value of the dollar in relation to America's major trading partners by some 50 per cent between 1980 and 1985. Consequently, US markets were flooded with cheap foreign cars, steel, textiles and high-tech imports. This brought an estimated loss of 2 million jobs in the short term and the prospect of further foreign penetration and job losses in the long term.[23] Since

US exports also became more expensive, America's share of world export markets continued to fall and the balance of trade, particularly in manufacturing, moved sharply into deficit.[24] Even after the dollar peaked in 1985, the trade deficit continued to widen to 3.5 per cent of GNP in 1987, until it fell to 2.3 per cent in 1988.

Increased competition in manufacturing from Japan, Western Europe, and newly industrialising countries, combined with greater automation, centralisation and rationalisation of production, accelerated the process of de-industrialisation in the United States. Since the 1950s, the country's basic manufacturing capacity had declined both absolutely, and in terms of its importance to the overall economy – from 30 per cent of GNP to 20 per cent in the 1980s. During the 1980s manufacturing's contribution to employment growth was also significantly less than its contribution to previous recoveries in the 1960s and 1970s. In the post-1982 recovery, the share of employment growth derived from manufacturing within the goods-producing sector was just 9 per cent compared with 23 per cent between 1961 and 1969 and 19 per cent in the 1975–80 period. By the time Reagan left office, only one in six civilian jobs was in manufacturing, compared with one in five in 1980. According to Bureau of Labor estimates, this decline is expected to continue at least until the end of the century despite the addition of many new jobs in high-tech industries and the continued growth of the services sector.[25] If the US is to balance its external trade, it will need to create another 5 million new manufacturing jobs by 1993.

A substantial part of the explanation for the further decline of manufacturing was the relatively static rate of investment as a percentage of GNP. Between 1981 and 1988, the overall rate of investment was the same (at 10.8 per cent) as it was between 1971 and 1980. It fell after 1985. Meanwhile personal consumption shot up: from 62.7 per cent of GNP in the 1960s and 1970s to 65 per cent in the 1980s (66.5 per cent in 1987–8).[26] Consequently, domestic business investment was a lower share of output in the United States than in any other major economy; less than half the share in Japan. A substantial part of the increase during the Reagan years was, moreover, financed from abroad and from military procurement. Meanwhile Americans spent a larger and larger share of output on consumer products and services. Coupled with only a modest rise in productivity (mean annual growth rates of real product per employee hour), from 0.6 per cent between 1973 and 1981 to 1.5 per cent between 1981 and 1988 compared with a 2.9 per cent rise between 1948 and 1973, this raises further doubts about the long-term competitiveness of the American economy.

The problems of social injustice, chronic budget deficits, low investment, foreign competition, a growing trade deficit, and de-industrialisation, seriously qualify the achievement of sustained economic growth and full employment since 1982. They also present significant difficulties for President Bush. How has he addressed Reagan's problematic legacy?

Bush and the legacy of Reaganomics

Although George Bush was elected on Reagan's coat-tails, the economic team in his administration is undoubtedly much less ideologically committed than Reagan's. Most are conservative Republicans, but pragmatic rather than devoted to any one set of economic doctrines; and most have had considerable experience of Washington politics, rather than the Sunbelt and the Hoover Institution. Guided by key economic figures like Richard Darman (OMB Director), Nicholas Brady (Treasury Secretary) and Michael Boskin (Chairman of the Council of Economic Advisers), it seems unlikely that Bush will pursue a grand strategy or unconventional economic ideas. He is more likely to make some minor mid-term corrections to Reagan's policies. Indeed, it is important to remember that it was Bush himself who, as a rival for the Republican Party nomination in 1980, once dismissed Reagan's policies as 'voodoo economics'. However, against this expectation of a cautious and pragmatic approach are the harsh realities of the political and economic situation. Reagan was re-elected in 1984 and Bush was elected in 1988 because the economy, for all its underlying problems, made most Americans more prosperous. Considered in this light, the temptations for Bush to continue with Reagan's 'conspiracy of make-believe' seem very compelling.

Undoubtedly, the budget deficit will remain the most pressing problem facing the new President and Congress. However, the deficit is so large and the political choices so difficult that, short of a crisis even worse than the stock-market crash of October 1987, the Administration and Congress will have little political incentive to reduce it further because the solution may be worse than the problem.

In his presidential campaign, Bush promised that he would not raise taxes. 'Read my lips', he told the electorate, 'no new taxes.' None the less, the Administration has promised to eliminate the deficit, in spite of Bush's plans to reduce capital gains tax and spend more money to achieve a 'kinder and gentler America' through greater provision for social and environmental needs. Bush's short-term budgetary plan, vaguely sketched out in his campaign, was for a 'flexible freeze', whereby spending on the military and domestic entitlement programmes would be allowed to increase with inflation but cuts would be sought in other unspecified areas.

Bush's budget for FY 1990, presented to Congress in February 1989, was also deliberately vague. Although the definition of a 'flexible freeze' was refined to include only those spending programmes which were not specifically identified as the President's priorities. Bush pointedly refused to say which programmes would be cut, hoping to leave that unenviable task to Congress. Figures produced by the Senate Budget Committee, however, showed that Bush's proposal would cut $13 billion in entitlements from Medicare and another $8 billion in discretionary domestic programmes; military spending would increase by $2 billion. As it soon became clear, the Administration aimed to achieve the $100 billion deficit target for FY 1990, as required by the Gramm—Rudman—Hollings Act, primarily through less painful revenue raising. This included extending payroll taxes for Medicare to all state and local employees not previously covered; increasing 'user fees' for certain government services; lowering capital gains tax;[27] various asset sales; and even more extensive use of creative accounting.

In April 1989, Bush successfully negotiated a much-heralded agreement with congressional leaders whereby $13.8 billion would be cut from the 1990 budget – including $4 billion from military spending and $2.7 billion from Medicare – and $14.2 billion found in revenue increases. However, like Bush's original budget proposals, the spending cuts included many accounting 'tricks' and one-off savings that will not be carried over into future years. Nearly half the $2 billion cuts in farm price-supports, for example, were to be achieved by making payments to farmers in FY 1989 rather than FY 1990; another $2 billion would be 'saved' by taking the postal service 'off-budget'. This sort of fudging, a major feature of budgeting since Gramm—Rudman—Hollings, fools no one. Neither does the trickery on the revenue side. Two-fifths of the proposed revenue 'increases' agreed between Bush and Congress included once-and-for-all proceeds from the sale of federal assets, as well as larger revenues anticipated from stronger tax enforcement. Both sides also agreed to find $5.3

billion in unspecified revenue increases without violating Bush's pledge against new taxes.

Judging from his 1990 budget, Bush was effectively emulating Reagan in gambling on substantial expansion to allow the American economy to grow out of its deficit. Although most economists, including the non-partisan Congressional Budget Office, do not accept the rosy economic forecasts on which the policy is based, the important question is whether, if the growth targets are achieved, they would most likely fuel rising inflationary trends in an already overheating economy and widen the trade deficit further. Indeed, these policies may already have set the White House on a collision course with the Federal Reserve and Wall Street, as well as Congress. By mid-1989 there was strong evidence of the Fed trying to *reduce* growth, in an economy already operating close to full employment and full capacity, by raising interest rates in order to hold down inflation and narrow the trade deficit. And added to all this is the recurrent cost of servicing $3,120 billion of accumulated debt which, in 1990 alone, will amount to 3 per cent of GNP.

Many commentators have described the economic climate as 'a recession waiting to happen'. In such an event, with the deficit so high, it would be difficult if not impossible to boost demand through new tax cuts or spending. By April 1989 Bush had scored a success in gaining congressional support for his budget without new taxes – at least not for a year. It may be, therefore, that with sufficient political skills and luck he can survive the basic fragility of the American economy through his term of office. However, there is not much left of Reaganomics – only a flicker here and there.

Notes

1 In 1960–73 GNP grew by 4 per cent per annum whereas in 1973–9 the rate was 2.3 per cent.

2 Paul R. Abramson, John H. Aldrich and David W. Rohde, *Change and Continuity in the 1980 Elections*, rev. edn, Washington DC, Congressional Quarterly Press, 1983, pp. 121, 148–9.

3 See Milton and Rose Friedman, *Capitalism and Freedom*, Chicago, University of Chicago Press, 1962; *Free to Choose*, London, Secker & Warburg, 1980; *Tyranny of the Status Quo*, London, Secker & Warburg, 1984.

4 The chief exponent of rational expectations theory within the early Reagan Administration was a former student of Friedman's, Beryl Sprinkel, Under Secretary of the Treasury for Monetary Affairs in 1981.

5 See *America's New Beginning: a Program for Economic Recovery*, Washington DC, 1981 — the basic reference document for the Administration's early policies.

6 Quoted in Isabel V. Sawhill and Charles F. Stone, 'The economy. The key to success', in John L. Palmer and Isabel V. Sawhill, eds, *The Reagan Record. An Assessment of America's Changing Domestic Priorities*, Cambridge, Mass., Ballinger, 1984, p.82.

7 Arthur Laffer, George Gilder and Jude Wanniski are the best known. Congressman Jack Kemp popularised the theory. In the early Reagan Administration, the supply-side view was represented by Paul Craig Roberts, Stephen Entin and Norman Ture. Until 1982 Ture was Under Secretary of the Treasury and Roberts was Assistant Treasury Secretary for Economic Policy.

9 This was Reagan's election promise. However, according to Roberts, Reagan 'did not mean that a balanced budget was his principal aim or a constraint that would dictate his economic policy'. Paul Craig Roberts, *The Supply-Side Revolution: an Insider's Account of Policymaking in Washington*, Cambridge, Mass., Harvard University Press, 1984, p. 90.

9 Dale Tate, 'Reagan economic plan nears enactment', *Congressional Quarterly Weekly Report*, 1 August 1981, p. 1371.

10 William A. Niskanen, *Reaganomics. An Insider's Account of the Policies and the People*, New York, Oxford University Press, 1988, p. 26.

11 These programmes, run by the states but financed in part by matching federal funds, include Supplementary Security Income (SSI) which provides cash for the poor who are elderly, blind, or disabled; AFDC; food stamps; and Medicaid (medical assistance for recipients of SSI and AFDC).

12 E.g. Social Security, Medicare (health insurance), veterans' benefits and services, general retirement and disability insurance, and federal employees' pensions.

13 Perry D. Quick, 'Businesses. Reagan's industrial policy', in Palmer and Sawhill, *The Reagan Record*, p. 297.

14 Marilyn Moon and Isabel V. Sawhill, 'Family incomes. Gainers and losers', in Palmer and Sawhill, *The Reagan Record*, p. 327.

15 Between 1970 and 1980, uncontrollable outlays in the budget (mainly index-linked payments to individuals) rose sharply, and they are expected to continue to do so.

16 See Peter M. Benda and Charles H. Levine, 'Reagan and the bureaucracy: the bequest, the promise and the legacy', in Charles O. Jones, ed., *The Reagan Legacy. Promise and Performance*, Chatham, NJ, Chatham House, 1988, pp. 118, 120.

17 See Roberts, *The Supply-Side Revolution*, especially ch. 7; David A. Stockman, *The Triumph of Politics: Why the Reagan Revolution Failed*, New York, Harper Row, 1986; Niskanen, *Reaganomics*, chs 2, 3 and 9.

18 William Greider, *The Education of David Stockman and Other Americans*, New York, Dutton, 1982. See also Sheldon Danzinger and Daniel Feaster,

'Income transfers and poverty in the 1980s', in John Quigley and Daniel Rubinfeld, eds, *American Domestic Priorities. An Economic Appraisal*, Berkeley, University of California Press, 1985; Thomas Byrne Edsall, *The New Politics of Inequality*, New York, W. W. Norton, 1984; Peter Gottschalk, 'Retrenchment in antipoverty programs in the United States: lessons for the future', in B. B. Kymlicka and Jean V. Matthews, eds, *The Reagan Revolution?*, Chicago, Dorsey Press, 1988, pp. 140–2.

19 When Reagan left office after six years of economic recovery, 12 per cent of blacks, 8 per cent of Hispanics (cf. 4.6 per cent of whites) and 30 per cent of black teenagers (cf. 16 per cent of all teenagers) remained unemployed. Women represented half the total number of workers wanting jobs but were discouraged from looking for them because they believed none were available.

20 Quoted in Thomas L. Muller, 'Regional impacts', in Palmer and Sawhill, *The Reagan Experiment. An Examination of Economic and Social Policies under the Reagan Administration*, Washington DC, Urban Institute, 1982, pp. 446–54. See also Peter Mieszkowski, 'The differential effect of the foreign trade deficit on regions in the United States', in Quigley and Rubinfeld, eds, *American Domestic Priorities*, p. 360, for evidence of the disproportionate employment benefits of increased defence procurement to the Pacific and North-East states.

21 In January 1989, unemployment rates in ten states (Alabama, Alaska, Arkansas, Kentucky, Louisiana, Michigan, Mississippi, Texas, West Virginia and Wyoming) remained at or above 8 per cent, whereas the rates in Nebraska and most states in New England were lower than 4 per cent. Even within otherwise prosperous states, such as California and Illinois, pockets of unemployment exceeded 10 per cent.

22 Henry J. Aaron, *et al.*, *Economic Choices 1987*, Washington DC, Brookings Institution, 1987, p. 23.

23 Quoted in Benjamin J. Cohen, 'An explosion in the kitchen? Economic relations with other advanced industrial states', in Kenneth A. Oye, Robert J. Lieber and Donald Rothchild, *Eagle Resurgent? The Reagan Era in American Foreign Policy*, Boston, Little Brown, 1987, pp. 126–7.

24 From 1981 to 1987, the US share of world export markets fell from 11.7 per cent to 10.2 per cent: US Congress, Office of Technology Assessment, *Paying the Bill: Manufacturing and America's Trade Deficit*, Washington DC, US GPO, 1988.

25 Richard W. Riche *et al.*, 'High technology today and tomorrow: a small slice of the employment pie', *Monthly Labor Review*, CVI, November 1983, pp. 50–8.

26 Measured by gross non-residential fixed investment. *Economic Report of the President*, January 1989, Table B-1.

27 Borrowing Reagan's supply-side rationale, Bush claims that the cut in capital gains tax will pay for itself by unleashing new investment and profits – a claim hotly disputed by the Congressional Budget Office which fears that it could cost billions of dollars in lost revenue.

US defence: the Reagan legacy and the Bush predicament

President Reagan came to office in 1981 with a clear mandate in the area of defence. Following his campaign statements, he promised to put right the Carter Administration's neglect of defence. In his eight years in office, he claimed to be following a defence policy that was consistent and dedicated to rebuilding US defence capabilities. Such a defence policy was deemed essential to support US foreign policy. My concern in this chapter is to look at the legacy he bequeathed to his successor. The central claim will be that reality was very different from the image Reagan portrayed, such that by the time he left office there was confusion and indecision over fundamental aspects of US defence policy.

This confusion applies to all parts of the defence realm, but we shall focus on the strategic dimension to illustrate the problem, rather than, say, focus on nuclear modernisation in Europe, notably the Lance issue, or on conventional, or chemical arms control. But the same features would be found in each – namely a lack of coherent policy, a dispute about the future direction of policy, and an emerging agenda of critical choices that had to be made sooner rather than later. In this light, the Reagan years left an agenda of unresolved policy dilemmas. This legacy has to be seen not only in terms of the projection of the Reagan Administration as determined and principled, but also in the context that the Administration did have eight years to solve the very problems of US defence policy that the Carter Administration had neglected.

The empirical focus of this chapter will be on the strategic arena, with four areas being looked at in some detail. They are: *first*, the defence budget; *second*, ICBM modernisation; *third*, the Strategic Defense Initiative (SDI); and *fourth*, the START negotiations. I will spend most time on the defence budget because this has ramifications for the other areas to be looked at, and also because it best indicates the problems facing President Bush. In each case I will look at the legacy of the Reagan Administration, in part by summarising the state of policy in each of the areas when the Reagan Administration left office, but mainly through an examination of the first six months of the Bush Administration's policy in each area. My reason for using the experience of the first six months of the Bush Administration is that the predicaments it faces illustrate graphically the confused legacy of the Reagan years.

The defence budget

There are two aspects of the defence budget that need to be examined, one obvious and well-documented, the other less so but of equally potential seriousness. The first is the sheer problem for defence caused by the need to reduce the budget deficit; the second is the impact of procurement decisions taken during the Reagan years on the defence budgets of the early to mid-1990s.

The nature of the budget deficit problem has been examined in the previous chapter. President Reagan, having come to power promising to balance the budget, presided over the largest and longest growth in the federal deficit in US history. When he left office, there were two particularly worrying budgetary problems: *first*, there was the accumulated national debt. Meeting the repayments on this debt accounted for some 7 per cent of federal spending in 1980; in 1988 it accounted for 14 per cent, and this is projected to grow to 16 per cent by 1995. The *second* aspect of the budget legacy is the federal budget deficit. The Gramm–Rudman–Hollings programme imposes a method of removing the deficit by FY 1993, and this contributes to the problems for the defence budget by imposing cuts in federal spending (to be shared fifty-fifty by defence and the other areas of the budget) if the President and Congress fail to agree on a budget that meets a specific budget deficit maximum figure for each FY. In FY 1990 this was $100 billion; in FY 1991 it was to be $64 billion.

Taken together, these two budgetary problems place massive constraints on US defence spending. The federal budget has to be so constructed as to ensure that the deficit falls by a given amount each year, and this implies either raising taxes or reducing expenditure. Neither Reagan nor Bush has been willing to do the former (although it seems inevitable that Bush will have to increase revenues, without calling it a raising of the taxation level in line with his 'read my lips' campaign statement). The only option, then, is to reduce expenditure by the amount needed after factoring in the growth in revenue created by growth in the US economy. In his first budget, Bush used an incredibly optimistic growth projection so that he could claim that the deficit would be under the Gramm–Rudman–Hollings $100 billion target ($99.4 billion is his projected deficit). In fact this growth figure is so optimistic that the actual federal deficit for the FY ending on 30 September 1990 is estimated to be $140 billion.[1] Now, the critical point here is that the FY 1991 budget will have to reduce this $140 billion deficit to $64 billion! This will put a massive squeeze on spending for that and subsequent FYs. The first Bush budget, then, was, in the words of Gordon Adams, a 'one-year exercise, whatever gets you through the night'.[2]

Furthermore, in reducing the budget deficit to comply with the Gramm–Rudman–Hollings plan, the President has little room for manoeuvre in terms of where to get the money from. This is because much of the budget, over 75 per cent, must be spent – it is unavoidable, committed expenditure. Deficit reduction has to come from the remaining proportion of the budget unless revenues are raised by tax increases or by economic growth, and most of this remainder (some 22 per cent) is defence expenditure.

The picture that results from even this brief summary of the budget is that President Bush faces a formidable predicament, one which will have considerable effects on the defence budget. It is well known that defence spending grew rapidly during the Reagan years. Although the turn-round in defence spending came in the last two years of the Carter Administration, it was the Reagan Administration that presided over the massive defence spending increases. The best indicator of this is the real rate of growth in the defence budget (net of inflation). The figures for FY 1976 to FY 1985 are shown in Table 5.1.

A simpler indicator is the percentage of GNP lavished on defence. The four Carter budgets averaged 4.9 per cent of GNP being spent on defence. In the Reagan years, this increased substantially, with an average of 6.0 per cent of GNP being devoted to defence expenditure (see Table 5.2). This is a considerable increase in the percentage of GNP devoted to defence, a rise of over 22 per cent, and of course was all the more in actual expenditure given the growth in US GNP in the period concerned.

Table 5.1   *Real growth in US defence spending*

Fiscal year	Percentage
1976	− 8.2
1977	1.9
1978	0.5
1979	4.0
1980	3.1
1981	4.8
1982	7.8
1983	7.3
1984	4.2
1985	9.5

Source: John Collins, *US–Soviet Military Balance, 1980–1985*, Washington DC, Pergamon-Brassey's, 1985, p. 296.

Table 5.2   *US defence spending as a percentage of GNP*

Fiscal year	Percentage
Carter	
1978	4.7
1979	4.7
1980	5.0
1981	5.2
Reagan	
1982	5.8
1983	6.2
1984	6.0
1985	6.2
1986	6.3
1987	6.2
1988	5.9
1989	5.7

Source: Report of the Secretary of State for Defense Frank C. Carlucci to the Congress. Fiscal Year 1989 Budget, Washington DC, Government Printing Office, 1988, p. 299.

Yet by the time he left office, even Reagan recognised that defence spending could not go on rising at the rate of the early 1980s. In his last defence budget, presented in January 1989, he asked for a modest 2 per cent real growth in defence expenditure as part of a $1.68 trillion five-year plan. His figures for FY 1990 and FY 1991 were $315.2 and $330.8 billion respectively (including Department of Energy military expenditure). Even this five-year budget trimmed $316 billion off the FY 1988 and FY 1989 five-year projections. Critically, this 2 per cent real-growth budget was immediately seen by most observers as impossibly optimistic given the budget deficit. It was no surprise, therefore, that Bush's first budget proposal, although based on the optimistic growth assumptions noted above, cut back on defence expenditure considerably.

In February 1989, Bush proposed a provisional budget, which included a freeze (in real terms) on defence expenditure for FY 1990, with real growth of 1 per cent for the next two FYs, and real growth of 2 per cent for FY 1993. This represented cutting the Reagan request from $315.2 billion to $309 billion. The programmes to be cut were not outlined in the announcement, and there then followed two months' negotiations between the armed services as to how the cuts should be implemented. The final budget proposal was announced in April 1989, following discussions between the President and Congress over the way to meet the Gramm−Rudman−Hollings deficit ceiling. The final budget proposed a further cut in defence expenditure, with a figure of $305.5 billion being proposed. The additional cuts meant that the Reagan proposal had been reduced by about $10 billion. The areas that received the most savage cuts were the Strategic Defense Initiative (SDI), where the Reagan proposal was reduced by $1 billion, and the B-2 bomber, whose procurement was delayed by one year, also saving $1 billion. More significantly, the Bush budget proposed considerable reductions in the five-year defence plan, with a total of $65 billion being cut for the period FY 1990−4. Although the cut of $7 billion in SDI funding in this period ($40 to $33 billion) received the most public attention,[3] it is important to note that this new level of spending on the programme still involves considerable increases over the figures for the previous five years; FY 1989 spending, for example, was $3.7 billion, compared to projected figures of $4.6 billion and $5.4 billion for FYs 1990 and 1991. In fact, the SDI programme is the programme least affected by the cuts.

However, even this reduction in the FY 1990 defence budget is not the end of the story, because many of the smaller projects to be cut have influential friends in Congress. This meant that in the hearings to ratify the budget, there were many who wanted to restore specific projects at the cost of others. The three projects that attracted most attention were the Navy's F-14 fighter, the Marine Corps V-22 Osprey troop carrier and the X-30 hypersonic plane.[4] Each of these was to be cancelled or curtailed under Defense Secretary Richard Cheney's budget proposal. Cuts in these and other programmes focused attention on the high-profile strategic programmes, such as SDI and the B-2 Stealth bomber.

In the debates on the budget the B-2 became the main target for reducing the defence budget still further, and for transferring funds into other programmes. The staggering cost of the B-2, at a programme cost of $70.2 billion, and a cost per plane of $570 million, made it an easy target. The House Armed Services Committee rejected the Bush budget proposal, reinstating the V-22 and the F-14 programmes, whilst cutting the B-2 programme by $800 million (from $4.7 to $3.9 billion) and the SDI programme by a further $1.1 billion (to $3.5 billion, plus about $400 million spent on SDI research but appropriated under the Department of Energy). This would create serious problems for the USAF, since cutting expenditure for FY 1990 by $800 million would add to the costs of procuring the bomber. The Senate, debating the budget in late July 1989, deleted only some $300 million from the request for the B-2, but with the crucial rider attached to the decision that the plane had to perform as intended before any more planes were authorised. The effect of the two levels of procurement accepted by the House and Senate would be to limit the numbers built in FY 1990 to two (House) or three (Senate).

The House of Representatives and the Senate ended up with rather different defence budgets, which had to be reconciled by negotiations at a conference of the two bodies. The critical areas of difference were the funding level for the B-2, as noted above, but also those for the SDI programme and the ICBM modernisation programme. On SDI, the Senate cut the President's request by only some $366 million whilst the House cut it to $3.1 billion, some $1.8 billion lower than the Bush request, and some $2.5 billion lower than the original Reagan request of January 1989. On the ICBM modernisation programme, whilst the Senate kept to the Administration's plan for funding the two missiles (the MX and the SICBM), the House cut the budget for the MX from $1.1 billion to $600 million, thus effectively ending the Administration's plans to rail-garrison the missile. This was a plan to mount missiles on trains, which would be garrisoned on USAF bases, to be dispersed on strategic warning of a possible imminent attack (a matter of a few hours). In a much more surprising move the House voted to cancel the SICBM, which had previously been the preferred system of Congress (so much so that it had become known as 'Congressman' rather than by its official name of 'Midgetman'). This vote was the result of an alliance between Republicans, annoyed with the reduction in MX funding, and liberal Democrats opposed to ICBM modernisation in what they saw as a new era of *détente*. Although these problems were resolved at the conference of the two bodies, they indicated the existence of very different views over how to allocate a declining defence budget.

Thus, even within the first six months of his administration, it has become clear that Bush faces serious problems in matching his defence budget to the sums available. This much is well known, and one can expect the next few years to witness more of the same. The FY 1991 budget proposal will, especially because of the Gramm–Rudman–Hollings requirements, be even more problematic, and things will get tighter each year after that. Particularly problematic will be cutting the 'favourite' weapons programmes of influential Senators and Congressional Representatives. The history of attempts to close military bases indicates the difficulties facing the Administration, and the very unsuccessful track record in cancelling major weapons programmes suggests very tough times ahead.

But there is a second aspect of the budget dilemma, an aspect that has received much less attention, but which promises to make things far more difficult. This is the effect of previous spending and procurement decisions on future defence spending requirements. There are two aspects of this, referred to as the 'bow-wave' and the 'stern-wave' effects. These refer respectively to the increased defence funding necessary as weapons programmes move from research to production, and the increases in expenditure needed as past spending commitments push up current spending. The critical point is that the Reagan Administration has left large bow and stern waves in the defence field.

This problem for the Bush Administration has been analysed in detail in a recent article by Gordon Adams and Stephen Cain.[5] They trace its origin to the shift from consumption to investment in the defence budget in the early to mid-1980s. As they note: 'Between FY 1980 and FY 1985, funds for DoD investment grew 104 per cent after inflation, while budgets for operations and maintenance (up 37 per cent) and for military personnel (up only 8 per cent) grew far more slowly. This rapid growth pushed the investment share of the defense budget from 38 per cent in FY 1980 to a peak of 48 per cent in FY 1985.'[6] This means that because Congress fully funds weapons programmes in one appropriation, large unspent, but committed, amounts have been built up. The simple implication of these commitments is that even when Congress cuts defence authorisations, actual spending will still increase, because of sums committed, but unspent, from previous budgets. The Congressional Budget Office (CBO) has estimated that despite cuts in budget authority in FY 1986 and FY 1987, actual defence spending rose by 6 per cent and 1 per cent in real terms respectively.[7] Furthermore, they estimate that 85 per cent of defence spending is now 'relatively uncontrollable', since, in addition to the 45 per cent of the budget that goes in personnel (payroll and pensions) costs, commitments now total about 40 per cent of defence spending in any one year. This means that the Secretary of Defense cannot touch this 85 per cent of the budget without cutting personnel or cancelling contracts.

But this is only one aspect of the stern-wave problem. The other main one is that this increased investment has been in more complex systems, requiring higher maintenance costs. The CBO has estimated that if the link between the cost of acquiring weapons and operating them holds, then operating costs will have to increase by an average of 3 per cent a year in the early 1990s simply because of the increased costs of maintaining and operating technologically more complex systems.[8]

As for the bow-wave effect, Adams and Cain point out that there are a large number of weapons programmes, started during the Reagan years, that are now about to enter production. Given the fact that defence research and development expenditure grew in real terms by 92 per cent between FY 1980 and FY 1989 (more than any other area of the defence budget), then the programmes involved create massive pressures on the defence budget as they move from the R & D phase to procurement. And, as they note, the size of the problem can be ascertained by the fact that 'on average' procurement and operational costs constitute 85 per cent of the costs of a weapons programme, the remaining 15 per cent covering the research and engineering stages.[9]

These two effects have serious implications for the defence budget. The CBO estimates that the Reagan modernisation programme will, as it moves to production, require a real growth in defence expenditure of 3–4 per cent a year in FYs 1990–4, even assuming that the SICBM

(Midgetman) is cancelled, and that SDI expenditure is held to 3 per cent a year growth.[10] As Adams and Cain point out, the gap between this requirement and a budget that merely kept up with inflation would amount to $180 billion by FY 1994. If defence spending could only be held constant (i.e. not increasing for inflation), then this gap would come to $310 billion by FY 1994, with the FY 1994 figure alone totalling $100 billion.[11]

To put it mildly, this situation would require drastic choices. Until now Defense Secretaries have dealt with stern- and bow-wave effects by a number of short-term measures. The most popular of these have been to use up the excesses of previous appropriations, many of which included inflated estimates for costs, to stretch out procurement cycles, and to cut maintenance and readiness funds. Yet each of these sources has now been virtually exhausted. Congress now insists on more realistic costings; procurement cycles are now stretched out so much that any increases could actually raise costs; maintenance backlogs have built up; and readiness levels are now at dangerously low levels. In short, these sources will not be as available in the Bush years as they were in the last few Reagan years. Moreover, the size of the problem is now so great that these measures are no longer of much help. In his first budget Bush effectively skirted around these problems by reducing defence expenditure in FY 1990, yet proposing that it increase in the following three FYs in real terms of between 1 and 2 per cent. The point here is that the reduction agreed in FY 1990 was achieved by slowing down programmes and cutting sustainability funds, with the clear assumption that the reductions would be compensated for by increases in later budgets. No real choices were made in the FY 1990 budget.

The predicament for President Bush is therefore that choices have yet to be made about priorities in the defence budget. The option of cutting everything a little will not suffice because the fundamental problem is that the programmes started by Reagan have yet to incur their main costs. Crucially, the short-term way of dealing with the problem that characterised the last few Reagan budgets and the first Bush budget cannot deal with the bow- and stern-wave effects that are now working their way through the system. President Bush has inherited a set of commitments that require an annual real *increase* of 3–4 per cent a year in defence spending, yet he also faces a budget deficit that has to be reduced to zero by FY 1993. To reiterate the most pressing problem: even if defence spending can be frozen in real terms, and not raided as a means of cutting the budget deficit, this will leave a shortfall totalling $180 billion by FY 1994 from the amount necessary to procure the systems already approved in successive Reagan budgets.

ICBM modernisation

Another area of the Reagan legacy that causes a serious policy predicament for President Bush is that of the modernisation of the US ICBM force. Reagan came to power having attacked Carter for allowing US strategic forces to decline. Specifically, Reagan spoke of the need to build up the hard-target capability of the US strategic arsenal, and this meant procuring a survivable and accurate ICBM force. Yet Reagan left office without having procured such a force, and with the debate over the nature of the ICBM force essentially the same as it had been when he came to office.

This 'problem' over the US ICBM force arose because of the Soviet deployment of three new ICBMs in the middle to late 1970s. These missiles, the SS-17, the SS-18 and the SS-19, were all accurate and MIRVed. In fact their accuracy was massively overestimated at the time,[12] but this claimed accuracy was accepted and became the basis of the fear in the late 1970s that the Soviets had the capability to destroy the US ICBM force. This was known as the 'window of vulnerability'. Candidate Reagan claimed that President Carter had done nothing to solve this potentially catastrophic problem.

When he came to office, Reagan promised to sort out the mess over the US ICBM force. President Carter had proposed deploying a new ICBM, named MX, in a multiple protective structure (MPS) basing mode. The idea was that the Soviets would have to target two warheads on each shelter, and, as it was proposed to have 200 MXs, each with 23 shelters, this would have required the Soviets to use 9200 accurate warheads, an ICBM figure far higher than the Soviets actually possessed. Nor did the notional 9200 allow for other types of targets that only these warheads could cover. The problem was that this plan was both expensive and environmentally harmful. Reagan vowed to drop the plan during his presidential election campaign, which left him with the problem of how to solve the vulnerability of the US ICBM force.

There is no need to trace the history of his administration's attempts to deal with the problem, since they have been well documented elsewhere.[13] It is sufficient to note that the initial decision was to scrap

MPS and place the missiles in existing Titan II silos. This was quickly modified so as to place them in existing, but superhardened, Minuteman silos. This was greeted with considerable scepticism in Congress, since, of course, the plan simply put newer missiles into the very silos that were supposed to be vulnerable. Within a year, the Administration came up with a new scheme, known as 'Closely-spaced Basing' (CSB) or 'Dense Pack'. This scheme received an even worse reception in Congress, since it seemed to reduce the survivability of the missiles, not increase it. As a result of this decision, Congress mandated the President, via the FY 1983 Appropriations Act, to find an acceptable basing mode before any more money was spent on the MX missile's deployment.

This led the President to set up a commission, with Brent Scowcroft – later Bush's National Security Adviser – as chair. The Scowcroft Commission was asked to recommend a course of action for dealing with the future of the ICBM force. In its report,[14] released in April 1983, the Commission solved the window of vulnerability problem by saying that it did not exist! It recommended that 100 MX missiles be deployed in existing silos, starting in 1986, and it also recommended proceeding with a new small, single-warheard ICBM, known as Midgetman. Research should proceed on both missiles and on ways to deploy them, allowing future decisions over whether to go ahead with more MXs in superhardened silos or with SICBMs in mobile basing modes to be taken when the future shape of the Soviet ICBM force, and the threat it posed, became clearer.

For the next five years, the Reagan Administration attempted to proceed with both missiles. The situation at the end of the Reagan period was that Congress had agreed only to 50 MX missiles, deployed in existing Minuteman silos. The Air Force wanted an additional 50 MXs, and proposed that the entire force be deployed in a rail-garrison basing mode. However, there was a central divide within the policy-making community. The USAF, and the Administration, preferred the MX to the SICBM, mainly for cost reasons. Congress, on the other hand, preferred the SICBM, because it was seen as enhancing strategic stability, whereas MX was seen as undermining it. This led to a series of budget clashes, as the Pentagon tried to omit funding for the SICBM, and maximise funding for the MX, whereas Congress tried to cut or even omit funding for the MX and increase it for the SICBM. By the end of the Reagan Administration there was no clear plan for the future ICBM force; indeed, in the FY 1989 budget Congress gave some money for the two missiles ($250 million each), but left it to President Bush to allocate the rest of the sum for ICBM development ($350 million) by 15 February 1989. Interestingly, he failed to meet that deadline, thus indicating that, despite the time it had had to make a decision, the new Administration could not easily do so.

The problem of what to do with the US ICBM force was addressed in a bipartisan report released in February 1989.[15] The working group that produced the report was co-chaired by Scowcroft and former Defense Secretary, Harold Brown, though Scowcroft cannot be associated with the outcome because he left to take up a post in the Bush Administration. It pointed out the fundamental difficulty facing the new President: the window of vulnerability already existed or would soon do so, and yet there seemed no easy way out of it. The working group saw three options. The first was to continue with the rail-garrison plan for the MX. This would cost a relatively modest $12 billion over its lifetime, but has the serious drawback that the amount of warning time needed to disperse the missiles might not be available. The second option was to deploy the SICBM on hardened vehicles – either in the northern US at existing military installations, or in the South-West on new installations. On receipt of tactical warning (a matter of a few minutes) the vehicles would disperse. The former would cost about $36 billion, the latter about $39 billion for lifetime costs. But basing in the South-West would give more warning time and would therefore make the system more survivable. These costs could be reduced by about one-third by putting two warheads on each launcher, but this would rule out South-West basing because of the reduced range that would result from increasing the payload of the vehicles. The final option was to develop a new basing mode, known as 'carry-hard', which involves placing the missiles in hardened capsules, which can then be moved between several thousand shelters. The cost of deploying 50 MXs in this mode would be $24 billion, and of deploying 500 SICBMs, $40 billion, each figure being for lifetime costs. The working group recommended that the President should end the long debate about the future of the US ICBM force by deploying the SICBM in the South-West and keeping the existing 50 MX missiles in silos, deploying them on a rail-garrison basis as funds became available during the 1990s.

The Administration's own thinking on the matter reflected the fact that there were different camps holding very different views. All, however, realised that the budget situation made it very unlikely that both ICBM programmes would be fully funded. It was this realisation that lay behind the USAF's recommendation that the SICBM be cancelled. It was seen as simply too expensive. The USAF estimates that the cost of deploying 50 MX missiles in the rail-garrison basing mode would be $5.4 billion, while deploying the same number of warheads on the SICBM would require a force of 500 SICBMs at a cost of about $38.5 billion. It was this thinking that led Defense Secretary Cheney to propose to the President in April 1989 that he proceed with the MX and cancel the SICBM.[16]

However, the President's decision, announced in late April 1989, was to proceed with both systems but in sequence. The Administration now intends to take the existing 50 MX missiles, currently based in silos, and redeploy them in a rail-garrison basing mode, becoming operational in 1992. The SICBM would be deployed from 1997, with 'at least 250 and maybe 500' deployed. This plan resulted in the Administration calling for $1.2 and $2.1 billion for the MX in FY 1990 and FY 1991, and $100 and $200 million for the SICBM in FY 1990 and FY 1991. SICBM funding would then rise to about $350 million a year by FY 1994.[17]

Nevertheless, this plan ran into objections in Congress, reflecting the divide on the issue that has plagued the debate for the last fifteen years. In the debates on the defence budget, some Representatives sought to increase funds for the SICBM, whilst others tried to delete funding for it altogether. The Pentagon finally agreed to increase Bush's proposed spending limits on the SICBM by about $947 million in FYs 1992, 1993 and 1994, but only as long as the funding for rail-garrisoning the MX was not reduced. Quite where this extra money for the SICBM will come from in an already problematic budget is not yet known.[18] Yet this did not prevent the House of Representatives from voting to cancel the programme in late July 1989, whereas the Senate agreed to fund the missile. The problem was sorted out at the House–Senate conference, but the picture looks much as it did during the Reagan years, and the Administration has yet to make a choice between the two ICBMs. It seems likely that both will continue to be funded, but it is equally likely that both cannot be deployed because of the costs involved. More saliently, there is a central linkage between the plans for the ICBM force and the US position at the START negotiations, where the US has taken an ambiguous position on the issue of banning mobile ICBMs. The obvious way forward is for the US to propose banning either all mobile ICBMs or banning mobile MIRVed ICBMs, and then to develop the appropriate US system. But, as we shall find out when we look at the US position on START, the problem simply re-emerges there as well. The ICBM modernisation plan, though, remains confused, and this looks likely to characterise the remainder of the Bush Administration.

The Strategic Defense Initiative

The SDI programme was very much the creation of President Reagan, and during his time in office about $16.2 billion was spent on the research programme. However, it was abundantly clear by the time he left office that the research programme would not achieve the goals that he had outlined in his famous speech launching the project on 23 March 1983. Then, he had called on US scientists to develop defensive systems to render Soviet ICBMs 'impotent and obsolete'. The academic industry that has followed the history of the SDI programme provides enough of a commentary to make any extended discussion here unnecessary.[19] The point I wish to stress is that by the time Reagan had left office, there were crucial decisions to be taken over the future of the programme. Reagan avoided these in the last few years of his administration, and Bush now has to take them.

What, then, was the situation of the SDI research programme when Reagan left office? The truth is that the programme was in a considerable state of flux, with no agreed role for the programme and an increasingly uncertain picture of what would constitute the first phase of deployment. The debate had moved on from the 'hardware' issues of the mid-1980s to 'software' issues. Whilst supporters and critics alike could agree that the hardware would 'work', albeit with very different estimates of what 'work' meant, they were divided on the issue of the reliability of the software. SDI officials remained confident that the software problems could be overcome by extensive testing, whereas critics viewed this as a generic limitation on the system's performance.

In the last year of the Reagan Administration, the programme received a serious setback with the release of an Office of Technology Assessment report on the software's reliability. It concluded that: 'there would be a significant probability ... that the first (and presumably only) time the BMD system were used in a real war, it would suffer a catastrophic failure'.[20] Moreover, this was not seen as something that could be resolved, since the problem was one of a generic limitation on the reliability of large-scale computer systems in the absence of *operational* testing.

By the time Reagan left office, no one believed in the ability of SDI to perform the role that he had advanced in his speech. The SDI Organization (SDIO) had put forward a deployment plan, one which called for a three-phase deployment starting in the late 1990s. But the levels of effectiveness envisaged made it much more of a point-defence than an area-defence system. A congressional estimate of the system's likely performance spoke of it being '16 per cent' effective against a Soviet attack.[21] The Joint Chiefs of Staff, in a classified statement of the minimum performance levels they would require before they approved the first phase of SDI, called for the system to be effective against 50 per cent of the Soviet SS-18 warhead force and 30 per cent of a first-wave attack of 4700 warheads.[22] This is far from the astrodome concept that Reagan spoke of.

What would the first phase of deployment look like? At the end of the Reagan Administration the SDIO's plan called for the deployment of a first phase containing the following elements:

Space-based Interceptor (SBI)
Boost Surveillance and Tracking System (BSTS)
Space Surveillance and Tracking System (SSTS)
Ground-based Surveillance and Tracking System (GSTS)
Ground-based Interceptor (GBI), previously known as the Exo-atmospheric Reentry Interceptor System (ERIS)

The critical point about this system is that it would rely solely on kinetic (i.e. propelled missile) weapons, with directed-energy (i.e. laser or beam) weapons having been downgraded in the research programme and only seen as being part of the *weapons* of the *third* phase of deployment, beginning in 2005–15!

Not only was this a very different kind of system than that commonly associated with SDI, and with a very much lower estimated effectiveness than presented by the President, but the cost of the system was the subject of fierce debate. The original (June 1987) SDIO estimate of deployment costs for Phase One was between $75 and $145 billion. In 1988, SDIO estimated the cost at $115 billion, only to be told by top Pentagon management that this was too high. SDIO came back in October 1988 with a cost of $69 billion. This reduction was achieved by a combination of reductions in the numbers of key systems (the number of SBIs was reduced by 51 per cent and of GSTSs, by 42 per cent); changing the technical requirements of the systems; and by using different cost-estimate models. Not surprisingly, this massive change in the estimated costs of Phase One caused considerable scepticism in Congress, with the common charge being that the real cost had been underestimated to get the system approved. This view was supported when the General Accounting Office reported that the SDIO had 'severely understated' the cost, which the GAO put at $120 billion.[23]

When Bush came to office he had to deal with four central questions about SDI. *First*, what was to be the role of ballistic missile defence in American strategy – partial missile defence or arms control leverage? *Second*, how much SDI expenditure can a declining budget stand? *Third*, should the Phase One deployment go ahead as planned? *Fourth*, should the US continue to abide by the ABM Treaty or move towards a broad interpretation of its provisions? At the end of his first six months in office, Bush had not answered any of these questions.

What he has done is to cut back the projected expenditure on the programme, as noted above, from $40 to $33 billion over the next five years. Yet he still envisages very large real increases in SDI expenditure and has stated that he will make a decision on the exact architecture of the system during his first term in office. The programme itself has undergone a major reorientation during the first few months of his administration as a result of two developments.

The first of these is the planned use of SDI systems in an anti-satellite (ASAT) role, following the difficulties the Pentagon had faced getting congressional funding for the previous ASAT system, the direct-ascent miniature homing vehicle. The first system involved, the MIRACL laser, was previously one of the leading contenders for SDI but had been downgraded in recent years.[24] In the longer term, the plan is to develop a directed-energy ASAT from technologies previously assigned to SDI roles, as well as to use some of the kinetic systems such as ERIS.[25] The clear indication is that directed-energy systems, having been downgraded by SDIO, are now set to reappear in an ASAT role.

The second, and more fundamental, development is that of the 'Brilliant Pebbles' concept. This has led to a re-examination of the SDIO's proposals for Phase One deployment. This concept calls for the deployment in space of thousands of small, cheap kinetic weapons. Each 'pebble' would be some three feet long, and weigh about 100 pounds, and would contain, in a small silicon chip, computing power the size of a current supercomputer to guide the system, via an optical sensor, to the targets – ICBMs in their boost phase. The project, which came out of the Lawrence Livermore Laboratory, has been in existence for only a couple of years, and has received little funding.[26]

The impact of the claimed promise of Brilliant Pebbles was to provoke a major review of the Phase One deployment plan. The head of SDIO during the Reagan years, Lt. Gen. James Abrahamson, said just nine days after he left the post that he favoured going ahead with Brilliant Pebbles rather than with the planned first phase. His reasons were mainly cost-based, since he estimated that Brilliant Pebbles could be deployed for around $25 billion. Moreover, it could, he claimed, easily meet the Joint Chiefs' minimum requirements.[27] The problem for Bush is that the concept of Brilliant Pebbles is currently just that – there is no hardware, and the critical issues of computing and control have yet to be addressed. Not only this, but there are several potentially serious generic problems with such systems, and these have only begun to be discussed in the literature.[28]

The result of the development of Brilliant Pebbles and the cuts in the planned budget for SDI has meant that the programme is now in as great a state of flux as ever. The Phase One plan has now slipped by about two years, with development of the systems to begin in 1994, not 1992, and interceptor production to start in 1998. Critically, the SDIO, under its new director, George Monahan, will now review the possibility of developing Brilliant Pebbles. Until this review is completed, in late 1989 or early 1990, there is no clear sense of where the programme is moving.

Finally, the President, as well as having to deal with fundamental questions over the nature of any SDI system and the added problem of how to pay for it, will also soon have to face the thorny question of whether or not to violate the 1972 ABM Treaty. While none of the planned tests of sensors for the next two years will violate the treaty, any attempt to deploy Brilliant Pebbles, or the original Phase One systems, will do so.

The START negotiations

The final area to mention is that of the negotiations over a new strategic arms control agreement. President Reagan, having come to office with a record of opposing every US–Soviet arms control agreement, left office with a signed and ratified INF Treaty, and with the basis of the START Treaty. Yet although the basic limits and sublimits of the agreement had been agreed, a number of issues remained.

The essential framework of the new strategic arms agreement is uncontentious. Each side has agreed to the following limits: 6000 accountable warheads on 1600 delivery vehicles; within the 6000 limit, no more than 4900 warheads on ICBMs and SLBMs; a sublimit of 1540 warheads on heavy (e.g. the SS-18) missiles; a sublimit of 3000–3300 warheads on ICBMs; bombers carrying SRAMs and gravity bombs are heavily discounted, with each bomber counting as carrying only one warhead.

This framework would not reduce warheads by 50 per cent, as is often claimed, since it omits SLCMs, as well as heavily discounting bombers carrying gravity bombs and SRAMs. It is estimated that the two sides will, even after complying with the terms of the treaty, field some 8000 to 9000 warheads on strategic systems, with the US having about 9000 and the Soviets having nearer 8000.[29]

Even then, there remain four main critical issues. *First*, Bush will have to decide what linkage he will accept between START and SDI. The Soviets have continued to insist that no START agreement can be signed without a commitment by the US to abide by the ABM Treaty. Although they became less vociferous about this, it remains one of the main stumbling blocks. At the summer session of the negotiations in 1989, the US failed to get the USSR to accept separate negotiations on space and defensive systems. On the US side, there is an evident division over this issue, with the Joint Chiefs arguing that the Administration should drop its insistence on the right to deploy SDI if this meant not getting a START agreement, whilst other agencies continued to press for this right.[30]

Second, there are the remaining unresolved minor issues in the draft treaty. It looks as if the two sides will be able to resolve the limits on ALCMs. The US has pressed for these to be discounted, since they are less threatening than ICBM warheads. Accordingly, they have proposed that bombers carrying ALCMs be given a nominal loading; the Soviets, on the other hand, have proposed that each bomber be counted as carrying the maximum that it could carry. Reports during the summer 1989 negotiating sessions indicated that the two sides were moving together on this issue, with the likely compromise being that each bomber would be counted as carrying the actual number it *was* carrying, which poses problems of verification and monitoring. Similarly, the issue of banning the SS-18 or any successors, much discussed in the US, appears to have been resolved, with the US deciding not to press for such a ban. Finally, the two sides appeared close to agreement on the size of any deployment areas for allowed mobile missiles.

Third, there still remain major unresolved issues. Chief amongst these are those concerning mobile missiles and limits on SLCMs. The mobile missile issue is particularly problematic, since it is intimately linked to the internal US debate over the relative merits of the MX and SICBM missiles. Under the Reagan Administration, the US formally proposed that all mobile ICBMs be banned, whilst still proposing to deploy MX and Midgetman. In the first few months of the Bush Administration, there has been discussion over whether to continue to hold out for such a ban, or whether to ban only MIRVed mobile ICBMs. Not surprisingly, those congressional figures who supported Midgetman support the idea of a ban on MIRVed mobile ICBMs, whilst those who want to rail-garrison the MX oppose such a ban. President Bush decided in June 1989 to drop the US insistence on a ban on mobile ICBMs as long as Congress funded both the MX and the SICBM. Of course, the problem is that if Congress does not agree to fund both systems, then the US position at the negotiations will probably change. The Soviets oppose a ban on mobile missiles, given the fact that they have already deployed both a MIRVed mobile ICBM system (the SS-24) and a single-warhead mobile ICBM (the SS-25).

The other main area of difference is over the limits to be placed outside the treaty on SLCMs. The Soviets have proposed limits of 400 and 600 on nuclear and conventional SLCMs respectively. The US, which plans to deploy some 4000 SLCMs (750 nuclear, the rest conventional), argued that the Soviet proposal cannot be verified, and therefore opposed any limits on SLCMs. There have been reports that the Soviets might change their position, possibly agreeing to a complete ban on nuclear-armed SLCMs,[31] but the issue has not been resolved at the negotiations.

The *fourth* problem for President Bush is the political acceptability of any agreement, given the 'bad press' that his predecessor gave to arms control. The likelihood is that there will be a tough battle to ratify any agreement, with particular attention being paid to verification. In this light it is important to note that the Soviets have already agreed to US proposals for trial monitoring of weapons deployment before an agreement is signed.

Finally, it appears that the US has now downgraded the START negotiations, preferring instead to place most emphasis on getting a conventional arms control agreement to cover Europe. The positive reason for this is the critical importance of the linkage between a conventional agreement and a short-range nuclear force (SNF) agreement in Europe; the negative reason is the difficulty in deciding on the

American position on the remaining START issues until the fate of the US ICBM modernisation and SDI programmes are known. The current situation therefore looks like one of START being on hold.

Conclusion

In all of the four areas that I have looked at, the same picture emerges. Reagan left behind unresolved issues, issues that Bush has yet to confront. Of course, any president leaving office will leave things to be tidied up by the successor, but in the case of the Reagan–Bush succession the picture is in reality one of central strategic and defence issues being unresolved. In each case Bush has to act soon. The defence budget, ICBM modernisation, SDI and START all need direction and leadership.

In his first six months in office, Bush has adopted a policy of deferring major decisions. In each of the areas I have examined, actual choices will have to be made *within* his first term of office. He cannot do what his predecessor did, that is, fudge and delay and leave the decisions to his successor. The problem of the defence budget simply has to be addressed as the Gramm–Rudman–Hollings targets become ever tighter; the ICBM modernisation issue is reaching a decision point as Congress looks like forcing a choice between the two systems within the very near future; SDI is undergoing a critical examination of its likely direction, and this will require a clear sense of its role in US defence policy; finally, the START negotiations are intimately affected by developments in each of the above areas, and decisions taken about the agreement will have massive implications on the future strategic forces of the US. All in all, the defence area is one in which it can accurately be said that President Bush faces genuine predicaments, ones that he will have to face in what may turn out to be his only term in office. This agenda of predicaments is not of his making; rather it is the defence legacy of the Reagan Administration.

Notes

1 *Aviation Week and Space Technology (AWST)*, 24 April 1989, p. 19.
2 Quoted in ibid.
3 *International Herald Tribune*, 24 April 1989.
4 See Pat Towell, 'Bush's cuts would take away hometown bacon', *Congressional Quarterly*, 13 May 1989, pp. 1136–41.

5 Gordon Adams and Stephen Alexis Cain, 'Defense dilemmas in the 1990s', *International Security*, XIII, 4, 1989, pp. 5–15.

6 Ibid., p. 6.

7 Cited in ibid., pp. 6–7.

8 *AWST*, 16 January 1989, p. 16.

9 Adams and Cain, 'Defence dilemmas', p. 8.

10 Ibid., pp. 9–10.

11 Ibid., p. 10.

12 See Steve Smith, 'MX and the vulnerability of American missiles', *ADIU Report*, IV, 1, 1982, pp. 1–5; Smith, 'Problems of assessing missile accuracy', *RUSI Journal*, CXXX, 4, 1985, pp. 35–40.

13 See John Edwards, *Superweapon: the Making of MX*, New York, Norton, 1982; Herbert Scoville, *MX: Prescription for Disaster*, Cambridge, Mass., MIT Press, 1981; Office of Technology Assessment, *MX Missile Basing*, Washington DC, Government Printing Office, 1981. For details of the missile's history, see issues of *Arms Control Today*, the best source on the debate.

14 *Report of the President's Commission on Strategic Forces*, Washington DC, Government Printing Office, 1983.

15 See 'Bipartisan consensus called for on strategic policy', US Information Service press release, London, 7 February 1989.

16 *International Herald Tribune*, 20 April 1989.

17 *Arms Control Today, May 1989, p. 21.*

18 *AWST*, 10 July 1989, pp. 23–4.

19 For a discussion of SDI see the two Office of Technology Assessment Reports: *Strategic Defenses*, Princeton, NJ, Princeton University Press, 1986; *SDI: Technology, Survivability and Software*, Princeton, NJ, Princeton University Press, 1988. See also Rip Bulkeley and Graham Spinardi, *Space Weapons*, Cambridge, Polity Press, 1986.

20 See Office of Technology Assessment, *SDI*, p. 4.

21 See the unpublished report by Douglas Waller and James Bruce, 'SDI: progress and challenges, part 2', 19 March 1987, office of Sen. William Proxmire, p. ii.

22 *AWST*, 26 June 1989, p. 30.

23 *AWST*, 3 April 1989, p. 45.

24 *International Herald Tribune*, 2 January 1989.

25 *Arms Control Today*, January/February 1989, p. 28.

26 This is discussed in *International Herald Tribune*, 26 April 1989; *AWST*, 20 March 1989, pp. 260–1; 3 April 1989, pp. 47–50. See also the discussion in the SDIO's *Report to Congress on the Strategic Defense Initiative*, Washington DC, SDIO, 13 March 1989, section 5.3.

27 *AWST*, 20 March 1989, p. 260.

28 See *AWST*, 22 May 1989, pp. 20–1.

29 The implications of a START treaty on US and Soviet strategic forces are discussed, respectively, by Michele Flournoy, in 'START thinking about a new US force structure', *Arms Control Today*, July/August 1988, pp. 8–14; 'START cutting Soviet strategic forces', *Arms Control Today*, June/July, 1989, pp. 14–21.

30 *International Herald Tribune*, 2 June 1989 and 10–11 June 1989.

31 Ibid., 14 July 1989.

The Bush Administration's foreign policy review

The transition from Reagan to Bush was widely expected to be smooth and efficient. It was believed that George Bush's experience as vice-president during the Reagan years would provide continuity and ensure that the new Administration would not have to go through the painful learning process that had plagued some of its predecessors. Bush was expected to 'hit the floor running', especially in matters of foreign policy and national security where his experience prior to assuming the presidency was far more extensive than any of his predecessors since Nixon. In the event, these expectations were disappointed. The President initiated a comprehensive review of foreign policy and strategy consuming most of the first half of 1989. This review, hampered by delays in filling crucial positions at the State Department and by the controversy over John Tower which left the Defense Department leaderless for nearly two months, provoked charges that the Administration had hit the floor and fallen flat on its face.

The Bush review of foreign policy became the target of much criticism, largely on the grounds that it led to a lack of initiative in a period when Gorbachev's diplomacy continued to have an almost hyperactive quality. While some of the criticism was justified, much of it failed to understand the purpose of the review. This chapter sets out to examine the rationale underlying the review, the way it was conducted, and its results. In addition, the analysis identifies the policy choices which emerged from the review and offers some overall reflections on the consequences of the review.

The origins and rationale

The review of foreign and strategic policy initiated by President Bush soon after coming to office was a response to domestic factors, international trends, and a general sense of uncertainty about the direction in which the United States should move as it entered the 1990s. It was a response to both problems and opportunities and came at a time when a stock-taking and prospectus were badly needed.

An important factor leading to the review was a sense that the United States faced difficult choices in its defence budget and needed to work out a much clearer sense of priorities than had been evident in the Reagan Administration. The Reagan legacy in defence was rather mixed. Although the President had succeeded in regenerating American military power and, during his first term, had mobilised considerable support for what was the largest peacetime increase in defence spending in US history, this had not proved sustainable. During the second term defence authorisations declined, but, as Steve Smith has shown in the previous chapter, the Administration had proved reluctant to make the difficult decisions that were necessary. It failed to make choices between competing defence programmes, moving ahead, for example, with both the B1-B and the new Stealth bomber, the B-2. It had also avoided a final choice between the SICBM, the Midgetman, and the MX missiles. The need to cut federal spending meant that such choices could not be avoided for much longer if the means and ends of United States policy were to be brought into harmony. Moreover, it was necessary for the new Administration to sort out its strategic posture in order to ensure that the US negotiating stance in START was consistent with its priorities. The President's National Security Adviser, Brent Scowcroft, in particular, was unhappy with certain aspects of the START negotiating position of the Reagan Administration, and felt that it was necessary to elicit alternative approaches. It was hardly surprising, therefore, that almost as soon as the election was over there was discussion of some kind of review of defence policy.

In the event, the review that was undertaken was much broader than envisaged in late 1988. Much of the initiative for this seems to have come from Scowcroft who, prior to taking office, suggested that a reappraisal of United States policy was overdue. This reflected Scowcroft's sense of unease with the Reagan Administration's foreign and security policy – an unease that was shared by a President-elect who was more pragmatic than his predecessor and generally seemed uncomfortable with visionary schemes. This was not entirely surprising. There had been a dichotomy between the first and second Reagan Administrations, especially in policy towards the Soviet Union. Moscow stopped being the centre of an evil empire and Mikhail Gorbachev became Reagan's partner in ambitious schemes for arms reductions. After pursuing a very confrontational policy based on an extensive programme of strategic modernisation and the President's Strategic Defense Initiative, the Administration had drifted into what was in effect a *détente* by default, yet had provided no serious intellectual rationale for the change in policy. The sense of vision, however, remained and the proposals for space-based defences became transmuted into plans for ridding the world of nuclear weapons through superpower agreement. Such grandiose schemes had little appeal to policy makers who, for the most part, were more pragmatic, more cautious, and less ideological than the Reagan people.

In many respects, the Bush Administration represented the return of the old foreign policy establishment. Key figures in the Administration such as Scowcroft and Lawrence Eagleburger, the Deputy Secretary of State, had considerable experience in government and approached foreign policy very much from a traditional Atlanticist perspective. From this perspective too, a policy review was essential. It was necessary to assess the implications for the Atlantic Alliance not only to Gorbachev's policies towards Western Europe, but also of the trends and developments in the Soviet Union and Eastern Europe. There was concern that Gorbachev might simply be pursuing the traditional Soviet objective of dividing the Western Alliance, albeit through more subtle means than any of his predecessors. And even if the Soviets' new thinking offered new opportunities to move towards a safer and more co-operative relationship, the US response had to be both considered and co-ordinated with its allies. In these circumstances, the case for what Bush termed a prudent reassessment appeared overwhelming.

Another factor, lurking in the 1988 election campaign, and which almost certainly helped to prompt the review, was uncertainty over the future role and responsibilities of the United States in view of growing concerns about US decline. Although the Reagan Administration had succeeded in restoring American strength and self-esteem, the new sense of confidence had something of a fragile quality about it and the popular success of Paul Kennedy's *The Rise and Fall of the Great Powers* highlighted the growing concern over the United States economy, and the belief that the regeneration of American military power had created a budget deficit of almost crisis proportions. The growth of the trade deficit also contributed to concerns that, in a remarkably short time, the United States had gone from the world's largest creditor nation to the largest debtor. While it was possible for the new Administration to take comfort from the fact that the Soviet Union was in the midst of a long-term, systemic crisis which threatens the very legitimacy of the Soviet state, the notion of decline was less comfortable when applied to the United States. Yet the rise of economic competitors in the shape of Western Europe and Japan suggested that the age of superpower dominance of the international system might soon be over. Consequently, there was a sense that the world was changing and that United States foreign policy might have to change too. At the very least, there was a need for reflection and reappraisal, rather than moving ahead with business as usual.

There were also important domestic considerations underlying the review. The Bush Administration confronted a difficult task in attempting to satisfy multiple constituencies. On the one side, it faced potential problems with the more conservative wing of the Republican Party which had been unhappy about Reagan's willingness to reach accommodations with the Soviet Union and had always been suspicious of George Bush. On the other side it faced a Democratic Congress and the need for a bipartisan approach both to heal the wounds of the bruising election campaign of 1988 and to ensure the effectiveness of United States policies. If the Bush Administration attempted to differentiate itself from its predecessor by adopting a more pragmatic approach on issues such as the Strategic Defense Initiative, it risked alienating the right. If it reverted to a more hard-line policy towards Moscow − which would delight the right − then it would alienate the Democrats in Congress and precipitate another period of turbulence and disorder in United States foreign policy-making. In these circumstances a thorough policy review had much to recommend it. Such a review would enable the Administration to establish its own position on a series of policies yet would avoid the impression that the President was either departing too abruptly from the policies of his predecessor or was following these policies too slavishly. Although this was not part of the official rationale, the review can be understood as an effort to legitimise the objectives of the new Administration and thereby provide a sound domestic base from which to operate a new foreign policy.

The review process

The first public indications that there would be a review of US foreign
policy surfaced in mid-January, although at this stage it appeared to
be primarily an idea being pushed by Scowcroft. During his confirmation hearings before the Senate Foreign Relations Subcommittee,
Secretary of State Baker affirmed that the Administration would engage
in a strategic review, but he offered no details. In fact, those details
had not been discussed by Bush's senior advisers, and the length and
scope of the review were not determined until two weeks into the
Presidency. The options before the Administration ranged from a quick
overview of current policy lasting no more than a month, to a
comprehensive review of American strategic interests and policy into
the next century which might last as long as a year. In the event, the
Administration opted from something that was more than a quick
stock-taking but was less than the fundamental and thorough reassessment that had been discussed. On 9 February, during a speech to
Congress, Bush announced that the results of the review would be ready
within ninety days.

This relieved those commentators who had expressed concern that
if the review lasted throughout 1989 it could effectively halt the
improvement of superpower relations. The target date of mid-May
meant that there would be a hiatus, but it would be acceptable. Indeed,
given the nature of the review, anything more rapid than this would
have been impossible. Although the review was not unlimited in scope,
it was certainly ambitious for a relatively short timetable. Its major
theme was US–Soviet relations, with particular attention being given
to conventional and strategic arms control negotiations and US force
structures in view of the 'apparent' changes occurring in the Soviet
Union. The review would also address US foreign policy on various
regional and international issues, including chemical and biological
weapons, proliferation of ballistic missiles, drugs, the environment,
Central America, and the Middle East.

The 'terms of reference' for the review were drawn up by the
National Security Council staff after informal discussions with the
President, Secretary of State James Baker, and Scowcroft. Although
Bush, at this stage, had not approved a final draft of the study directive,
the main shape of the review of policy towards the Soviet Union was
apparent by 9 February. According to one report this was to consist
of three elements: a basic 'strategic overview' of policies towards the

Soviet Union which would also consider US military objectives in Europe given the changes in the Soviet Union and Eastern Europe as well as in the Atlantic Alliance; an analysis of the United States strategic force structure and the modernisation programmes that were required; and an effort to identify the appropriate United States position in both strategic and conventional arms control negotiations with the Soviet Union.[1]

Given the complexity of this task, and the inevitable bureaucratic and organisational rivalry, it was necessary to use inter-agency groups to review specific issues. The enterprise as a whole was co-ordinated and consolidated by the staff of the National Security Council. This fitted in with the new President's philosophy. Among Bush's first moves as President was a restructuring of the foreign policy decision-making apparatus, with special attention given to the NSC and its staff. As well as returning to the original conception of the National Security Council as a small and streamlined advisory body (whose statutory members are the President, the Vice-President, and the Secretaries of State and Defense, but which invariably also includes the National Security Adviser), Bush created a second 'deputy' council under the chairmanship of Robert Gates, the Deputy National Security Adviser. This committee consists of: Gates, the Vice-Chairman of the Joint Chiefs of Staff, the Deputy Director of the CIA, the Undersecretary of Defense for Policy, and the Undersecretary of State for Political Affairs. It can also include, when necessary, the Deputy Secretaries of State and Defense. This second committee is important in that it is able to take some of the strain off the principals, yet consists of people within the departments who have sufficient seniority and importance to carry weight with the principals. Furthermore, it contains representatives of the Joint Chiefs of Staff and the Central Intelligence Agency and therefore was in a particularly strong position to co-ordinate the political and military strands in the review.

Although officially under Scowcroft's direction, the majority of the co-ordination work for the review was carried out by the council of deputies under Gates. The NSC staff co-ordinated and distilled the many studies undertaken throughout the bureaucracy. The Departments of State and Defense provided the main inputs, but contributions were also elicited from other agencies, various 'think tanks' such as the RAND Corporation, and former policy-makers such as Henry Kissinger. Their reports were then reviewed by the Gates Committee and approved for submission to the full National Security Council and President Bush.

The review began in early February amidst serious problems. The Administration could not embark on new initiatives before the review was completed, yet the review itself was hampered by a lack of personnel in both the State and Defense Departments as well as by the scope and comprehensiveness of the process. The debate in the Senate resulting in the rejection of John Tower as Secretary of Defense left the Defense Department leaderless for nearly two months, a development which exacerbated the difficulties of filling lower positions.

This was all the more critical because the Defense Department had a significant role to play in the review. There were several outstanding issues relating to force structure. These included mobile missiles, strategic defence, and the Stealth bomber. Even when Richard Cheney was finally confirmed as Secretary of Defense, the difficulties did not disappear. Cheney's immediate preoccupation was the defence budget for the forthcoming fiscal year. The fact that the budgetary request had to be completed prior to the review not only meant that several major decisions had to be finessed, but also that continued funding was requested for weapons systems which may never be deployed.

At the State Department too, key positions were not yet filled. Because of the Tower fiasco, the Administration was very slow in nominating people, conducting lengthy reviews of potential appointees to ensure that they were free of taint. Moreover, when choices were made and people nominated, the hard right in the Senate, led by Senator Jesse Helms, slowed the confirmation process, creating even longer delays. The process was so slow, in fact, that members of the State Department were still being confirmed in mid-June.

In spite of these problems, the review period was one of intense activity. In late February, Secretary Baker reported that there were twenty-eight foreign policy reviews being undertaken within the State Department. President Bush had requested reviews of US–Soviet relations, the position and policies of Mikhail Gorbachev, a variety of regional issues, international issues, arms control, and military force structures, and wanted them completed in a ninety-day period. By the first week in April, three of the most important papers on the Soviet Union, Eastern Europe, and Western Europe, had been submitted to the National Security Council. They were among only a handful of studies completed before mid-April.

Part of the reason for this was that considerable time was consumed by two issues. One was the future of Gorbachev and whether the United States could expect him to remain in power in the short and medium terms. The other was what to do about Eastern Europe. This debate centred around a highly controversial proposal by Henry Kissinger, who contended that the United States and the Soviet Union should attempt to reach a comprehensive political settlement in Europe. The Kissinger plan envisaged an easing of Soviet control and an explicit policy of military non-intervention by the Soviet Union in Eastern Europe (i.e. an effective and explicit abandonment of the Brezhnev Doctrine) in return for a pledge by NATO not to take advantage of this to interfere in Eastern Europe or to undermine Soviet security in any way. The scheme for a grand political settlement was rejected by the new Administration for several reasons. Part of the problem was that it appeared to demand United States complicity in keeping Eastern Europe under Soviet control, albeit a more tenuous form of control than in the past – something that smacked of a second Yalta. A further objection was that Soviet control over its satellites was diminishing in any event and there was therefore no reason why the United States should offer anything in return. These considerations led to the rejection of the Kissinger proposal in favour of a policy of differentiation which was designed to encourage diversity but not discord in Eastern Europe. The approach was less bold and dramatic than that proposed by Kissinger, but was more in line with the overall sense of prudence and pragmatism exhibited by the Administration in its first few months. Indeed, these qualities were clearly discernible throughout the review and were evident in the conclusions that were reached.

The conclusions of the review

Although the review yielded no overall policy document or comprehensive analysis of the challenges that the United States will face through the 1990s and beyond, it was clear from the statements that were made by the President and key advisers in mid-1989 that the review had resulted in what might be described as a cautious optimism about East–West relations. The major conclusions of the review were 'status quo plus' in orientation. They suggested that the US should not make major changes to any of its policies and that it should play a wait-and-see game with the Soviet Union and Eastern Europe. The approach was neutral and it was concluded that the United States should neither facilitate nor harm the processes of reform occurring in the Soviet

Union. This was essentially a compromise between a fairly hard-line Department of Defense and a much more moderate Department of State, crystallised by Scowcroft's own conservatism. Towards the end of the review, however, this caution became a source of frustration to President Bush who may have been unhappy with visionary policies although he nevertheless wanted some bold initiatives. Because these initiatives were lacking, the Bush foreign policy was once again criticised as ineffective.

Despite the 'status quo plus' orientation of the review, however, it answered many of the basic questions that the Bush Administration posed. Initially the focus was on Gorbachev and his ability to remain in power. This was somewhat ironic given that United States presidents are elected for only four years at a time. Irony aside, however, the review concluded that Gorbachev was secure in his position for at least three to five years and that the Bush Administration would have to deal with him. At the same time, the review rejected the idea that US policy should be designed to keep Gorbachev in power, advocating instead that Bush adopt a policy aimed at promoting US self-interests, neither deliberately helping, nor hurting the Soviet leader.

On issues of arms control, however, the review was less conclusive. Indeed, in early May, Bush was becoming more and more frustrated as the review process failed to elicit any new initiatives on conventional arms control. Signs of its failure to produce results had already been apparent in early March with the opening of the Conventional Forces in Europe (CFE) talks in Vienna. Both State Department officials involved in the negotiations and the White House acknowledged that no policy planning had been done at the high levels of Administration prior to the opening of the talks. From the flurry of activity that occurred after Secretary of State Baker returned from Moscow in mid-May, it appears that the review never actually formulated any new policies on conventional arms control. The new initiatives announced by President Bush at the NATO summit were generated by a small group of top advisers working together after the Baker visit to Moscow.

On issues involved in the Strategic Arms Reductions Talks (START) negotiations, the review did not proceed much faster. Nor were the initial results conclusive. Despite the resumption of the START negotiations on 19 June, the Administration had not completed studies that it had begun in March and April about the outstanding issues. Included among these issues was that of Soviet SS-18 missiles that are capable of carrying far more than their stated number of ten warheads.

Additionally, there were questions concerning both the mobile and heavily MIRVed Soviet SS-24 missiles and the US position of a ban on mobile missiles. The review examined compromises which either did not ban mobile missiles or which banned only MIRVed mobile missiles. Nuclear-armed sea-launched cruise missiles (SLCMs) were also studied. Limitations on SLCMs were reviewed because of the perceived differential between the threat they pose to the heavily populated US seaboards and the threat they pose to Soviet cities inland. SLCMs are also problematic because of the similarity between US nuclear and conventionally armed versions. Also under discussion were rules for counting air-launched cruise missiles (ALCMs) since these could radically alter the number of deployable warheads if the rules do not match actual bomber capabilities. Finally, the strategic review's discussions examined the Strategic Defense Initiative, the ABM Treaty, and their role in the START negotiations.

In many cases, this review, National Security Review 14 directed by Arnold Kanter, reopened matters that had been settled by the Reagan Administration. The reason for this was the belief, especially of Scowcroft, that the Reagan START positions and the Air Force posture which favoured MX over Midgetman had failed to address adequately the vulnerability of US land-based missiles. The dilemma for the Bush Administration was whether to accept positions it deemed less than perfect, or reopen them, with the possibility that the Soviets would reopen others and a treaty signing would be delayed.

In what appears to be at least partly a delaying tactic to allow more time to address these concerns, the Administration tabled a 'try before you buy' pre-treaty verification scheme aimed at establishing functional accurate verification techniques before a treaty is signed. It was hoped that such a plan would facilitate the ratification process by allaying concerns over verification difficulties. Critics, however, contended that this proposal would only slow the negotiations and delay their conclusion. Yet this was consistent with the Administration's priorities. The Bush Administration put the START Treaty on the back burner while giving far greater impetus to the CFE negotiations. Indeed, it was only in late September 1989 that the United States announced that it was prepared to relax its demand for a ban on mobile missiles – conditional upon congressional funding for the MX and Midgetman. The delay was symptomatic of differences amongst the agencies and departments involved, and the difficulties that stemmed from the interdependence between negotiating positions, where the executive is dominant, and force structure decisions, where the funding process gives Congress a decisive voice.

Indeed, arms control matters could hardly be settled before the results of the review of military force structures. Yet because of the late start of Secretary Cheney and his staff and the rapidly approaching budget deadlines, the review of force structures became subordinate to the budget process, where Cheney was asked to cut approximately $10 billion dollars from the Reagan request. Bush did make a decision on the land-based mobile missile in late April as the budget deadline approached. His decision, however, was effectively a non-decision, providing for continued funding for both the MX and the Midgetman. Cheney and the Air Force had supported the MX, while Scowcroft supported the Midgetman. The decision by Bush to back both missiles, therefore, was based at least partly on the political necessities of compromise within his administration as well as the need to pressure the Soviets on the issue. Yet the issue remained controversial in Congress. The House was sympathetic to the MX but opposed to Midgetman while the Senate leaned in the opposite direction. The worst position for the Bush Administration would be to negotiate a START agreement which permitted the deployment of mobile missiles, yet to find that there was insufficient congressional support for US deployment of such systems. In these circumstances, the treaty would stand little chance of being ratified. By making the modified START position dependent on congressional backing for its modernisation programme, however, the Administration has almost certainly improved the chances of congressional support for the MX and Midgetman programmes.

Other force structure decisions eclipsed by budgetary imperatives in the first part of 1989 included SDI and the B-2 Stealth bomber. These programmes were funded by the Bush Administration, although at lower levels than in the Reagan budget. Their role in the force structures has been somewhat played down for the moment, but in both cases, doubts about the programmes remain. This is especially true of SDI where the Bush Administration has significantly altered the goals and has delayed deployment decisions into the second half of the 1990s at the earliest.

Where the review had the greatest immediate impact on US foreign policy was in the various regional issues that face the United States. In Central America, the Administration, following its review of the issue and working closely with congressional leaders through March 1989, abandoned the Reagan Administration goal of displacing the

Sandinista Government of Nicaragua, opting instead to work with the nations of Central America in supporting intensified peace efforts. Although non-military funding of the Contras would continue until February 1990, the new approach not only represents one of the more obvious shifts from the more ideological approach of the Reagan Administration but is also designed to obtain bipartisan support.

In Eastern Europe, the results of the review suggested once again that the United States should engage in a policy of 'status quo plus'. While acknowledging that significant changes were taking place in Poland and Hungary, the review recognised that US policy towards Eastern Europe faced serious constraints. The United States should do nothing which would give the Soviet Union a pretext to re-establish its grip in Eastern Europe. Nor should the United States adopt policies which would encourage nationalistic movements to rise in Eastern Europe. It was acknowledged that reform rather than revolution is the key to the continued loosening of the Soviet bloc. Accordingly, the review led the United States to adopt a renewed policy of differentiation within Eastern Europe, encouraging political and economic reform in those countries where it was already occurring.

On the Middle East, Secretary Baker reaffirmed the determination of the United States to engage in a pragmatic attempt to secure peace and democracy for all parties. His statement recognised, as in Central America, that the regional states themselves were of utmost importance and that high-visibility American initiatives would not succeed if the basis for their success did not already exist among the Arabs and Israelis. In addition, Baker made clear that the United States was not opposed to an increased Soviet presence in the Middle East diplomatic field, so long as that presence was constructive in nature.

Despite their obvious implications for US foreign policy, the conclusions of the review were never presented in a single document. Instead, the completed studies were used to generate a series of five speeches given by President Bush during April and May 1989. Bush gave the first speech to an audience in Michigan on 17 April. Its topic was Eastern Europe, and the President made clear his commitment to encouraging the kind of change that was occurring in Poland and Hungary and to promoting reform elsewhere. Because of the changes that were under way in Poland, especially in relation to the role and legitimacy of Solidarity, Bush proposed a list of items through which the United States would help the Polish economy. These included the easing of Poland's repayment schedules, authorisation for the Overseas

Private Investment Corporation to operate in Poland, allowing Poland to work with the International Monetary Fund (IMF), support for educational, cultural and training programmes, supporting debt for equity swaps by business and non-profit organisations, and continuing to support International Finance Corporation loans to the Polish private sector. Overall, Bush announced that the US would use a policy of differentiation in Eastern Europe, helping those nations which undergo significant liberalisation and political reform. There would, however, be no repetition of past mistakes in Western financing of Eastern Europe. No money would be lent unconditionally, and no help would be given unless sound economic processes were used in Eastern Europe.

The second speech was at Texas A. & M. University on 12 May. The speech focused on US–Soviet relations, and the President made clear that the United States wanted to go beyond containment and 'welcome the Soviet Union back into the world order'.[2] He indicated that the review of superpower relations completed by the Administration had identified an unprecedented opportunity to improve US–Soviet relations and transcend traditional patterns of conflict. The United States now sought 'much more than simply containing Soviet expansionism – we seek the integration of the Soviet Union into the community of nations'. That this could be contemplated was the result of the success rather than the failure of the containment policy and the changes that were taking place in the Soviet Union. Bush contended that his goal was both bold and ambitious and would require strength, patience and a sweeping vision on the part of the United States. At the same time, the Soviet Union would also have to take positive steps. These, it was contended, should include reductions in its forces in Europe, continued liberalisation in Eastern Europe, co-operation with the West on regional problems, permanent respect for human rights and democratic pluralism within the Soviet Union, and a willingness to address global and transnational problems such as drugs and the environment. As well as this general road map for the improvement of superpower relations, Bush renewed President Eisenhower's call for an 'open skies' agreement, arguing that this should be explored, on a broader, more intrusive and more radical basis. Greater openness of this kind would enhance confidence and reveal the Soviet commitment to change. As an incentive for the Soviet Union to move in the directions indicated by the United States, Bush held out the possibility that if Moscow relaxed its emigration laws he would work with

Congress for a temporary waiver of the Jackson–Vanik Amendment, thereby opening the way for the Soviet Union to obtain most favoured nation status. Apart from open skies and a possible waiver of Jackson–Vanik, the speech had few specifics. Nevertheless, it revealed that even though the review had resulted in the 'status quo plus', the 'plus' was far from insignificant. The Bush Administration, as a result of its review, had embraced what could be described as a policy of co-operative engagement with Moscow, a policy that was far removed from the competitive strategy that Bush had talked about during 1988.

The third speech in the series – on 21 May before an audience at Boston University – focused on the relationship between Western Europe and the United States. Emphasising that the relationship was based on culture, kinship and shared value, President Bush acknowledged that, in the past, United States policy had been somewhat ambivalent towards a more united Europe – an ambivalence that had more recently been accentuated by concerns over 1992. The Administration though was convinced that 'a strong, united Europe means a strong America' and accordingly, Bush welcomed 'the emergence of Europe as a partner in world leadership'.[3] He argued too that new consultative mechanisms were required to ensure that this partnership worked effectively. The President also applauded European co-operation on security issues, especially the role of the Western European Union (WEU) in the Persian Gulf, while reaffirming that Europe remained important to the United States and that US ground and air forces would be maintained in Europe as long as they were needed and wanted. The President also warned of the dangers of complacency in the West, and reiterated the importance of the nuclear elements in NATO's force structure. Improvements in East–West relations in Europe would continue, but should be accomplished through a 'deliberate step-by-step approach'. In spite of this cautionary note, the President made clear that he placed a high priority 'on negotiating a less militarized Europe, one with a secure conventional balance at lower levels of forces'.[4]

The President's final speech in the US, before his trip to the fortieth anniversary NATO summit in Brussels, was made at the Coast Guard Academy on 24 May. The speech concentrated on broad US security interests and reaffirmed the commitment to free markets, and to the search for a more stable relationship with the Soviet Union. Bush reiterated the goal of integrating the Soviet Union into the international community and argued that this held tremendous promise for stability.

He called upon the Soviet Union to be more open about its military expenditures while also emphasising that the United States should maintain its military strength and move ahead with the deployment of mobile missiles. In addition, Bush acknowledged that there were growing threats to stability in the Third World as a result of the proliferation of ballistic missiles and chemical weapons.[5]

The most dramatic initiatives of all, however, came during the President's visit to Europe for NATO's fortieth anniversary summit. At the summit Bush unveiled a plan to speed up the conventional force negotiations in Europe. The President also accepted the inclusion of aircraft – something that the Warsaw Pact had been demanding and NATO resisting – and called for a reduction in United States and Soviet forces in the Atlantic to the Urals zone to a common ceiling of 275,000. These ideas were also laid out in the President's speech on 31 May in Mainz, West Germany, in which Bush called for an end to the cold war and the division of Europe. As a major step in this process the Berlin Wall should come down. In many respects the statement was the most optimistic of all the foreign policy addresses that Bush had given and the President set out a vision for a Europe in which there was political freedom in the East, a Berlin without barriers, a cleaner environment, and less militarisation.

Although some of the details were still lacking, the series of speeches given by Bush had revealed the main themes in the Administration's policy both towards Western Europe and the Soviet Union. What then can be said about the review? To what extent did it succeed in meeting the initial objectives of the President?

Analysis of the review

The visit to Europe was widely hailed as a great success for Bush. His initiative on conventional force reductions had shown that good public relations was not the exclusive preserve of Mr Gorbachev, and had provided the way for a compromise in NATO on the issue of short-range nuclear forces and arms control. At the same time, the Bush initiative seems to have taken place in spite of the review process rather than because of it. In March, when the conventional force negotiations opened in Europe, there were reports that the US position had been given little or no high-level attention and that the President had not provided any sense of direction.[6] Nor did the review seem to offer very much on this. The crucial shift in the Bush position seems to have come partly from the visit to Moscow by Secretary of State Baker in early May. Going with the stated intention that he would 'test the new thinking' in Moscow, Baker returned very impressed with Soviet seriousness about improving relations. Gorbachev's plans to make deep cuts in Soviet forces in Europe struck a particularly responsive chord with Baker and subsequently with the President. The United States' response, that was unveiled in Europe, was worked out in mid-May by a small group of advisers that included Baker, Cheney, Scowcroft, Gates, Undersecretary of Defense Paul Wolfowitz, the Chairman of the Joint Chiefs, Admiral William Crowe, and his Vice-Chairman, General Herres, and Chief of Staff John Sununu. Discussions were held during the President's vacation in Maine and subsequently in Washington where the final details were thrashed out. Gates and Undersecretary of State Lawrence Eagleburger were then sent to Europe to brief the Allies prior to the summit.[7]

The fact that the conventional arms control initiative resulted from the President's discussions with a small group of advisers rather than from the formal review process was seen by critics as an additional indictment of the review. Many commentators argued that it was unnecessary, that it put off crucial policy decisions, and delayed continuation of Reagan's policies on arms control and security. Overall, the review was seen as too slow and as engaging policy planners in lengthy studies of foreign policy that prevented them from acting on current policy problems. It was criticised for resulting in a slow transition from Reagan to Bush, and for attempting to get visionary policies out of pragmatic people. To what extent, though, does the review deserve these criticisms?

It is clear that such arguments are not groundless. There were reports that the President himself was dissatisfied with the conclusions of the review and especially its failure to provide new and creative ideas. Furthermore, the President reportedly changed the language of some of the speeches, making them much more positive about Gorbachev. On the other hand, the President should not have been surprised at the lack of originality from a bureaucracy which, by its very nature, prefers tradition, routine, and orderly procedure to innovation and creativity. The need for compromise amongst different groups with different interests and divergent perspectives also militates against bold initiatives.

Perhaps an even more telling criticism of the review is that in so far as it did provide ideas such as the reintegration of the Soviet Union into the international community, there was little sense of how this might be done or of the problems that could arise. The objective may be far more difficult to implement than it was to formulate. Similarly, the reaffirmation of American interests in Western Europe and the desire for co-operation does little to ease the problems that are likely to arise in managing the Atlantic Alliance during the 1990s. Bush may have accepted the principle of more equal partnership, but an 'orderly devolution' of power and responsibility from the United States to Western Europe could still prove elusive.

Other criticisms, however, are less persuasive. The claim that the review took too long is particularly unfair. It is hardly surprising that a comprehensive review of US foreign policy took ninety days to complete. The magnitude of the effort required for a comprehensive overview of the kind the President wanted would have cast doubt on any review that had taken less time. And to suggest that the United States cannot take ninety days to ensure that its foreign policy has a basic coherence and sense of purpose in the light of changing circumstances seems inappropriate to say the least.

Moreover, the review provided time for the Administration to get both its foreign policy team and its decision-making structures into place. Although the shortages of people at the State and Defense Departments hindered the review, they might have had more serious ramifications if the Bush Administration had attempted to launch major foreign policy initiatives. Indeed, a major benefit of the review was that it enabled the Administration to avoid any ill-advised foreign policy ventures during its first few months. In attempting to distance themselves from their immediate predecessor, new presidents sometimes attempt to introduce new policies too soon. Furthermore, lack of experience can sometimes result in ill-fated initiatives such as Kennedy's Bay of Pigs fiasco or the Carter Administration's deep arms cuts proposal. By undertaking a comprehensive review and attempting to sort out the highly diverse policies of his predecessor, Bush managed to avoid such mistakes.

A closely related advantage of the review was that it enabled the Bush team to develop its expertise and become more familiar with the existing policy agenda. The team was characterised by people knowledgeable about foreign and security policy, but who now had an opportunity to become more familiar with the precise details of the arms control negotiations and regional security issues.

The review also gave Bush an opportunity to establish a domestic consensus behind his foreign policy. His initial caution towards the Soviet Union satisfied the right, which had been unhappy with Reagan's apparent collaboration with Gorbachev. On the other hand, while Bush requested continued funding for the B-2, the MX, and SDI, again satisfying the right, he also cut Reagan's defence budget – a move that was welcomed by a Democratic Congress. Bush displayed a similar ability to find compromise positions in his policy towards Central America. He moved away from the Contras (and accepted the Sandinista Government), but also secured continued humanitarian aid from Congress. His domestic base was further strengthened by the bipartisan praise over his initiatives at the NATO summit and his resounding support from US public opinion.

But perhaps the most important result of the review has been the subtle shift of attitude towards the Soviet Union among Bush and his top advisers. After the election campaign and during the period preceding his inauguration in January, an increasingly hawkish line towards the Soviet Union raised doubts about the desire of the new Administration to keep US–Soviet relations moving in the direction mapped out by Reagan and Gorbachev. Statements by leading members of the Bush team suggested considerable scepticism about change in the Soviet Union. During his Senate confirmation hearings, for example, Baker noted that: 'However fascinating the twists and turns of *perestroika* may be and however riveting the details of decline as reported in Soviet newspapers, the Soviet Union remains a heavily armed superpower'.[8] He acknowledged the change in Soviet rhetoric, but claimed that 'the force structure and policies that support far-reaching interests and clients have not changed commensurately'.[9] Scowcroft appeared even more sceptical. He stated his belief that the cold war was not over and that Mikhail Gorbachev was seeking to buy time for his domestic reforms by causing divisions within NATO.[10] Secretary of Defense Cheney, too, was wary of Soviet intentions. At one point, he upset both the President and the Soviet Union by suggesting that the United States should remain vigilant because Gorbachev was likely to fail and be replaced by a hard-line leader.

By the end of the review, though, those attitudes had undergone subtle, but important, shifts. Baker and Bush were both becoming convinced of the seriousness of Gorbachev's attempts at reform even before Baker visited Moscow in early May. Although Baker was clearly convinced of Gorbachev's seriousness during his visit to Moscow, there are indications that he was moving in this direction before the visit.

His remarks in a speech on 5 May acknowledged that dramatic changes were occurring in the Soviet Union and that they were going beyond rhetoric: 'in a number of places, words have turned into realities'.[11] The withdrawal from Afghanistan and Gorbachev's unilateral troop cuts in Europe and the Far East were examples of this. After his visit to Moscow, Baker became even more convinced about Gorbachev's seriousness on conventional arms control.

While Scowcroft's views of late are less visible, there is no doubt that the initiatives on conventional and nuclear arms control being proposed by the Bush Administration have at least his stamp of approval. Cheney's views, too, have shifted since he came into office. At a NATO defence ministers' meeting soon after the NATO summit he indicated that the United States could capitalise on Gorbachev's new policies and enhance security. In late June, Cheney acknowledged that 'There is clearly a lot of evidence on the table that we are dealing with a less hostile and less threatening Soviet Union'.[12]

But even without any major new initiatives or the other benefits described above, the review was far from a failure in its outlook for US foreign policy. What is recommended is not a visionary policy based on sweeping proposals for a new world order, but a policy which accepts the need to come to terms with the ways in which the world has changed and is changing. What is suggested is not that United States policy should be accommodating because the Soviet Union has changed its nature, but that it should go 'beyond containment' because the Soviet Union is changing in positive ways which should be encouraged. The Bush Administration is ready to broaden the agenda with the Soviet Union and to accept a Soviet role in solving global problems so long as that role is constructive. Indeed, the Mediterranean summit with Gorbachev in early December 1989 confirmed the common interest of the superpowers in seeking stable reform in central Europe.

A similar approach is evident in West–West relations. Bush is ready to broaden the agenda with Europe as well, encouraging the development of economic and political union. This is more than just pragmatism. It is a vision of the world which recognises the erosion of bipolarity, and simultaneously acknowledges that the Europeans, in partnership with the United States, can play a valuable role in addressing the world's regional and international problems.

Perhaps most important of all, the Bush review has recognised that the United States cannot impose its visions on others. A 'kinder and gentler' world can only be achieved through close co-operation with other nations, whether they be global or regional players. The review did not produce a vision, but it did produce vision. It allowed the Administration to discern present trends and future possibilities and crystallised the underlying rationale which will guide the Bush Administration in its efforts to both manage and accommodate change.

Notes

1 See D. Oberdorfer, 'US moving to review Soviet policy', *Washington Post*, 9 February 1989.

2 President George Bush, 'Address at Texas A. & M. University', 12 May 1989, official text, US Information Agency.

3 Bush, 'Boston University Commencement Address', 21 May 1989, official text, US Information Agency.

4 Ibid.

5 Bush, 'Remarks to the Coast Guard Academy', 24 May 1989, official text, US Information Agency.

6 See, for example, J. McCartney, 'Non-nuclear talks near, and Bush is not ready', *Philadelphia Inquirer*, 2 March 1989.

7 See D. Lauter, 'Gorbachev plan for deep cuts in forces sparked Bush's arms policy initiatives', *Los Angeles Times*, 30 May 1989.

8 See *International Herald Tribune*, 18 January 1989.

9 Ibid.

10 Ibid., 23 January 1989.

11 Secretary of State, James Baker, 'Address to CSIS', 4 May 1989, official text, US Information Service.

12 *Christian Science Monitor*, 27 June 1989.

Glasnost and Soviet political reform under Gorbachev

To discuss Soviet political reform under Mikhail Gorbachev we need to consider a number of questions: what has Gorbachev been trying to do; what were the obstacles he confronted; how has he responded to those obstacles; and how successful has he been? This chapter will focus on the institutional structures of the Soviet Union and the extent to which Gorbachev had to change those structures in order to succeed. It looks especially at those reforms which relate to democratic procedures and federalism, and argues that the constitutional changes were significant as a prerequisite for economic restructuring.

What is Gorbachev trying to do?

An appropriate starting point in assessing Gorbachev's objectives is to examine a Soviet citizen's analysis of the situation as it appeared nearly four years after Gorbachev became General Secretary of the CPSU in March 1985. Andrei Sakharov was interviewed in December 1988 for the *New York Review of Books*, and his comments raise detailed questions about Gorbachev's aims.[1] A dissident who became a Supreme Soviet Deputy, Sakharov had hopes of reform, and initially welcomed the advent of Gorbachev. On the other hand, Sakharov expressed impatience with the slowness of the transition process and sought to push on towards a fully democratic Soviet Union. His comments need to be read in this light. He considered Gorbachev to be an improviser in the Khrushchev mould, without long-term goals other than those he professes. This is an important comment in view of some cynical Western assessments of Gorbachev as a kind of political conjuror who is trying to deceive the West by sleight of hand, while having a secret agenda identical to that promoted by all previous Soviet leaders, namely, to take over the world. Sakharov pointed out that Gorbachev was responding to a crisis. Gorbachev understood that change was desperately needed in the Soviet Union, but that the political structures were too rigid to enable significant economic reform to occur.

In this respect Sakharov expressed disappointment because of the extent to which by the late 1980s Gorbachev failed to fulfil his early promises. He characterised Gorbachev as a compromiser, a politician who had made deals with his opponents. These opponents had subverted Gorbachev's initiatives. Thus Gorbachev's problem, according to Sakharov, was to undermine the compromises to his own and the country's advantage. However, in Soviet politics there remains a constant temptation to try to achieve democratic change through undemocratic methods, in particular the traditional purge. In fact, in April 1989, after Sakharov was interviewed, Gorbachev purged a sixth of the CPSU's Central Committee.[2] This was obviously a cause for celebration among reformers in that it got rid of some dead wood. But at the same time it was a cause for anxiety in that the method was undemocratic. Similarly, the candidates for the Central Committee's share of the new Soviet Parliament were presented in a way which precluded choice for the Committee members, except to vote against a candidate.[3] Such procedures raise doubts about Gorbachev's commitment to democracy. He appears to be easily pushed back on to traditional CPSU methods.

Sakharov also complained that Gorbachev's constitutional reforms did not recognise pluralism. The Head of State, simultaneously General Secretary of the Party, remained in absolute control with the power to issue directives having the force of law. Further, Sakharov criticised the two-stage system for electing a new Supreme Soviet, a process which he considered undemocratic (though the US president is also elected through an electoral college). Sakharov also noted that the Popular Fronts of the Baltic Republics were not allowed to nominate candidates for the 1989 election. In the event, however, results indicated that, in spite of this handicap, Popular Front activists obtained a majority by being disguised as independents.[4] Finally, Sakharov was unhappy about the undemocratic nature of the Press Laws, Public Assembly Laws and the new Public Order Act.

Sakharov's comments are worth recalling because they posed fundamental questions about how, and to what extent, Gorbachev would transform the Stalinist administrative command system. Sakharov argued that partial reform could be worse than no reform at all because the process of reform itself would create a crisis. To a degree, Gorbachev would be able to use the crisis to push forward his reforms, but without careful management the situation could get out of control. The difficulties of transforming an arthritic system can be illustrated by a typical Soviet anecdote. One has to imagine former Soviet leaders sitting together in a train passing through the Soviet Union, when suddenly it stops. Lenin leaps up and shouts: 'shoot the driver!' The driver is shot but the train stays put. Then Stalin jumps to his feet demanding: 'shoot one in five of the passengers!' This is done and the train moves forward a little before coming to a halt. Khrushchev then leaps up and says: 'it's all the fault of our previous leaders. Let's try two drivers – one for each side of the train.' After more desultory movement the train stops again. Brezhnev remains slumped in the corner and says: 'let's pull down the blinds, open a bottle of vodka, and pretend the train is moving!'

Gorbachev's answer was to blame the passengers for the lack of movement and tell them to get out and push. Perhaps one of the most fascinating of his actual pronouncements occurred in a speech to representatives of the mass media just before conducting a purge of officials in September 1988. He argued that it was necessary to rid the public consciousness of its faith in a 'good tsar', an all-powerful centre imposing restrictions and establishing order from above.[5] Gorbachev saw the development of the Soviet Union as stemming from populist demands and criticism from below. The way forward for the Soviet economy was to introduce market mechanisms because the economy had failed to produce goods that people wanted. For supply to respond to demand, the needs of Soviet citizens would have to be communicated. And hence the people must operate in a system in which they did not fear the consequences of articulating their demands. A precondition of market reform, therefore, had to be a corresponding reform of the political system. Thus *perestroika* – the rebuilding and transformation of the Soviet Union – would only be possible in a climate in which *glasnost* was possible, and that would hinge on political change.

Glasnost has frequently been mistranslated in the West, and is wrongly thought to derive from the Russian word *glaza* – meaning 'eye'. It has thus been interpreted as involving the opening of everything to public scrutiny. But 'openness' is an inaccurate translation. The new concept of *glasnost* comes from the Russian word *golos*, which means 'voice', and in many ways is merely a substitute for the Communist Party's traditional call for *kritika* – criticism and self-criticism.

In a climate of *glasnost* the Soviet people should be able to speak up and make clear their requirements. It is only in this way that their local leaders and the political system can become properly responsive.

Glasnost, I think, continued to be regarded by Gorbachev as a way of preserving the essential institutions of the Soviet system, whilst reining-in their zones of control. There is an element of contradiction about the policy. Gorbachev is not prepared to abolish the vanguard Party, but in promoting the concept of *glasnost* he attacks the basis of the Party's legitimacy.

Obstacles to political reform

The Communist Party rules because it claims a monopoly of the ability to decide the correct way to go forward. Sometimes it appears to be claiming a monopoly of truth. This is not quite correct. It claims a monopoly of methodology and of the ways of deciding which is the best policy.[6] But if the people know more than the Party, or if it has been misinterpreting the people's demands, then there are doubts about the Party's claim to legitimacy. Gorbachev will have to find a new doctrine of Party legitimacy at the same time as defining a new relationship between, on the one hand, the Party and the soviets, and on the other the relationship between the Party and the economy.

Thus the role of the CPSU and its institutions present the major structural problem, though of course Gorbachev derived his own power from the way the institutions were set up. In brief, the process is that the CPSU's Congress meets every five years to examine the economic plan and elect a Central Committee to run the Party's affairs between Congresses. In turn the Central Committee elects a Politburo and a Secretariat. In theory, the Politburo acts as the supreme policy-making institution, but it also co-ordinates the work of the top Party and State bodies (the Party Secretariat and the Presidium of the Council of Ministers). The relationships are shown in Figure 7.1.

The Secretariat, headed by the General Secretary, carries out personnel policy and co-ordination of the various branches of policy making. In effect the Party Secretariat continually interferes in the workings of the economy. It acts as the source of political input to the administrative process, and also appoints people to key positions. Each Secretariat, and they exist in every territorial administrative unit, has a *nomenklatura*, a list of positions to which favourites are appointed. Thus, historically, a general secretary determined the appointments

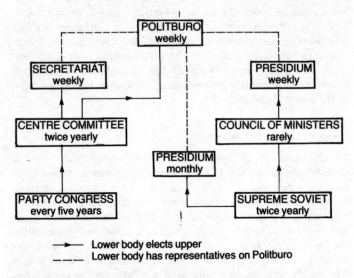

Figure 7.1 *Government structure before the Gorbachev reforms*

of those who would one day make up the Central Committee, and re-elect him. General secretaries have used this power to bring in a number of cronies to ensure their own security. It was most marked in the Brezhnev period when it seemed that just about everyone who had been in Brezhnev's class in the Dnepropetrovsk Engineering Institute in 1931 held high office of one kind or another.[7] This 'Dnepr Mafia' and its network was an example of the 'cronyism' running throughout the system. Needless to say, Gorbachev himself emerged from a group, known as the 'Stavropol Mafia', headed by Mikhail Suslov, a hard-line ideologue in Brezhnev's Politburo.[8]

In sum, the General Secretary has traditionally been the most powerful man in the Soviet Union, controlling the power of patronage, setting the Politburo's agenda, and summarising its decisions. The similarities with the power of the British Prime Minister are quite striking. Gorbachev, however, has set about restructuring the political apparatus. Ironically, if he succeeds he will have to create for himself a separate basis of power and legitimacy.

Gorbachev's initiatives

The Politburo which Gorbachev inherited in 1985 was split between a Leningrad faction and a Siberian group. Some of the latter were former General Secretary Konstantin Chernyenko's followers whilst others were associated with Prime Minister Nikolai Ryzhkov. The Leningrad officials appear to have joined the Politburo because they had knowledge of the USSR's defence and high-technology industries which are concentrated around their city. By contrast, the Siberians derived their expertise from the energy industry. To begin with, Gorbachev appeared to try to hold the balance between the two factions. In his first year, he seemed uninterested in appointing members of his own mafia, though he expanded the Politburo, shuffled responsibilities, brought in Yegor Ligachev, Eduard Shevardnadze and Boris Yeltsin, and dropped three members of the 'old guard', including Grigory Romanov. Then throughout 1987 a bitter struggle in the Party hierarchy forced Gorbachev to adopt a conciliatory line towards his conservative critics, chief of whom were Ligachev and the head of the KGB, Viktor Chebrikov.

The turning point for reform came at a special Party Conference in June 1988, which Gorbachev called to set a new political agenda and to pave the way for sweeping personnel changes in the Politburo and the Party's Central Committee. At the end of September Gorbachev retired President Andrei Gromyko and the Chairman of the Party Control Commission, Mikhail Solomentsyev, as well as three candidate members in the Politburo. He brought in two of his own cronies – Vadim Medvedev as Secretary for Ideology and G. Razumovsky as head of the Commission for Cadres Policy, and introduced A. Biryukova and A. Lukyanov (a close associate of Gorbachev) as candidate members (see Table 7.1). This was hailed by reformers as a coup, but it was a partial one. The conservatives Ligachev, Chebrikov and the Ukrainian Party boss, Vladimir Shcherbitsky, continued to sit on the Politburo.

However, one of the outcomes of the CPSU's Central Committee plenum, held on 30 September 1988, was an instruction to the Politburo to create a new structure for the Party apparatus, better suited to the process of *perestroika* at national and local level. Its significance was not fully appreciated in the West, but the first stage was the creation of six commissions at national level to consider future policies and to replace the existing committee structure. Indeed, the Politburo,

Table 7.1 *Politburo membership, 30 September 1988*

Full members

M. S. Gorbachev	General Secretary & President
Ye. K. Ligachev	Secretary & Chairman, Agriculture Commission
V. M. Chebrikov	Secretary & Chairman, Legal Commission
V. A. Medvedev	Secretary & Chairman, Ideology Commission
V. P. Nikonov	Secretary & Vice-Chairman, Agriculture Commission
N. I. Ryzhkov	Prime Minister
V. V. Shcherbitsky	First Secretary, Ukraine
E. A. Shevardnadze	Foreign Minister
N. N. Slyunkov	Secretary & Chairman, Social & Economic Commission
V. I. Vorotnikov	President, RSFSR
A. N. Yakovlev	Secretary & Chairman, International Commission
L. N. Zaikov	First Secretary, Moscow

Candidate members

A. P. Biryukova	Deputy Prime Minister
A. I. Lukyanov	Deputy President
Yu. D. Maslyukov	Chairman, State Planning Commission
G. D. Razumovsky	Secretary & Chairman, Cadres Policy Commission
Yu. F. Soloviev	First Secretary, Leningrad
N. V. Talyzin	Deputy Prime Minister
A. V. Vlasov	Prime Minister, RSFSR
D. T. Yazov	Minister of Defence

itself, seemed to divide into two groups: one contemplating long-term strategies, and the other administering current policy. Gorbachev supervised current Party personnel policy, whilst Razumovsky looked into its future. Medvedev was charged with long-term ideological policy, whilst Gorbachev probably kept a hold on immediate requirements. N. Slyunkov was responsible for social and economic policy in the long term, Biryukova and Nikolai Ryzhkov on a day-to-day basis. Two members were on the Agriculture Commission. The conservative Ligachev was given long-term agricultural policy, and Nikonov daily management, though the inherent tension in having two Agriculture Commissioners in the Politburo was surprisingly resolved in Ligachev's favour when Nikonov retired in September 1989. Yakovlev dealt with long-term international and perhaps defence policy; Foreign Minister Eduard Shevardnadze dealt with immediate issues. Finally, Viktor Chebrikov was in charge of long-term legal policy, while the Minister of Internal Affairs and the head of the KGB coped with these matters in the short term.

Next, in April 1989 Gorbachev purged the CPSU's Central Committee of a sixth of its members, mostly 'pensioners' from the Brezhnev era and some of them former Politburo members, including former President Gromyko, former Prime Minister, Nikolai Tikhonov, a former Vice-President, Vasily Kuznetsov, and the corrupt Azerbaijan Party boss, Geidar Aliyev. This minor 'massacre', or what Gorbachev called 'a serious regrouping', signified his increasing confidence and a determination to establish support for reform as the key to preferment. Curiously, after the September 1988 Politburo 'purge', the complexion of the Central Committee's Secretariat had become more evenly balanced between reformers and conservatives whereas previously it had slightly favoured Gorbachev. His supporters, Biryukova and Lukyanov were relieved of their Secretariat posts when they entered the Politburo. The conservative Chebrikov, still on the Politburo but no longer in charge of the KGB, joined the Secretariat, though only for a year (see Table 7.2).

One explanation, made plausible by the reorganisation of the apparatus, including the Politburo, is that Gorbachev was preparing to completely bypass the Secretariat's power to interfere in the workings of the economy.[9] Indeed the removal of Shcherbitsky, Nikonov and

Table 7.2 *CPSU Central Committee Secretariat, 30 September 1988*

M.S. Gorbachev	General Secretary
V.M. Chebrikov*	Commission for Legal Policy
L.N. Zaikov	Also First Secretary, Moscow
Ye. K. Ligachev	Commission for Agriculture
V.A. Medvedev	Commission for Ideology
V.P. Nikonov*	Commission for Agriculture
G.D. Razumovsky	Commission for Party Builders & Cadres Policy
A.N. Yakovlev	International Policy Commission
N.N. Slyunkov	Commission for Socio-economic Policy
O.D. Bakhlanov	Military Industries

* Resigned 20 September 1989

Chebrikov from the Politburo a year later, in September 1989, brought about a new equilibrium in the balance between state and Party representatives at the top. For the first time since the immediate post-Stalin era, the state *apparat* had a clear majority over the Party (if candidate members are included).

The tension in the higher councils of the Party was reminiscent of a struggle in the period 1953–7 when Khrushchev made little progress with economic reforms. Then, in a fit of impatience, Khrushchev abolished the central ministries and replaced them with territorial economic councils.[10] It seemed that Gorbachev might be following an almost Maoist policy of 'throwing stones' and 'mixing sand and soil', confusing the lines of authority at the top.[11] Perhaps he hoped that the confusion would embolden the people involved in everyday policy-making at the factory and local level to assert themselves. The extent to which this proves successful will depend on the calibre of managers and the capacity of trade unions to respond to workers' needs.

Accompanying these changes in personnel and Party structure were Gorbachev's proposals for important constitutional reform.[12] Plans had already been under some discussion, but they were eventually unveiled at the special Party Conference in June 1988.

First, there was to be a new Congress of People's Deputies comprising 2250 members, some of them freely elected. This would meet once a year as a rule, tackle important constitutional questions, and elect a new Supreme Soviet and its Chairman.

Secondly, the new Supreme Soviet would operate on a permanent basis. This was significant because the old Supreme Soviet had met twice a year for five days at a time, merely to rubber-stamp legislation. The announcement indicated that the new 542–member legislature would operate with full-time 'parliamentary committees'. Like the old Soviet it would consist of two chambers – one comprising representatives from various nationalities and one consisting of representatives from the Union as a whole, whose chairman, Yevgeny Primakov became a candidate member of the Politburo in September 1989, thus enhancing the institution's power. But it was not explained how these people would be elected to each chamber. The Congress of People's Deputies would, however, act as an arbitrator between the Chamber of Nationalities and the Chamber of the Union.

Thirdly, there would be a Constitutional Review Committee, the members of which would have ten-year terms with the object of 'guarding the constitution' in order to create 'our own socialist system of checks and balances'. As the phrasing suggests, Gorbachev's interest in constitutional change did not mean that he would slavishly copy the United States or a European system. His speech to the Supreme Soviet did, however, call for a clear-cut separation of functions of the Party and the soviets, for legal reforms, and for judges and assessors to be elected for fixed ten-year terms. Figure 7.2 gives an outline of the new governmental structure.

The 1989 elections

The most exciting aspect of the reform package was the announcement that although a third of the seats in the Congress would be reserved for representatives nominated by public organisations, two-thirds would be directly elected (on the usual Soviet basis that, to win,

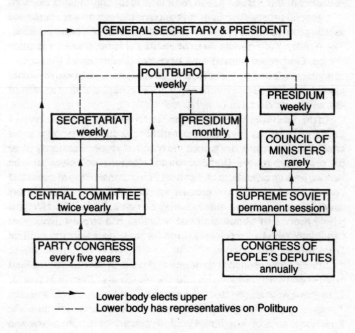

Figure 7.2 *Government structure after the Gorbachev reforms*

a candidate would have to obtain an absolute majority of 50 per cent plus one vote). Moreover, there might be several candidates for single-seat electoral districts. The complex procedures culminated in the March–April 1989 elections, during which official candidates faced opposition on the hustings, a novelty which attracted the attention of the rest of the world.

Of the 750 seats reserved for public organisations, 100 were to be nominated by the CPSU, 100 by the trade unions, and 75 each by the Komsomol, the Soviet Workers' Committee, and the War and Labour Veterans' Organisation. Other organisations were to nominate the remainder, varying from 20 for the Academy of Sciences down to 2 for the All-Union Conference of Fish Farmers. These could all have been elected in a competitive fashion but there were only 880 candidates for 750 seats. The Academy of Sciences, with 20 seats, held an election for its nominees, and 8 out of 23 were elected on the first round. A feature of this election was to recur later in the constituency elections – a general protest vote against those candidates who were perceived as being foisted on the Academy in the old manner of a beauty contest. The Academy of Sciences, like the electors at large, wanted a genuine choice. Gorbachev himself may have had doubts about the type of candidates selected by the official organisations. Conservatives would almost certainly be over-represented in this group, and they would not favour the acceleration of *perestroika*.[13]

In the direct constituency elections for 1500 seats, problems occurred in 275 of them. In 76 of those constituencies fielding three or more candidates, no contender gained the required absolute majority of 50 per cent plus one vote. In these, run-off elections took place between the two leading candidates. A further 199 were single- or two-candidate constituencies where voters crossed out names, thereby preventing any candidate achieving an absolute majority (see Table 7.3). Here the whole process of nomination and selection had to start again, and candidates who had previously stood for these seats were disqualified from further participation.

The elections produced some major shocks. In the RSFSR, the First and Second Party Secretaries and the Mayor and Deputy Mayor of Leningrad were all rejected; so were the First Secretaries of Karelia, Tyumen, Chita, Perm, Tomsk and other *oblasts*. In the Ukraine, the First Secretaries of Voroshilovgrad, Transcarpathia, Chernigov and Lvov were rejected. They had all been presented to the electorate unopposed, and the outcome in the Ukraine was widely regarded as

Table 7.3 *The election process in 1989*

Candidates nominated (January)	7531	
Candidates selected from these (March)	2895	
Constituency elections (March–April):		
with 1 candidate	384 ⎫	of which rerun
with 2 candidates	953 ⎬	199 (15%)
with 3 or more candidates	163	76 (47%)
Elected constituency seats	1500	275
Seats for public bodies	750	
Total	2250	

Source: Keesing's Contemporary Archives, 1989, pp. 36512–13.

a protest against the procedure rather than necessarily as a protest against the candidates themselves. Indeed the First Secretary of Voroshilovgrad had been considered as a possible Gorbachev protégé. In Belorussia, the Party bosses of Gomel, Mogilev and Minsk were also victims. A similar pattern occurred in Central Asia. In Armenia there was a significant boycott of the polls.

In some places only half of the electorate turned out, a clear protest against the old way of doing things. People wanted a choice between candidates and were frequently denied it. On the whole, abstentions probably benefited Gorbachev because they indicated the need for genuine democratic process. Conservatives who had accepted nominations in uncontested situations were affected particularly, and the losses sustained by officials in the Ukraine can be taken as a sign that the voters wanted more reform rather than less.

Success for Gorbachev?

It is difficult to reach a definitive conclusion about the elections because so many seats were uncontested. Even where there was a contest, it is unclear how much voters really understood the extent to which candidates differed on issues. However, there were clear indications that electors favoured contested elections. In this sense the results reflected popular support for *glasnost* and a demand that the 'old guard' allow it to work fully. On balance Gorbachev did well out of the rejection of conservatives.

But what of the threat from radicals? A spectacular victory in Moscow for Boris Yeltsin, the charismatic radical reformer, was seen in the West as a slap in the face for Gorbachev, because the latter had been pressured to expel Yeltsin from the Politburo for indiscipline in 1987. However, one should consider Gorbachev's advantage in being able to demonstrate to conservatives that support for immediate radical reform had grown dramatically since Yeltsin's expulsion. The Moscow result enabled Gorbachev to appear as a moderate and play the General Secretary's traditional role of power-broker.

The conservatives may have felt that the situation was one of Gorbachev's own making but, equally, it was difficult for them to resist the argument that there was little choice but to accept the need for reform. After the purge of the CPSU's Central Committee in April 1989 Gorbachev continued his offensive, and at the height of the coal strike in June 1989 referred to the appeal of 'leftist demagoguery'. To answer it the local Party cadres would have to stop lagging behind in the quest for *perestroika*.[14] Then, on 20 September, after a six-month delay, he capitalised on the popular verdict by removing another five members of the Politburo, among them Shcherbitsky and Chebrikov, the last of the Dnepropetrovsk Mafia, and the Leningrad boss, Yuri Soloviev, defeated in the March–April elections (see Table 7.4).

However, there is a qualification worth making. In Leningrad, as elsewhere, results reflected activity by protest groups who were prevented from registering their own candidates for the election. The existence of such groups threatens Gorbachev's intention to maintain the Communist Party's monopoly of power. The future of non-Communist politics will be an important test of *glasnost*. If Gorbachev really wants the free expression of views, he will have to accommodate groups organised to exploit *glasnost*. They will either have to be hijacked by the Party or allowed to operate freely. In the long run, this implies a multi-party system in fact if not in name, though it is far from clear how much political pluralism Gorbachev would be prepared to countenance.

In fact, after the elections, the CPSU accounted for a higher proportion of the Congress of People's Deputies than in the previous Supreme Soviet. The radicals amounted to only about one-tenth of the Congress. On the one hand this could be seen as a public endorsement

Table 7.4 *Politburo membership, 20 September 1989*

Full members

M.S. Gorbachev	General Secretary & President
Ye. K. Ligachev	Secretary & Chairman, Agriculture Commission
V.A. Medvedev	Secretary & Chairman, Ideology Commission
N.I. Ryzhkov	Prime Minister
E.A. Shevardnadze	Foreign Minister
N.N. Slyunkov	Secretary & Chairman, Social & Economic Commission
V.I. Vorotnikov	President, RSFSR
A.N. Yakovlev	Secretary & Chairman, International Commission
L.N. Zaikov	First Secretary, Moscow
V. Kryuchkov	Chairman, KGB
Yu. D. Maslyukov	Chairman, State Planning Commission

Candidate members

Ye. Primakov	Chairman, Supreme Soviet Chamber of the Union
B. Pugo	Chairman, Party Control Committee
A.P. Biryukova	Deputy Prime Minister
A.I. Lukyanov	Deputy President
G.D. Razumovsky	Secretary & Chairman, Cadres Policy Commission
A.V. Vlasov	Prime Minister, RSFSR
D.T. Yazov	Minister of Defence

of the Party in the Gorbachev era. On the other hand it reflected lack of genuine choice of candidates after the electoral commissions had whittled down more than 7500 nominees to 2895. There was not enough of a true choice presented to the electorate to allow it to deliver a verdict on *glasnost* or *perestroika*. Voters were not really presented with genuine choice between the old and the emerging ways. The electorate seemed willing to be mobilised but lacked opportunities for true political participation.

The televising of the meetings of the Supreme Soviet certainly demonstrated the existence of a great deal of interest in politics. Recorded highlights had to be broadcast in the evenings because there was a tendency for people to stop work to watch proceedings when they were scheduled during the day. Issues of social and economic reform were beginning to clarify, and the establishment of 'parliamentary committees', operating on a permanent basis, held out the prospect of a significant expansion of democratic procedures.

The first duty of the Congress which met on 25 May 1989 was to elect deputies to the two chambers of the Supreme Soviet and the post of President (i.e. Gorbachev). Radicals were no doubt disappointed that few of their number were elevated. The historian Roy Medvedev was the only Moscow radical to be elected to the Chamber of the Union. Initially, Yeltsin was the only nominee for the Chamber of Nationalities who failed to get elected, though the undemocratic device of asking an obscure delegate from Siberia to stand down in his favour eventually enabled the Muscovite to sit alongside Sakharov as a leader of the radical bloc.

Elections being arranged for local soviets and for the 1994 Supreme Soviet will provide a clearer indication of the extent of Gorbachev's political success, especially as nominated seats are to be abolished in the 1994 polls. But the balance sheet shows that Gorbachev had certainly attacked several problems bequeathed by Brezhnev.

First, he had overcome the crisis of gerontocracy. By the end of the 1980s the average age of the Politburo had moved down to the early sixties, whereas in Brezhnev's time it was in the middle seventies. Younger people were beginning to attain positions of power throughout the system, and Gorbachev presumably hopes that they will have new ideas for solving the problems of the Soviet Union.

Secondly, Gorbachev attacked the crisis of stagnation. It was almost as though nothing much had happened in politics after 1976. But no one could describe the Soviet Union as stagnating politically under Gorbachev. On the contrary the problem was whether the Soviet Union would become too volatile for its own survival.

Thirdly, Gorbachev confronted the crisis of corruption. In Brezhnev's last years many officials and leaders grew increasingly corrupt. Yuri Andropov attempted to bring them to court before he was incapacitated by ill health. Gorbachev indicated his determination to continue in this vein by nominating a notable Kazakhstan vigilante, Gennady Kolbin, to head a new People's Control Commission to combat bureaucratic inefficiency. In the climate of *glasnost* there were even calls to investigate Ligachev for corruption, and it was publicly hinted that Shcherbitsky had been involved in scandal.[15]

Federalism

However, a more serious problem facing Gorbachev is continuing unrest among ethnic and national groups. *Glasnost* not only allowed ideas to be expressed about changing politics and the economy, it also brought into the open the tensions that underlie the edifice of Soviet federalism. In the Baltic Republics, for example, Party officials won at the polls only where they identified with the Popular Fronts or where Fronts withdrew from contests. The elections delivered a resounding verdict for autonomy, if not independence. Gorbachev may have succeeded in placing himself in the centre of the Soviet political spectrum, but he has to deal with radical nationalism as well as with extreme reformers and anti-reformers. The Chamber of Nationalities is likely to be a tense forum, and it would be a minor miracle if it could deal effectively with fragmentation of the Soviet Union.

The dangers posed by such unrest became apparent in the communal violence in the Caucasus during 1988–90, particularly over the issue of whether the Armenian-populated enclave of Nagorno-Karabakh should become part of Armenia rather than Azerbaijan. Also, an attempt by Gorbachev's hardline opponents to exploit situations to discredit his administration may have been behind a local decision to use troops and poison gas against nationalist demonstrators in Tbilisi, Georgia, in April 1989.

Allied to the unrest is the problem of demographic imbalance. The bulk of industry is in European Russia; resources are in Siberia; and the fastest growing population is in Central Asia. Gorbachev has to deal with this equation without making racial problems worse. Indeed, one of the interesting phenomena of the post-Brezhnev period has been the revival of Russian nationalism. Brezhnev followed a policy of trying to represent the minority nationalities in the Politburo. For years Arvid Pelshe was a token Latvian and there were always a couple of token Muslims. But the period since 1985 has witnessed a resurgence of Great Russian Chauvinism, partly encouraged by the overwhelming Russian composition of the Politburo.[16] Two of Gorbachev's tasks may be to get the Russian population to accept internal immigration by Muslims and to safeguard the rights of Russian minorities in the Republics.

But it is important to appreciate that the character of nationalist demands varies from Republic to Republic, and that a case-by-case approach is likely to be more realistic than any blanket solution. In the Ukraine, for example, the Popular Front, known as Ruch, has more limited objectives in terms of autonomy than the Baltic Popular Fronts.[17] Indeed, in September 1989 Shcherbitsky went so far as to allow Ruch to hold public meetings in Kiev, an indication of his waning power in the Politburo from which he was ejected that same month.

The Baltic Republics, however, demand at least economic, if not political independence, and perhaps secession. They have always had some say over culture and language but from 1988, as in Yugoslavia, they began asking for control of the profits made by their enterprises. The Baltic Republics claimed that they were subsidising the rest of the Soviet economy. However, to allow them to retain a larger proportion of their profits would affect areas such as Central Asia which are subsidised from central funds. Reduced economic investment in the Muslim Republics would exacerbate their existing grievances.

To deal with the nationalities problem, the CPSU published in *Pravda* (17 August 1989) proposals for discussion by the September 1989 plenum of the Central Committee. Accordingly, the powers of All-Union (federal) and Republican institutions were to be defined. The Union's competence would include political structure, defence and security, foreign policy, general economic and political problems, and overall development. Republics would be allowed to have overseas representatives but not in contradiction with All-Union interests and policies. The Army would have status as both a multinational and an All-Union institution, its bases and deployment to be decided by the Union in agreement with the Republics. The Republics would have residual powers, that is, other areas not voluntarily surrendered to the Union. Disputes over competence would be resolved by the Constitutional Review Committee, acting as a constitutional court.

Although the Republics might cavil at their 'residual power' status, history has shown that residual powers allow for policy making in unforeseen areas which cannot be given readily to an authority endowed with specific powers. In trying to limit the scope for contention, the CPSU also proposed the writing of a new treaty or 'Declaration of the Union of Soviet Socialist Republics' to replace that of 1922 (and presumably of 1940 when the Baltic Republics supposedly voted for incorporation into the USSR). This will be an acid test of the viability of restructured federalism. Gorbachev has to establish and legitimise procedures governing relations between the Republics, and yet it is conceivable that a Republic's parliamentarians might refuse to sign a new treaty. Even so, a treaty will not sort out the problems of displaced persons and territorial claims. A separate set of proposals directed at smaller authorities, *oblasts* and *okrugs*, aimed to increase their representation on the soviets of the Republics in which they are situated. Their consent to any boundary changes would have to be obtained, outstanding disputes being settled by the USSR's Congress of People's Deputies.

In economic matters, the Republics will own land and resources. Enterprises will be divided between All-Union institutions, Republics, communes, co-operatives, social organisations and workers' collectives. They will make agreements with each other, with the Republics, and with the All-Union ministries under rules laid down by the Union. Individual agreements will deal with the distribution of foreign earnings, and the intention seems to be to develop a body of case-law to determine such relationships. In general, the Republics will be allowed to choose their own economic methods, taking account of 'the principles of economic effectiveness and social justice'. Whether capitalism can be 'socially just' may well exercise the brains of the Constitutional Review Committee! To overcome the problems of less developed areas, Republics will have to contribute to a fund for their support and for the alleviation of disasters. But there appeared to be no ready answers to questions about tax rates, and collection, payment and distribution of proceeds.

In politics, the CPSU Central Committee resisted a proposal to make the CPSU and other 'social organisations' simultaneously All-Union and autonomous in the Republics, arguing for centralisation at the expense of autonomy. But the Parties in the Republics will need independence and the right to argue with Moscow. Otherwise, if they do not represent popular views, non-Party candidates will be elected to the Republic legislatures which will then follow the Hungarian and Polish models. In a further proposal, the RSFSR would create institutions clearly distinct from the All-Union ones. The RSFSR has been the only Republic without its own Party (though at various times it has had its own bureau in the Central Committee), and so the proposal implies the formation of a Communist Party for the RSFSR. Finally, in a measure inspired by Estonian attempts to disenfranchise new Russian immigrants, there would be 'no privilege or discrimination on grounds of nationality, religion, language or period of residence'. *Inhabitants* of a Republic are both *citizens* of that Republic and the USSR.

All these proposals will have to be transformed into detailed legislation, and although the measures were accepted in principle, with small amendments, by the Central Committee in September 1989, it is clear that many nationalist battles lie ahead.

Conclusion

The success of political reform will depend very much, however, on the extent to which it expedites economic reform. Gorbachev has to provide consumer goods to offer the population incentives to work harder. Although there is a link between the political and economic restructuring, in some ways political reforms were the screen behind which the plan for economic reform had been devised. As the next chapter suggests, the most important aspect of the plan was price reform. Without a rational price structure the USSR will not be able to operate a market system or any form of competition, but Gorbachev's group shied away from implementing it in 1988–9. Similarly, *perestroika* and reform in the factories was only beginning, and a sytem of leasing on collective farms was still to be put into practice. Gorbachev's removal of political dead wood should facilitate restructuring, but the time when it will begin to take effect will almost certainly be during the Five-Year Plan commencing in 1991.

At the end of the 1980s, then, Gorbachev had entered a critical period. He had aroused opposition to his policies without having improved living standards. He could blame conservative forces, but the public was growing impatient for the benefits of the Gorbachev approach. If these are not forthcoming, nostalgia for authoritarian methods may increase. Indeed, in 1986 the author was told on the proverbial Leningrad tram: 'what we need in the Soviet Union is someone like your Margaret Thatcher. There is a true heir to Stalin.'

Notes

1 'An interview with Andrei Sakharov', *New York Review of Books*, XXXV, 22 December 1988, pp. 28–9.

2 *Pravda*, 26 April 1989, p. 1, *Current Digest of the Soviet Press*, XLI, 24 May 1989. Seventy-four full members and twenty-four candidate members declared: 'it is necessary for us, in the interests of the cause, to relinquish our authority as members of the CPSU Central Committee'.

3 Fifty-two candidates were elected unanimously. Ligachev was the least favoured candidate, securing only 78 out of 641 votes. Electoral Commission Report, *Pravda*, 19 March 1989, pp. 1–2.

4 *Keesing's Contemporary Archives*, 1989, pp. 36512–13.

5 *Pravda*, 25 September 1988, pp. 1–2.

6 A discussion of the Party and policy-making can be found in R. J. Hill and P. Frank, *The Soviet Communist Party*, London, Allen & Unwin, 1986, pp. 92–5.

7 T. H. Rigby, 'Old style congress – new style leadership', in R. F. Miller, J. H. Miller and T. H. Rigby, *Gorbachev at the Helm*, London, Croom Helm, 1987, p. 31.

8 D. R. Kelly, *Soviet Politics from Brezhnev to Gorbachev*, New York, Praeger, 1987, pp. 61–2.

9 *Keesing*'s, 1988, pp. 36355–6.

10 R. Medvedev, *Khrushchev*, Oxford, Blackwell, 1982, pp. 114–15.

11 S. Schram, ed., *Mao Tse-Tung Unrehearsed*, London, Penguin, 1974, p. 295.

12 Gorbachev's report to the USSR Supreme Soviet, in *Pravda*, 30 November 1988, pp. 1–3.

13 *Keesing's*, 1989, pp. 36512–13.

14 *Guardian*, 20 July 1989, p. 10.

15 A warning of what could happen to Shcherbitsky was given in *Pravda*, 30 August 1988, p. 6, in an account of the career of Brezhnev's son-in-law who was subsequently imprisoned for accepting bribes.

16 Sakharov also discusses this, see note 1.

17 Jonathan Steele, *Guardian*, 10 May 1989, p. 19; 9 September 1989, p. 8.

The politics of *perestroika* and the Soviet economy

Mikhail Sergeyevich Gorbachev needs to be a better politician than economist, and his economic reforms cannot be understood outside of their political context. This is precisely the complaint of Western (and some Soviet) economists, however: the economic component of *perestroika*, or restructuring, remains fettered by political constraints. Among scholars who analyse recent events in the Soviet Union, political scientists tend to be impressed by the change that has occurred, while economists are more likely to be pessimistic on account of the change that has *not* occurred. Throughout this chapter, economic concerns and their political context for the Soviet leadership will be considered.

Part of the reason behind the cool reception for the Soviet economic agenda is the perception that the economy is still on a 'treadmill of reforms'.[1] Every Soviet leader since Stalin has introduced changes with grand fanfare but little success. The general goal of this so-called tinkering, especially the Kosygin reforms introduced in 1965, was to increase efficiency by decentralising economic management, but no measures to date have been consistent and stringent enough to quicken the pace of the Soviet economy for long.

Although the treadmill analogy is useful as a reminder that proposals for economic reform are nothing new in the Soviet context, it provides little explanatory power for the increasing pragmatism of economic reform in the 1980s. The 'basic theses' of economic *perestroika*, although far from being realised, are indeed radical. Along with the familiar call for cutting back the powerful government ministerial structure, the 1987 programme included proposals for greater enterprise autonomy and major changes in the pricing system.[2] In conjunction with a law to phase in self-financing for factories, this package of reform measures looked far more comprehensive than its predecessors.

Perhaps the failure of previous, weaker, reform efforts had at least served to convince the current leadership that more drastic measures were necessary.

The other notable component of the new round of economic reform was the Soviet Union's willingness to consider measures toward integration into the world economy, including an overture to the members of the General Agreement on Tariffs and Trade (GATT) in 1986. The United States rebuffed that effort, probably in part because of cynicism about the 'treadmill' nature of reform in the Soviet system. What is this system that has proven so resistant to change, and may remain so despite the farthest-reaching proposals for economic reform since the 1920s?

Stalinism: economics of control

To look behind the programme of *perestroika* involves some explanation of how it came to pass that the Soviet Union, one of the two world superpowers in the second half of the twentieth century, found itself in the 1980s facing what Gorbachev himself called a 'pre-crisis' situation. Western scholars would be more blunt in assessing the damage that Stalinist methods of economic management had done over a sixty-year period, but those methods had a certain amount of effectiveness in establishing the USSR as a major world presence.

In 1928–9, after Stalin had marginalised his political opposition, the Soviet Union embarked upon the course of agricultural collectivisation and an emphasis on heavy industry that has determined its economic structure to the present day. At that time, even after the economic respite provided by Lenin's relatively market-oriented New Economic Policy (NEP), the road to global status seemed impossibly strewn with the debris of the First World War and a ruinous civil war. Although the country recovered somewhat during the mid-1920s, society having agreed with Nikolai Bukharin's injudicious but accurate assessment of the NEP as an opportunity to 'Enrich yourselves!', the standard of living lagged far behind that of the developing West.

One of the key issues of debate within the leadership was at what pace the country should industrialise. Stalin used the threat of foreign invasion to push through his preference for industrialisation at breakneck speed, emphasising the need to catch up with the West and especially with the United States. A typical book jacket of the time depicted a chart with the gross national product for the United States dropping precipitously after the Depression and remaining near zero, in contrast to the Soviet Union's soaring projection.[3] The emphasis on competition continued under Khrushchev, who claimed that the USSR would match and in a few years surpass the US in milk, butter, and, most absurdly, meat production. Brezhnev shifted the focus back to the military, and fulfilled the pledge in that sector. In this period, even reducing the 'urban bias' in favour of the peasantry had centred on industrial production for the countryside.[4] The economic system remained until the end of the 1980s strongly biased toward what might be termed economic 'building blocks', that is, heavy industry, rather than the 'trimmings' of consumer-oriented production.

Administration from the centre − a command economy − in fact functions rather well for certain types of projects. If a strong government sets a goal and then allocates resources towards it regardless of cost, it is possible to have large-scale achievement in a short period of time. Thus, Stalin began some of the gigantic projects that were to herald an obsession with size. The Moscow underground might be the best in the world, but it was built at incalculable cost on such a tight timetable that buildings on the surface were known to collapse as workers 'stormed' beneath them. Time pressure from priority state orders reinforced a bias toward big, heavy industry products.

But the cost to the country of Stalin's methods was grave enough to cause Western and now some Soviet scholars to assert that the programme of rapid industrialisation left the country worse prepared for war or any other trauma than a more moderate plan would have done. One reform-minded academic believes that the German invasion occurred partly because Stalin had so weakened the country.[5] And certainly the legacy of the Stalin years, with the stress on central economic control, left the Soviet Union even further behind its Western counterparts in terms of standard of living.

Most of the Brezhnev Politburo (no member of which remained after 20 September 1989, except for Gorbachev himself) would have granted consumer desires little role in the functioning of the economy. But the 1980s bore out the prediction that 'although Soviet leaders can ignore societal preferences concerning the economy, they do so at their own peril'.[6] A lack of economic achievement seems to have eroded the ability of the Communist Party to govern effectively.

Perfecting the plan

Maintaining centralised economic control has historically remained more salient than the concepts of consumer preference and profitability which drive Western market economies. The mechanism by which the centre expresses its preferences is the Five-Year Plan, supplemented by generally more realistic annual plans. The plan has proved a crude but not ineffective means of stimulating production, as attested to by the complaint of a coal miner following the summer 1989 strikes: 'The plan hangs over our heads like the sword of Damocles. Produce! Produce!'[7]

For all its unpopularity and misdirected signalling, the pre-eminence of planning remained little challenged. Even at the ground-breaking Congress of People's Deputies in 1989, Gorbachev resorted to strangely hybrid phases like 'a full-blooded socialist market' to express the idea that although a market component is especially necessary to bring 'the Soviet economy into the world economy', planning is considered an essential part of Soviet socialism.[8]

Drawing up the plans is the task of a much-maligned government agency, Gosplan. As can be determined from an enthusiastic 1931 description, Gosplan faces no easy task: 'Under socialism the whole economy of the country becomes a huge single enterprise ... the anarchy of economic life has disappeared and its place has been taken by conscious determination of all the processes of production.'[9] Gosplan's information in setting plan quotas has to come from the enterprises themselves, which thus have every incentive to keep production low and to under-report, if necessary.

The plan has been the means by which the Soviet Union governs investment. One major difference between the Stalinist planned economy and a consumer-oriented one is a question of the timetable involved: the Soviet Union has put a huge percentage of its production into investment, something like one-third, whereas most West European countries allocate about one-fifth of their GNP toward investment. The high Soviet figure comes at great cost to the consumer sector, and is most clearly manifested by chronic shortages of essential foodstuffs and of housing.

The welter of paperwork issued in Moscow also cannot enforce quality production, and the result is empty shops or shops with goods no one wants. Having authorities decide what to produce instead of unleashing the force of consumer demand is one problem, but the other is that incentives for workers to produce marketable goods are squeezed out. Quality control tends to focus on sporadic visits by government officials, undertaken more vigorously and enforced since Gorbachev became General Secretary, but none the less inadequate.

One of the economic effects of production to satisfy a target rather than the consumer is what Western economists ominously call a 'monetary overhang'. The savings deposits of Soviet citizens are extremely high, representing the pent-up purchasing power of the Soviet consumer. A mere 8 per cent of savings is estimated to be in the form of disposable personal income,[10] guaranteeing a network of shortages unless prices soar high enough to soak up a larger percentage of savings. Hyperinflation is a far from benign solution, however, and other approaches will be required to avoid social unrest.

Despite these problems, the plan-dominated system set up by Stalin to emphasise heavy industry continued to produce satisfactorily, if erratically, for the first years of Brezhnev's rule. Rather than controlling for quality, quantity was increased; rather than conserving materials, input was increased: the economy was expanding, and thus the essentially wasteful method of trying to control production from the centre was able to continue.

It was in the oil crisis of the mid-1970s that the Soviet Union faced a great modern economic challenge, and the leadership's refusal to rise up to that challenge meant economic stagnation. Oil prices fell, and the USSR lost billions of roubles in revenue that it had counted on; in addition, the agricultural harvest repeatedly failed to meet production targets. The poor standard of living tolerated by citizens, which was almost a point of pride after the devastation of the Second World War, had become the source of chronic social discontent. Using a war of more than forty years ago as an excuse for late-1980s retarded economic development became increasingly unsatisfactory. And the truth about historical events, if known, would show that this lop-sided pattern of growth might not be justified either as a wartime measure or a peacetime plan.

This is a rough sketch of the situation that Gorbachev inherited. He probably came to power as the result of frustrated pressures for reform that built up under Brezhnev, but even those who wanted change did not agree on how much and of what kind.

The anti-alcohol campaign

Gorbachev began in 1985 with more conservative types of reform that would rock the boat gently and, so it transpired, prepare it for rougher waters. The first major move was the anti-alcohol campaign, combined with a call for greater discipline.

The central leadership had for years lambasted alcoholism, poor work performance, and absenteeism from the workplace. Yuri Andropov, during his brief tenure as General Secretary, began to put some muscle into these complaints. Gorbachev took the next step, a big one, by focusing on alcoholism as a major social problem, and he proceeded to 'narrow the gap between words and deeds': many shops selling liquor were closed, all others kept shorter hours, beer bars were closed altogether, and production of vodka and wine for domestic consumption was drastically reduced.

By the time these measures were introduced, Soviet social statistics had become truly alarming. The important indicators of life expectancy and infant mortality shown in Tables 8.1 and 8.2 measure up poorly in comparison with other industrialised countries, and reflect a generally inadequate health-care system. The life expectancy for Soviet men was nearly ten years less than the average in most European countries and the United States, and that for women about five years less. The overall infant mortality rate averaged two to three times higher; all large nations have a regional disparity in health care, as evidenced here, but Soviet Turkmenia still has one of the highest infant mortality rates in the world.

These figures are influenced by the very high rate of alcohol consumption (among other social and environmental problems), estimated by one expert at 15–16 litres of absolute alcohol per person of 15 years of age or older.[11] Indeed, 'the antidrinking campaign

Table 8.1 *Average life expectancy, USSR*

	1971–2	*1978–9*	*1983–4*	*1986–7*
Men	64.5	62.5	62.6	65.0
Women	73.6	72.6	72.8	73.8

Sources: Narodnoe khoziastvo SSSR za 70 let; Narodnoe khoziastvo SSSR, 1987.

Table 8.2 *Infant mortality rates, USSR*
              (per 1000 live births)

Soviet Union	25.4	Latvia	11.3
Armenia	22.6	Lithuania	12.3
Azerbaijan	28.6	Moldavia	25.9
Belorussia	13.4	Russian Republic	19.4
Estonia	16.1	Tadzhikistan	48.9
Georgia	24.3	Turkmenia	56.4
Kazakhstan	29.4	Ukraine	14.5
Kirghizia	37.8	Uzbekistan	45.9

Source: Narodnoe khoziastvo SSSR, 1987.

could not have started too soon. By any comparative, historical, or world health standard, the Soviet Union by the mid-1980s was facing an alcohol problem of truly crisis proportions.'[12]

At first the campaign was received favourably by some of the population at large, as the problem of alcoholism was recognised to be a very serious one. In time, however, as stringent measures continued unabated and were combined with two counter-productive price increases, the average citizen became angry that he or she could not obtain a bottle even to celebrate a birthday.

Higher prices fuelled an already flourishing illegal trade and caused a significant jump in vodka production by means of stills at home or even in the workplace. Stories began to surface in the media about deaths from drinking raw or contaminated liquor, and the health problem meant to be addressed by the campaign came to be counter-balanced by the dangers associated with drinking home-brew or even toxic substances. Shops sold out of perfume and, more problematically, sugar, used to promote fermentation in illegal stills. In the autumn of 1988, with the anti-alcohol campaign virtually abandoned, the supply of sugar had to be rationed for the first time since the Second World War.

Ironically, a major source of state revenue had been vodka sales. Gorbachev stated that this loss would be made up for by increased work productivity, and there was an initial improvement in work performance. But it has been estimated that the loss in revenue from reduced vodka sales at least equalled the cost to the Soviet Union of the fall in world oil prices in the 1970s, over 40 billion roubles. A well-intended campaign had spun out of control.

The economic underpinnings of the anti-alcohol campaign are discussed here at length because they provide an example of the difficulties of bold reform. The politics and economics of the Soviet Union tend to swing in extremes, since pressure from the centre has to be exerted very strongly in order to have any effect. A leader like Brezhnev who does not particularly desire change can let inertia carry things along and 'muddle through' problems on a piecemeal basis. A reform-minded Soviet leader, on the other hand, faces the problems of economic and social dislocation resulting from his efforts to introduce change, however necessary.

Radical reform

By 1988, more unsettling plans had been unleashed. In very broad terms, Gorbachev's economic reforms can be described as an uneasy compromise between trying to introduce business on a profit-making basis and using plan indicators. Western economists criticise his reforms because they do not see market mechanisms as being compatible with strong state control. Certainly the case of China offers evidence that half-way reform measures might result in neither mechanism functioning properly, a 'dismantled planned economy with uncoordinated, unlinked, and imperfect markets existing here and there for individual goods'.[13]

However, an all-or-nothing attitude overlooks the political constraints within which a general secretary operates, and for a long time led the cynics to believe that nothing was changing in the USSR. The politically realistic policy of gradual economic change is not ideal, of course, because it means some measures will contradict others and firms will become adept at avoiding harsh market mechanisms. The struggle is to replace the relatively benign personalistic system of the past with hard budget constraints.

Incremental economic reform, while probably the only path that would not mean extreme social upheaval, none the less has another major shortcoming. The longer Gorbachev requires for his plans to be fully implemented, the more time his opponents have to sabotage the delicate change-over.[14] Every step of the way for both economic and political reform appears to have involved intense discussion at top levels, and public speeches of Politburo members are often quite openly in disagreement.

One of the conservative figures in evidence is Politburo member

Yegor Ligachev, whose functions within the Secretariat of the Party Central Committee were cut back in 1988. Those he lost included the important area of supervision of ideology, and he was left supervising only agriculture. Gorbachev himself held the latter post in the Brezhnev Politburo, and must know that being in charge of agriculture in the Soviet Union is a thankless task. Agriculture is in fact an important ideological battleground as well as the *bête noire* of the Soviet economy. Six years after the introduction of the very expensive Food Programme, the agricultural picture remained grim: Soviet production of grain per capita was higher in 1988 than in many Western nations, but the Soviet Union remained a net importer of agricultural products.[15] The rate of spoilage for fruit and vegetables was by one estimate as high as 60–80 per cent, and for grain, about 25 per cent.[16] Yet measures aimed at increasing the incentive of farmers to market their products, and even mild attempts to address problems with the infrastructure, met with stiff resistance. Gorbachev's efforts to find enthusiasts for leasing of the land, a much-fêted campaign to make the peasant 'the master of his own house', continued to receive a lukewarm reception in 1989.[17]

Even a minor victory for would-be agricultural reformers (the announcement that farmers would be paid in hard currency for production above the previous year's level to save on grain importation), none the less continued a bad incentive structure by penalising 1988's good producers. More significant structural alteration in agriculture would probably mean reversing collectivisation (as the Chinese have done). If Gorbachev's 'attempt to challenge past ideological precepts should be considered an important aspect of his [agricultural] reform strategy',[18] then it is indicative of major resistance to agricultural reform at the highest levels.

But differences in the top leadership regarding economic and political change reflect deeper social conflicts. Even at the level of the Politburo, 'Hiring and firing, homilies from the General Secretary, general injunctions to shape up, and patchwork reform schemes will not suffice to produce economic efficiency.'[19] A leader who retains cautionary voices in the Politburo may do so as a kind of check, because persuading that body to support radical reform requires the same kind of battle as must be fought society-wide.

The short fuse of price reform

This chapter began with mention of Gorbachev's ability as a politician. It is much more important than his skill at economics, for a good economist would long ago have introduced measures that would be intolerable politically. The single most important change that experts agree must come to the Soviet Union is the same change that has caused trouble in Eastern Europe: price reform.

Prices in the USSR have the fundamental problem of not reflecting market value. Food prices have always been controlled, to the extent that it is cheaper to feed animals bread than to feed them unprocessed wheat. The practice of buying bread to feed animals led to a law against it, but not to economic measures to make it impractical. Controlled food prices mean that prices for other goods shoot wildly upward, with the result that a pair of shoddy boots might cost 200 roubles, or about a month's wages.

Inflationary pressure introduced by controlled prices, as well as other economic distortions, mean that consumer demand is unmet *and* goods are not sold. The kind of equilibrium at which supply and demand meet cannot send signals to producers in the Soviet Union because they are satisfying the state's plan, not consumer demand. The old Soviet saying, 'They pretend to pay us and we pretend to work', could be expanded to 'We pretend to produce goods and they pretend to sell them'. This lack of purchasing power and the resulting lack of incentive promotes low worker productivity, poor quality production, and a very bad match between supply and demand.

The general secretaryship of the Communist Party of the Soviet Union is said to be the most powerful office in the world, but even a general secretary cannot effectively dictate economic change. Gorbachev first mentioned the explosive words 'price reform' in early 1987 and brought up the necessity of having realistic prices. To the Soviet consumer, who already could not find meat and until late 1988 drink, this meant what the campaigns of their leaders always mean: more work for fewer goods. The Soviet socialist system at least provided cheap basic foodstuffs, and now Gorbachev was speaking of removing even this.

It did not take long for Gorbachev to feel the backlash of public opinion, and even though he insisted that workers' wages would rise to meet increased costs and the prices of manufactured goods would fall, he had to back down on the idea of price reform. By 1989 reform-minded economists in the Soviet Union changed their tune as well, and called for price reforms in two or three years instead of immediately.[20] Some of these economists are brave social scientists who called for reform even under Brezhnev; it appears that they, too, assessed the political and social risks of introducing price reforms too quickly.

On the other hand, forces which oppose Gorbachev and his far-reaching plans for change may have found that one route is to let him sink along with his most radical schemes. Some argue that the extremism of the anti-alcohol campaign was partly due to over-zealous implementation that was bound to alienate the average citizen. Certainly price reform proved to be an explosive issue in Eastern Europe and holds vast potential for social unrest in the USSR. There is by no means agreement on how to salvage the economic situation, and it is inevitable that a reformer will be blamed for the temporarily harder times that occur as reforms are tried out.

Some sabre-rattling

One of the unhappiest sectors of Soviet society is the military, as R. C. Plummer suggests in Chapter 10. Although the strength of the military in Soviet politics should not be overestimated − after all, a less reformist figure than Gorbachev might well have been selected if the military had sufficient influence over the civilian world − it none the less constitutes a large part of society. Two milestones in the handling of the military came in 1989: the first announcement of a 'real' defence budget[21] and the promise of a 14 per cent cut in overall defence spending by 1991.

The last Soviet politician to trim the military was Nikita Khrushchev, and this combined with his other reforms created a coalition of opposing forces strong enough to recommend removing him. Gorbachev waited in order to tread carefully when pruning Soviet defence expenditure; it is clear that he wanted the relative efficiency of the defence sector to encompass consumer production. A great many consumer items were reassigned to the military industrial sector,[22] and a number of managers who made their mark in efficient military production were transferred to the civilian sector.

But Gorbachev could hope for little short-term benefit from a reallocation of economic resources to civilian production. Although Soviet defence expenditure is high by world standards and re-channelling the vigour of, for example, R & D should eventually affect the output and quality of civilian goods, even a significant allocation is quickly swallowed up by the ever-hungry civilian sector.[23] A proposal to cut expenditures on defence by half by 1995 was made contingent upon the result of disarmament talks,[24] but international support for arms and troop reductions might sooner keep the wounded tone of some military leaders to a tolerable volume than have an effect on the production of consumer goods. 'The benefits of thorough-going economic reform are likely to require some time in materialising, while the costs in the form of inflation and unemployment will be more immediate.'[25]

The many controversial economic changes, however gradual, are not springing from a vacuum. It is unrealistic to believe that Gorbachev materialised in Soviet political life as a sort of alien force who wants to run a Western country. He is very much a product of the Soviet system. Because of this, Western analysts disagreed initially about the degree of sincerity behind his reform efforts. Once it became clear that he was taking genuine risks in order to introduce a far-reaching programme of economic, social and political reform, the attention shifted to predictions about how long he would last. Although the latter is an interesting question, a more important one is what are the forces behind Gorbachev, the forces that will lie in wait for another reformer if need be?

Many of the reformers are about Gorbachev's age, in their fifties and early sixties. They were strongly influenced by the relatively tolerant Khrushchev era, thus proving the importance of one reform period for the next. Gorbachev appeared to keep this in mind, as one of his biggest and most successful social initiatives was the encouragement of more honest writing on Soviet history (which included a number of largely positive reassessments of Khrushchev). There was also an explosion of programmes that take advantage of the more open climate to sponsor Soviet scholars, even young students, on visits to the West. In the likely event that Gorbachev and his allies fail to achieve all that they want, the seeds are being planted for the next reform period to swing even further toward profound change.

This is because the forces that drove Gorbachev to radical reform include the need for the Soviet Union to reconcile its past history of rigid economic management and strong central control with the complexity of modern society. The leadership requires accurate information about social conditions and the public must be able to satisfy at least minimal needs. This does not necessarily require a Western-style democracy or Western-style capitalism, and it is unlikely that the Soviet Union will come to resemble those systems all that closely. What it could mean is a more flexible political agenda, permitting citizens to express their concerns and get results. At least a portion of the Soviet leadership recognises that consumer interests are not something alien to the state, but rather an integral part of a nation's performance.

The 1989 coal strike

Should anyone have required further proof, the coal-miners' 'scream of despair'[26] in the summer of 1989 brought home the point: citizens are finding their voices with a vengeance. The grim conditions under which miners live were evident in the thirty-seven-point programme from the strike committee of the Ukrainian Donetsk Basin, which included:

- All miners are to be provided with their own flat within ten years.
- A review of soap quotas by the authorities.
- Resolution ... on the question of water, gas and electricity supplies to the villages and settlements.
- Workers are to be provided with good quality food in accordance with medical regulations.[27]

Gorbachev termed the strike an even more serious challenge to the country than Chernobyl and a grave blow to the economy.[28] He had already addressed the miners of the Donetsk Basin to much the same effect in February 1989:

The slightest hitch in one region or component rapidly affects our general position. Just imagine if such stoppages were to begin in a republic like the Ukraine ... at this time it is necessary to maintain production at the required level. Turning the country around ... will take time.[29]

The Western press made much of Moscow's acquiescence with the miners, which included permitting earlier legislative elections and a wage increase. Some commentators went so far as to suggest that Gorbachev had all but dared the miners to act, an odd perspective on the relationship between politicians in power and strikers. It was true, however, that to have the Russian Republic experiencing serious consumer unrest might persuade those dragging their feet that radical change was necessary, a point that the Soviet media rallied around.

Whether everyone agreed that that change should be *perestroika* was another matter: some of the miners' demands, for higher wages and an end to the co-operative movement, were in contradiction to key economic components of the reform effort.

Deputy Prime Minister (and economist) Leonid Abalkin rightly noted that in working out a settlement with the miners for higher wages and pensions, the government opted for immediate 'political stability' despite the long-term economic costs.[30] Increasing wages was highly undesirable without a concomitant price increase, but wage policy provided recourse for a leadership with few bonuses to hand out. That is one of the reasons why wages remain out of control.[31] Another of the miners' demands in conflict with *perestroika*, the call to halt the 'inegalitarian' co-operative movement, was side-stepped. Although the miners and many other social groups oppose the co-operatives on the grounds that they (often illegally) buy inputs at state-controlled prices and then sell the finished product at a profit, Gorbachev continued to defend the importance of a quasi-private sector.

Why the situation exploded when it did is an important question. A sharp increase in coal production since Gorbachev's accession in 1985 reflected the regime's need for foreign currency, but also served to aggravate festering social problems. Some of the strike committee leaders cited the open debate in the new legislature, which had a television audience of many millions, as inspiration: a sort of 'Why shouldn't we be heard too?'[32] A balanced evaluation of the reasons behind social unrest needed to include the more open political climate, but that in turn provided the outlet for, rather than created, strong pressure for improved living conditions.

That the strike should occur in the coal industry is perhaps not surprising. Although a large share of resources had been devoted to improving technology in the coal industry, it remained 'the branch of the energy sector in which the USSR is comparatively most backward ... The Soviet Union reports employment of around a million persons in coal mining compared with 159,000 persons in the United States, who produce somewhat more coal.'[33] This retarded economic development can be explained by the lack of incentive to innovate, the channelling of funds to tackle immediate bottlenecks (thus contributing to inadequate research and poorly tailored solutions), and, perhaps most importantly, the slim likelihood that a bad political decision will be reversed by its economic consequences.[34] An inefficient work environment is not likely to foster comfortable living, especially when virtually the same authorities are responsible for both.

Another factor contributing to unrest in the extractive industries was the now common knowledge that fossil fuels are critical exports, earning approximately 70 per cent of all Soviet hard-currency income from sales of non-military goods.[35] In a uniquely Soviet twist to worker grievances, the Donetsk Basin miners sought to put their region on a self-financing basis, rather than seeking protection from the market as would be rational in a capitalist economy. This demand was not met, but the price of coal, which was artificially low, does appear to have increased.

Populist pressure

Prior to the ground swell of activism that led to the miners' strike, nationalism and environmentalism were the two social concerns that surfaced most readily in response to the chance for public expression. The former is a great problem for the Soviet empire and may yet contain the seeds of its destruction. Nationalist uprising affected the allocation of resources in much the same way as the miners' strike, in this case with considerable resources directed to the troubled region of Nagorno-Karabakh. Although it is unlikely that any areas will spin out of Soviet control in the near future, it requires an expert hand in Moscow to keep nationalism from becoming actively anti-Soviet.

Environmentalism provides another compelling example of behaviour by ordinary citizens which affected central planning (mostly through the mediation of the intelligentsia). A plan to redirect Siberian rivers with a huge complex of hydroelectric dams was the subject of a ground swell of public complaint that eventually made itself heard in the highest corridors of power. The project has been postponed indefinitely.

These are examples of the failure of centralised planning to take costs into account, be they environmental costs or otherwise. The fact that citizen pressure may eventually act as a counterforce to central planning is very important to the political and economic growth of the Soviet Union. Despite the difficulties faced by Gorbachev and the increasingly divided Soviet Union over which he presides, his lifting of social controls to the extent that opposing voices can be heard is the most positive development in the modern Soviet state.

The economic implications of these changes are far-reaching for a socialist nation. The leadership admits that poor economic performance is more than anything else due to the lack of economic incentive provided by the system and to excessive expenditure on heavy industry. Although central planning will not be scrapped, the annual plans appear to be more responsive than in the past: the 1989 plan cut state investment for the first time since the Second World War.

A primary goal of the leadership is to improve the standard of living, and clearly this could not be done in isolation. Building up trade relations with the West means that the quality of production has to reach a competitive level. The number of joint ventures with foreign partners rose rapidly,[36] as did the number of schemes which Soviet economists proposed in order to bring foreign goods or foreign currency into the economy. Scholars in the East and the West recognise that the precarious state of the economy jeopardises every aspect of reform. 'So long as material shortages get worse rather than better and there is no improvement in the standard of living for the average Soviet citizen, the continuation of political reform cannot be taken for granted.'[37]

One of the more desperate proposals to get goods to the consumer is to import billions of dollars worth of consumer goods to mop up excess savings.[38] Although in 1989 the Soviet leadership let the economy shoulder a net debt burden over twice that of 1984, worth about US$27.3 billion,[39] it is unlikely to renounce fiscal caution and risk a much higher level of foreign indebtedness.

Even so, the urgency of offering at least some consumer satisfaction was underscored by Alexandra Biryukova's visit to Britain in the summer of 1989. A candidate member of the Politburo with responsibility for the consumer sector, Biryukova visited eight cities and ordered some 1.7 million pairs of shoes, 50 million pairs of tights, and vast quantities of soap, toothpaste, razor blades and instant coffee.[40]

Measuring progress

It is clear that the Soviet Union is experiencing a long-overdue shift to domestic priorities, and Gorbachev's success or failure in overseeing this change will have a great deal to do with whether or not the USSR becomes a member of the world economic community. Soviet exports cannot remain hinged upon raw materials such as oil and gold (export of the latter increased in value by 400 per cent between 1984 and 1986),[41] which are subject to high extraction costs and fluctuating prices. Economic reform depends on institutionalising pressure for quality production of competitive goods; periodic campaigns by the leadership are a poor substitute for economic incentives.

Soviet reformers want to enlist international organisations in their battle. Although the United States had warmed to Soviet mention of GATT membership by 1989, bilateral economic integration took priority over multilateral moves. The Bush Administration's approval of sales of personal computers to the Soviet bloc was a pragmatic move, recognition both of the 'real big dollars out there'[42] and the readiness of most manufacturers to consider essentially low-level, out-of-date technology to have few potential military uses.

Evaluating the success or failure of Gorbachev's economics depends very much on the standard used.[43] Should the results so far be measured against those of the Brezhnev era? Or the reform experiences of other Communist countries? Or against Gorbachev's 'floridly reformist rhetoric'?[44] It is only by the first standard that Gorbachev's economic programme emerges triumphant, and even then with the caveat that the supply of food and goods to consumers actually worsened after *perestroika* began.[45] Other socialist countries, most notably China and Hungary, have moved much further in the implementation of economic reform. Such major issues as currency convertibility remain problematic for all of these economies, however.[46]

Measuring economic achievement against Gorbachev's statements introduces an important political consideration. He is a masterful tactician, and will often float an idea several times before attempting to introduce it as policy. It is also typical for general secretaries to use economic projections as a means of inspiration. Gorbachev, like every other general secretary, has to settle for less. Whether his inclusion of political reform and consumer pressure in the official Soviet system can make the difference in economic reform remains to be seen. Certainly Gorbachev is acutely aware of the truth behind populist politician Boris Yeltsin's pronouncement: 'You have to take into account the impatience of people. If people had seen results in their standard of living, they would have believed in *perestroika* with all their hearts and souls.'[47]

It is none the less no mean achievement to throw open so many doors in a 'poorly built house'[48] in order to examine its faults and attempt to correct them. Western economists might advise blowing up the whole structure and starting anew, but the Communist Party bears too much responsibility for creating the present arrangement to oversee its demolition.

Notes

1 The phrase is Gertrude E. Schroeder's, 'The Soviet economy on a treadmill of "reforms"', in US Joint Economic Committee, *The Soviet Economy in a Time of Change*, Washington DC, Government Printing Office, 1979, pp. 312–40.

2 'Osnovnye polozheniya korennoi perestroiki upravleniya ekonomiki', *Pravda*, 27 June 1987, pp. 2–3.

3 V. V. Obolensky-Ossinsky, *Social Economic Planning in the USSR*, Schiedam, Netherlands, De Eendracht, 1931.

4 Stephen K. Wegren, 'Gorbachev's agricultural reforms', presented to the Social Science Research Council Workshop on Soviet Domestic Politics, University of Toronto, June 1989, p. 20.

5 A. P. Butenko, *Sovetskaya Belorussia*, 16 December 1987, p. 3, available in English in *Current Digest of the Soviet Press*, XXXIX, no. 50, pp. 6–7.

6 Ed A. Hewett, *Reforming the Soviet Economy: Equality vs. Efficiency*, Washington DC, Brookings Institution, 1988, p. 35.

7 *Sotsialisticheskaya industriya*, 8 August 1989, p. 2.

8 Report to the Congress of People's Deputies, Moscow television, 30 May 1989, translated by *Foreign Broadcast Information Service*, SOV-89-103S, Daily Report Supplement, 31 May 1989, pp. 55, 60.

9 Obolensky-Ossinsky, *Social Economic Planning*, pp. 11, 12.

10 *PlanEcon Report*, V, nos 6–7, p. 5.

11 Vladimir G. Treml, 'A noble experiment? Gorbachev's antidrinking campaign', in Maurice Friedberg and Heyward Isham, eds, *Soviet Society under Gorbachev*, Armonk, NY, M. E. Sharpe, 1987, p. 53.

12 Ibid.

13 Jan Prybyla, 'China's economic experiment: back from the market?' *Problems of Communism*, XXXVIII, January–February 1989, p. 8.

14 For a pragmatic discussion of this and other difficulties with economic reform, see Jerry F. Hough, *Opening up the Soviet Economy*, Washington DC, Brookings Institution, 1988.

15 For trade figures, see Food and Agricultural Organisation of the United Nations, *The State of Food and Agriculture 1987–88*, pp. 136, 138, 140, 142; calculation of per capita grain production is based on the CIA estimate for agricultural GNP, 1988.

16 John Hardt, speaking at the Kennan Institute, Washington DC, 28 November 1988.

17 Understandably, Gorbachev attributed the sluggish response to local

bureaucratic resistance (see, for example, *FBIS*, as cited, p. 50) without mentioning the unwillingness of peasants to risk joining a programme that might be halted.

18 Wegren, 'Gorbachev's agricultural reforms', p. 52.

19 Timothy J. Colton, 'Approaches to the politics of systemic economic reform in the Soviet Union', *Soviet Economy*, III, 1987, p. 161.

20 This group includes economists Nikolai Shmelyev and Leonid Abalkin, both of whom are quoted in the text on other aspects of their economic visions. They have come to sound more like Politburo member Nikolai Slyunkov, head of the Central Committee Economic Department, on the subject: 'Suffice it to say that a price reform is absolutely necessary. But it needs meticulous preparations.' (Interview, *Novosti* Press Agency, 1988.)

21 Gorbachev named the figure of 77.3 billion roubles for 1989 in his report to the Congress of People's Deputies (*FBIS*, as cited). This is rather lower than the CIA's estimate, but not the first time that this general secretary's statistics more closely resemble Western figures than those provided by the Soviet central statistical bureau.

22 Certain consumer items were already produced by the defence industry. Television sets and radios are examples, though neither offers much evidence that the tighter quality control exercised over military output carries over to production for the civilian sector.

23 Rowland T. Maddock, 'The Soviet defence burden and arms control', *Journal of Peace Research*, XXIV, 1987, pp. 385, 386.

24 Vladimir Lapygin, speaking on behalf of the Supreme Soviet Committee on Defence and State Security, Moscow World Service, 31 August 1989. (Translation provided by *FBIS*, SOV-89-170, 5 September 1989, p. 89.)

25 Maddock, 'The Soviet defence burden', p. 386.

26 During an unruly session of the legislature, Yuri Golik, elected to the Congress of People's Deputies from the Siberian mining city of Kemerovo, called the strikes 'A scream of despair from the Soviet people'.

27 As reported by the Ukrainian Central Information service, cited in the *Guardian*, 24 July 1989. The demands are similar to those of the striking Siberian miners.

28 *Washington Post*, 25 July 1989, pp. 1, 18.

29 *Izvestiya*, 24 February 1989, pp. 1–2.

30 *Washington Post*, 25 July 1989, p. 18.

31 *PlanEcon Report* (V no. 17, p. 3) indicates that average wage increases, figured at less than 1 per cent in the plan, were approximately 9.4 per cent in the first quarter of 1989.

32 *Sotsialisticheskaya industriya*, 8 August 1989, p. 2.

33 Robert Campbell, *Soviet Energy Technologies*, Bloomington, Indiana, Indiana University Press, 1980, p. 99. Although these employment figures referred to the 1970s, worker productivity remained very low comparatively in the 1980s.

34 Ibid, pp. 236–44.

35 Ed A. Hewett, *Energy, Economics, and Foreign Policy in the Soviet Union*, Washington DC, Brookings Institution, 1984.

36 Compared with the five joint ventures registered in the second quarter of 1987, some 174 were initiated in early 1989. (*PlanEcon Report* V no. 17, p. 8).

37 Archie Brown, 'Political change in the Soviet Union', *World Policy Journal*, VI, Summer 1989, p. 469. Brown adds that this need not reflect upon Gorbachev's ability to stay in power.

38 This is a pet proposal of Nikolai Shmelyev, a radical economist and member of the Congress of People's Deputies.

39 CIA estimates show a steady climb of indebtedness since Gorbachev became general secretary, reaching an estimated US$41.7 billion by 1988.

40 As reported by *The Times*, 31 July 1989, p. 1.

41 CIA estimate: the value of gold sales rose from US$1 billion to some $4 billion.

42 Ed Black, vice-president of the Computer and Communications Industry Association, *New York Times*, 19 July 1989, pp. 1, D4.

43 The standards which follow were suggested by Timothy Colton, 'Approaches to the politics …', p. 148.

44 Ibid.

45 Nikolai Shmelyev, 'Novye trevogi', *Novyi mir*, no. 4, 1988, p. 161.

46 Although Soviet commentators recognise the importance of convertibility, a remarkable level of mistaken conclusions are in evidence. Professor G. Matyukhin, for example ('Convertible rouble: what does it take?', *Pravda*, 10 May 1989, p. 4) sees little connection between price reform and convertibility, citing other mechanisms that would work only between market economies.

47 Interview in the *New York Times*, 9 June 1989, pp. 1, 6.

48 Historian Yuri Afanasyev, a radical reformer and deputy to the Congress of People's Deputies, supplied the analogy; personal interview, April 1988.

'New thinking' and Soviet foreign policy

This chapter presents an overview of theoretical and practical developments in Soviet 'new thinking'. However, it will also argue that the world in general and the NATO nations in particular confront an unparalleled and possibly short-lived opportunity to collaborate with the USSR in the transformation of international relations in ways more in keeping with the problems of the twenty-first century.

What is 'new thinking'?

This question is not as easy to answer as it appears. Conventionally, the phrase is associated with Gorbachev's foreign policy reforms, as the terms *perestroika* and *glasnost* are with his economic and political reforms. Increasingly, however, the concept of 'new thinking' has gained wider currency within the USSR not simply as a term for foreign policy reform, but as a characterisation of the new 'spiritual culture' that the Gorbachev administration wishes to inspire in the hearts and minds of Soviet citizens. Soviet social scientists speak about 'old thinking' and 'new thinking' as being representative of socio-pyschological types.[1] The phrase 'new thinking' therefore has a resonance for the Soviets which goes beyond the conventional Western appreciation of it. And it is as well to bear this in mind, since it means that the international and domestic aspects of 'new thinking' often interact in ways that are not immediately obvious to the outside observer.

Secondly, of course, much of the 'new thinking' is not particularly new. In Soviet terms some of its central elements, notably, 'peaceful coexistence', owe a great deal to Khrushchev, as Gorbachev himself has noted.[2] And in international terms, many of the concepts now becoming common currency in Soviet discourse, concepts like 'global interdependence', have been around for years. However, what is new is that these concepts are not only making an appearance in the CPSU's discourse, but that Gorbachev's combination and recombination of old and new is producing a new conception of international relations which completely overturns the one bequeathed to him.

Finally, however, it must be said that the phrase 'new thinking' cannot be understood in purely literal terms. Like much political rhetoric in any language, it is not simply a description of existing practice, but simultaneously points to an ideal – what 'ought' to occur – and acts as an exhortation and invitation to the target audience to participate in the achievement of that ideal. Gorbachev uses the term not just to describe what his administration is engaged in, he also intends it as an invitation to dialogue. It would therefore be a mistake to read the phrase too literally since, quite apart from being tempted to try for easy but unhelpful definitions, one is likely to lose the resonances of the word 'new' with its suggestion of process, openness and lack of limits.

That said, the depth and seriousness of Gorbachev's innovations in foreign policy and the logic which appears to be unfolding in his 'new thinking', cannot be fully appreciated unless one first pays some attention to the situation bequeathed him from the past.

Sources of 'new thinking'

To begin with, it is worth stressing that 'new thinking' is not simply a product of the Soviet inability to pay for the arms race. Its sources are to be found in a much deeper complex of problems which are both domestic and international in origin.[3]

Domestically, the USSR is undergoing a crisis of systemic proportions which touches on all aspects of society. In his book *Perestroika*, Gorbachev paints a grim picture of drastic economic decline, social degradation, political and moral alienation of Party and people, and makes no bones about asserting that any delay in introducing reform could have led, 'in the near future' to 'serious social, economic and political crises'.[4]

Ironically this situation has not arisen entirely for want of reform. On the contrary, the process of economic reform at any rate has been almost continuous since Khrushchev first attempted a partial de-Stalinisation of society in the fifties. However, all previous attempts have manifestly failed to achieve anything, except perhaps further disorganisation of the system, largely because they have been too limited and piecemeal. Thus the Stalinist 'administrative-command' economy still remains essentially intact, and all attempts to move from extensive to intensive growth have been frustrated by the lack of any plausible incentives. In fact, the introduction of 'market' indicators, like profit, have only disorganised matters further by enabling the peripheries to disobey the centre even more than they do already.

On the other hand, the lack of political and social reforms has had even more disastrous effects. Creativity in all spheres of activity, including foreign policy, has been largely stifled or exiled to the periphery of the system by the overweening arrogance of the Party and its officials. Knowledge within the system became a matter of learning the rules of the game, which resulted in the destruction of theory, the corruption of information flows throughout the system, and the perpetuation of conformist mediocrity, especially in the social sciences – all of which Gorbachev has vigorously condemned.[5] Alienation pervaded society almost in direct relation to the increasing education and sophistication of the Soviet population and the increasingly grotesque formalism of the Soviet political establishment. Consequently Soviet citizens turned to alcohol, corruption, crime, or internal emigration on a massive scale.

Even in the context of a more favourable international environment, a domestic crisis of such proportions would eventually have forced the Soviet élites to the conclusion that the USSR's identity as a 'great power', and therefore their own power, rested on a fragile domestic base that required immediate and concentrated attention to prevent it from disintegrating completely. In such circumstances, the obvious and logical function for Soviet foreign and defence policies, and Gorbachev has made no secret of the fact, is to create the international conditions for domestic reform.

However, the international outlook for the USSR was poor when Gorbachev came to power in 1985. Developments across the board were demonstrating that the basic assumptions of Soviet 'old thinking' were not only out of touch with reality but were damaging Soviet national interests. On the defence side, the achievement of strategic parity with the USA in the 1970s proved a hollow victory, since it provided the USSR with no more bargaining power than before at the same time as the costs of sustaining this military competition increased almost exponentially. Similarly, the search for total military security which had engendered it proved to be equally illusory. By the beginning of the 1980s it had become increasingly obvious, that preparing for the contingency of world war only made world war more likely.[6] One conclusion from Soviet history was therefore becoming graphically clear. The search for absolute military security could only be maintained at the cost of economic, political and social insecurity – all of which had now come to represent far more substantial threats to the integrity of the Soviet state than world war.

Other aspects of the international situation reinforced this conclusion. The Soviet search for equality with the US, and their basic 'inferiority complex' *vis-à-vis* the United States,[7] encouraged Soviet politicians to play the superpower game on US terms with fairly disastrous results. Attempts to win influence and support in the post-colonial countries, whether through aid, trade, or arms sales, not only proved immensely costly but produced little return. The lack of Soviet integration into world financial markets and its lack of access to such instruments of 'Northern' control as the World Bank and International Monetary Fund, proved to be a particular source of weakness, because it meant that, unlike the USA, the USSR had no effective control over its debtors. Moreover, the search for equality also resulted in disastrous foreign policy actions, notably the invasion of Afghanistan, which both undermined the USSR's standing in the post-colonial world, reinforced Western propaganda about the Soviet threat, and imposed further drains on the Soviet economy. On the other hand, the 'post-industrial' revolutions in the capitalist countries demonstrated that the USSR was not only failing to keep up with the capitalist states, but was actually falling behind. As Bialer has remarked, this 'visible and rapidly growing technological gap severely wounded the national pride of the Soviet political élite, creating a psychological shock of immense intensity'.[8] This had a two-pronged effect. On one side, it showed beyond doubt that without fundamental change the Soviet system would stand no chance of catching up, let alone keeping up, with the capitalist democracies. On the other side, it also demonstrated that the old Stalinist simplicities about the historic inevitability of capitalist crisis and socialist victory were not only empirically unsustainable but produced a grotesque complacency which was gravely damaging to Soviet national interests.

Finally, on the 'ideological front', Soviet 'old thinking' exacerbated and reinforced old-style Soviet heavy-handedness. In particular Stalinist 'two-campism' with its simplistic black-and-white view of the world and its in-built mechanism of coercion and control blinkered the very people who wielded it to their own advantage. It was, of course, politically functional. The Manichaean scenario of global class struggle between socialism and capitalism enabled successive Soviet leaderships not only to identify 'friend' and 'foe' rather easily, but to condemn anyone who disagreed with the Soviet Party line, within or outside the USSR, as a 'class enemy'. However, such Manichaeism when coupled with a history of international isolation and invasion also facilitated the development of a 'zero-sum game' conception of national security, and of a simple 'us' and 'them' conceptual scheme, which crippled the ability of the Soviet political élite to be creative in its search for policies and friends. Any manifestation of 'diversity' among people, no matter how harmless, was to be construed as potentially antagonistic to Soviet interests and therefore opposed. 'Unity' was reduced entirely to a question of uniformity − otherwise known as 'monolithic unity around the Party line'. And 'co-operation' of any meaningful sort became unthinkable, since class enemies could not co-operate and 'true' socialists did not need to, being already all of 'one mind' as represented by the Party.

Khrushchev attempted to modify this 'old thinking' thereby laying some of the groundwork for Gorbachev. Thus, he envisaged the possibility of a diversity between peoples which might not be antagonistic − hence his concept of 'different roads to socialism'. He also envisaged the possibility of long-term co-operation with capitalism, hence his policy of 'peaceful coexistence'. However, Khrushchev did not abandon the Stalinist conception of global class struggle and consequently did not entirely eliminate the seeds of 'two-campism'. As a consequence, the practice of 'different roads to socialism' did not survive the first manifestations of real difference in the socialist community in 1956, any more than the 'thaws' within the USSR did; and 'peaceful coexistence' was increasingly marginalised by the developing hostilities of the cold war. As a consequence the CPSU's conception of 'total security', at the expense of the rest of the world if necessary, was not fundamentally altered.

Changes in style and substance

In the five years of his tenure as General Secretary, Mikhail Gorbachev's 'new thinking' has cut a widening swathe of destruction through this inheritance, although it has clearly not severed all connections with the past.

Changes in the style of Soviet foreign policy were the most immediately visible results of Gorbachev's accession to power. Indeed, the new Soviet consciousness of the importance of public relations and the speed with which they mastered the international media circuits, had dramatic effects from the start. Moreover, the language of policy statements, both domestic and foreign, became much less stilted and Aesopian, and much more straightforward and businesslike.

Although institutional and personnel changes did not happen as immediately in the foreign policy area as they did in domestic matters, they were nevertheless fairly dramatic when they did come. Perhaps the most dramatic change from the point of view of the outside world – although hardly unexpected – was Andrei Gromyko's removal from the Foreign Ministry after almost thirty years as Foreign Minister and his replacement by the unknown, but evidently incorruptible Georgian ex-police chief, Eduard Shevardnadze in July 1985. This was not simply a change of face but effectively constituted an end to the dominance of the Foreign Ministry in foreign affairs. Equally interesting was the return of the veteran Soviet ambassador, Anatoly Dobrynin, from the USA to head the International Department of the Central Committee in 1986. Although he was replaced in 1988 by Valentin Falin, head of the Soviet news agency Novosti, his return to Moscow after years in Washington was an indication of the extent to which Gorbachev was interested in promoting people with expertise and experience to crucial decision-making positions.

Personnel changes were accompanied by structural changes. Not only was the long predominance of the Foreign Ministry fatally undermined, but its internal structure was reorganised to reflect the geopolitical realities of the post-war world. The departments of the Party's Central Committee Secretariat, including the International Department, were also streamlined and reorganised. Significantly, two of the Central Committee departments involved with international relations – the departments concerning relations with the socialist countries and foreign cadres abroad – were absorbed into the International Department, and their combined personnel considerably reduced. This had the institutional effect, for the first time, of placing the USSR's relations with the other socialist states, including the East European states, on the same footing as its relations with the rest of the world. Before, they were treated more like outlying provinces of the USSR itself.

Although their possible long-term effects are by no means certain, these changes of personnel and institutional structure are clearly significant. The extent to which the institutional 'mobilisation of bias' influences incremental day-to-day decision-making, information 'gate-keeping' and policy agenda-setting, all of which materially influence the overall policy-formulating environment, cannot be underestimated. In the old days, this institutional 'mobilisation of bias' worked against the reformers, now it is beginning to work against the conservatives. This does not, of course, fully guarantee Gorbachev's position, but it will make it increasingly difficult to dislodge the thinking that he has unleashed as time goes on.

'New thinking' is not a matter of style and presentation only, but has also increasingly become a question of substance. The most interesting development, from both the theoretical and political points of view, has been the accumulating evidence which suggests that Gorbachev is completely reversing the Manichaean scenario bequeathed to him.

As already remarked, Khrushchev laid some of the foundations for the elimination of 'two-campism' back in 1956. However, Gorbachev is now taking the crucial steps that Khrushchev did not take. The growing Soviet preoccupation with the question of 'interdependence', coupled with Gorbachev's increasingly explicit attempts to de-emphasise the importance of class for the understanding and management of domestic and foreign affairs are undoubtedly eliminating the central conceptual planks of Soviet 'two-campism' and of the antagonistic 'bad faith' model associated with it.

As with much else, the Soviet appreciation of global interdependence did not begin with Gorbachev but first emerged in the mid-1970s. At that time the discussion of interdependence by scientists and politicians produced considerable tension between those who insisted on the continued importance of the 'class approach' to all problems, and the proponents of 'globalistics' who asserted, logically enough, that global problems required an 'all human approach'. During Brezhnev's last years this tension was side-stepped by means of the political assertion that the two approaches should be made to complement each other. However, this did not entirely resolve the tension since it was maintained that global problems would continue to be the object of competition as well as of co-operation between the capitalist and socialist systems.[9]

Gorbachev, however, is now eliminating this tension by elevating the significance of interdependence and effectively removing class from the argument, without actually rejecting the theory of class struggle altogether. He is achieving this in two interrelated ways.

On the one hand, he is explicitly rejecting the Stalinist uses to which the theory of class struggle has been put, while not denying its value as a theory of social dynamics. Thus, for example, he has condemned its political exploitation as an instrument of repression by Stalin. 'Any attempts to justify ... lawlessness by political needs, international tension or *alleged exacerbation of class struggle* in the country are wrong', he states in *Perestroika*, thus undermining one of the crucial coercive instruments which the CPSU has always used to control dissent both within the USSR and in Eastern Europe.[10] He has also un-compromisingly rejected the 'enemy image' which was both cause and effect of the mutual 'two-campism' of the cold war. At the same time, however, Gorbachev has not denied that classes continue to exist as objective entities in the world, nor has he denied the relevance of class analysis. However, he is insisting that class is no longer of universal relevance.

On the other hand, Gorbachev is elevating the general idea of interdependence to the point of making it a universal principle, on the basis that nuclear weapons and global environmental crisis impose objective limits on the possibilities for class confrontation and general antagonism in the international arena.[11] At the 19th Party Congress in June 1988, for example, he argued that 'common human values' took absolute priority over class interests in the conditions of the late twentieth century.[12] In short, Gorbachev has used the issues of interdependence and imminent global catastrophe to relativise the question of class almost completely.[13]

This is clearly a development of enormous significance, because it effectively eliminates a central source of antagonism from Soviet thinking, and because it has considerable implications for the remainder of the old neo-Stalinist 'world view'.

For example, it has been accompanied by a comprehensive recon-ceptualisation of capitalism. The old thesis that capitalism is in general crisis and condemned by history to collapse under the weight of its own contradictions has become completely unsustainable in the light of all the contrary evidence. The result has been a gradual revision of the Soviet analysis of capitalism, which now recognises its dynamism, its technological and productive capacities, and the importance of its democratic forms as barriers to Western militarism.[14] The latter has by no means been lost sight of, but the nature of the threat and of the defence required to meet it have themselves been undergoing significant revision.

It has also been accompanied by a considerable change in the working definition of 'peaceful coexistence'. Gorbachev has abandoned the notion that 'peaceful coexistence' is a 'specific form of class struggle', and it no longer appears as such in the 1986 edition of the Party Programme. This is more far-reaching than it may at first appear. It means that the old conception of 'peaceful coexistence' in which economic, political, ideological and international relations between capitalist and socialist states were conceived of as being sites of 'class struggle', and therefore always potentially antagonistic, is now being superseded by a conception of coexistence in which such relations are to be entirely based on co-operation and mutual advantage. This suggests, as Bialer has noted, that 'the idea of a Soviet-orchestrated world-wide victory of socialism, even without a war, is being abandoned'.[15] As Gorbachev remarked in *Perestroika*, 'it is essential to rise above ideological differences. Let everyone make his own choice, and let us all respect that choice.'[16]

As this last statement implies, this new (and historically unique) Soviet emphasis on community and mutuality has led to the explicit acknowledgement that unity and co-operation can only be based on the recognition and legitimation of diversity. This acknowledgement was particularly noticeable in Gorbachev's United Nations address delivered in December 1988. Where difference and diversity were once perceived to be intrinsically antagonistic, Gorbachev spoke of them as being positive attributes of human existence. 'Differences often acted as barriers in the past. Now they can develop into factors of rapprochement and mutual enrichment.' As he pointed out, however, this demands 'respect of others' views and stances, tolerance, the ability to learn how to coexist *while remaining different*'. It 'needs goodwill *not to see the alien as bad and hostile*'. In short, it requires a 'good faith' rather than a 'bad faith' model of others' intentions and behaviour. Moreover, since 'specific interests underlie all differences between social systems, ways of life, and value preferences', such differences not only have to be acknowledged, they also have to be empowered. The 'principle of freedom of choice' for all nations (but it implicitly follows for individuals as well) therefore becomes 'a universal principle [which] knows no exceptions'. By the same token, any policy of intervention in another country's affairs should become unthinkable. Gorbachev speaks of 'unity through variety' and, in his

UN speech, referred positively to 'that kind of co-operation, that we might call creativity or co-development'.[17] It is clear from the generality of what he says that what Gorbachev intends is a conception of 'unity' and 'co-operation' which is not based on coercion but on a negotiated balance of interests achieved through dialogue and aimed 'at the essence of problems, not at confrontation'.[18]

This does not mean that the current Soviet administration has any intention of relinquishing its right to promote the USSR's national and international interests, but it does mean that Soviet interests could be open to negotiation, redefinition and even, where necessary, abandonment. Alexander Bovin stated the logical extreme of the argument as early as June 1987, when he wrote that

Compromise is the air without which constructive policy will choke ... Of course, each partner has a limit for concessions determined by the supreme interests of state security and commitments to allies. But to a significant extent *this limit is subjective*. It is determined not by interest 'in itself', but by precisely how a given interest is understood and formulated.[19]

The politicians do not put matters so starkly, but they have certainly suggested that Soviet objectives are to be viewed much more flexibly in future.[20] Defence policy is an obvious example.

The new Soviet appreciation of the relationship between diversity and interdependence has been accompanied from the beginning by substantial revisions in military doctrine and security policy. Gone is the obsession with military security regardless of cost and impact. Gone also is the search for total security at the expense of virtually everything else. The new Soviet sensitivity to the legitimacy of the 'other point of view' has reinforced the realisation already bearing down on them in 1983–4 that ever-greater military preparations against the possibility of war only increase its likelihood. It has sensitised the Soviet leadership to the genuine security fears of the NATO nations and to their own share of responsibility for the arms race. The result has been a comprehensive call for the construction of common security régimes, both at the global level and in terms of regional security régimes, which not only abandon the self-defeating 'zero-sum game' approach to national security, but go beyond narrow military considerations to encompass co-operative political, economic and diplomatic relations on the basis of the 'expanding-sum game'.

Policy outcomes

The practical outcomes, in terms of policy and diplomacy, of such conceptual changes will inevitably take longer to materialise, not least because they are partly reliant on the active collaboration of the international community. However, where Soviet action has been less dependent on reciprocal responses from other countries change has been rapid, especially by comparison with the past.

One obvious practical result of the new Soviet preoccupation with interdependence, has been the heightened Soviet willingness to co-operate with and strengthen the power of such international forums as the United Nations, and to engage much more overtly in finding co-operative solutions to regional problems. Soviet participation in international efforts to end the Gulf War and achieve peaceful solutions in Angola, Namibia and Cambodia, not to mention the unconditional Soviet withdrawal from Afghanistan, stand out as tangible examples.

'New thinking' has also been visible in renewed superpower summitry and the revitalisation of arms control negotiations as well as in developing Soviet attitudes towards Europe.

Arms control

There have been several significant developments here quite apart from the actual arms reductions achieved.

First, the USSR has now acknowledged the importance of openness in the conduct of military and international affairs. Although there is still a long way to go, the USSR has been much more forthcoming about publishing defence data, monitoring war games and so on. Even more significantly, it has also acknowledged the central importance of verification procedures based not on national means but on 'bilateral and/or international inspection on site', which include random inspections and cover the destruction or storage as well as the deployment of weapons systems.[21] As a consequence of the INF Treaty signed in December 1987 there have already been several intrusive on-site inspections by both Warsaw Pact and NATO investigation teams. Indeed, its verification procedures may prove to be the Treaty's greatest success.

Secondly, the new Soviet awareness of threat perception has also been expressed in their consideration of asymmetrical force reductions. For example, they have indicated a willingness to contemplate cuts in strategic weapons (under START) which might well fall below the figure of 50 per cent first mooted at the Geneva summit in November 1985.[22] Similarly, Gorbachev has announced the unilateral reduction of Soviet conventional forces in Europe by 500,000 men along with their associated weaponry. This overture – advanced at the UN in December 1988 – was followed by unilateral troop reduction proposals on the part of some of their Warsaw Pact partners. More recently still, Gorbachev has held out the prospect of unilateral reductions in short-range nuclear forces, provided NATO is willing to get SNF talks under way.[23]

Thirdly, the Soviet desire for arms control and generalised 'new thinking' has prompted a new flexibility and sophistication which is quite out of keeping with traditional Soviet diplomacy. Most obviously, Gorbachev has consistently sought to dictate the terms of international debate and to set the pace and agenda for reform, rather than simply reacting to US proposals and terms as in the past. By launching a whole series of major initiatives – the unilateral ban on nuclear weapons testing in 1985–7, the November 1985 Geneva proposals, the January 1986 plan for total disarmament, the October 1986 Reykjavik package, the INF negotiations, and so on – the USSR has sought to offset its bargaining weaknesses by keeping the US and NATO off-balance and by occupying the 'moral high ground'. This the USSR has mostly succeeded in doing, not least because Soviet negotiators have demonstrated a willingness to compromise, for example over SDI, and to be tactically flexible, for example in talks on the relationship between intermediate-range, strategic and space-based weapons systems. By contrast the US and NATO responses have seemed slow, unimaginative and often casuistic.

There is no doubt that these initiatives in great part reflect a Soviet desire to change the international rules of the game to their benefit, but as MccGwire argues, the 'fact that Gorbachev's proposals promote Soviet objectives does not exclude them from also being in the interests of the West'.[24] On the contrary, the new Soviet openness to compromise and negotiation offers the capitalist democracies a unique opportunity to address some of the imbalances that are gradually ruining their own economies – excessive arms spending being only the most obvious.

Western Europe

An emphasis on mutuality and compromise has also been a common theme of Gorbachev's policies towards Western Europe. The Soviet concept which has attracted most attention has been the notion of the 'common European home'.

The concept initially appeared during Gorbachev's first visit to London in December 1984, so it is by no means completely new.[25] In many respects, it is no more than a metaphor for the general idea of community, so those observers looking for 'blueprints' are tending to miss the point. However, it does articulate various strands of Soviet policy towards the region.

At one level, it reflects a long-standing Soviet desire for greater economic integration between the EC and Comecon, since this has always provided one obvious avenue for ameliorating the rigours of domestic economic reform. Increasingly, however, and uniquely for the USSR, Gorbachev has also evinced considerable interest in creating and expanding political, cultural and social ties with Western Europe. In his speech to the Council of Europe in July 1989 Gorbachev listed a whole series of issues on which the USSR would be interested in pan-European co-operation, ranging from a pan-European express railway to co-operation on human rights.[26] Gorbachev has also indicated Soviet readiness to become involved in the activities of the Council of Europe, including co-operation with the European Convention and the European Court of Human Rights. Along with Poland, Hungary and Yugoslavia, the Soviet Union was accredited observer status by the Council. This means that it will be sending thirty-six members of the new Supreme Soviet to the Council's Assembly. Undoubtedly, these closer political connections are partly intended to help economic integration, but even so they will clearly transform Soviet relations with Europe in the long term.

The concept also reflects Soviet awareness that Europe is the original seat of the superpower confrontation and that Western Europe proved most unwilling to relinquish the policies of *détente*, even when Soviet–US relations were at their nadir. From the Soviet perspective it therefore appears likely to be the most productive channel for the military and political elimination of cold war thinking.

This does not mean, however, that the USSR is engaged in the old policy of 'divide and rule' generally ascribed to it. Gorbachev made it clear from the outset that he had no intention of continuing the

Soviet obsession with the US relationship and wished to expand the USSR's horizons. The Soviets were equally aware from an early stage that the forces 'which bind ... and unite Western Europe and the USA are ... stronger than those which divide them'.[27] So attempts to divide NATO can hardly be much of a Soviet concern, especially when it is one so-called Soviet tactic for which Western leaders always claim to be on the look-out. In any case, evidence suggests that they might prefer the opposite. The Soviets have often looked to Western Europe to exercise a moderating influence on US foreign policy excesses, and this was certainly the case under Reagan. Moreover, both Gorbachev and his advisers have explicitly said that the notion of the 'common European home' is not intended to freeze the US out of Europe. On the contrary, it has been suggested that the 'common home' is an extension of the Helsinki process and therefore includes its thirty-five signatory states with, of course, the US and Canada among them.[28]

By the same token, however, the Soviets have made it plain that they will not tolerate any conception of the 'common home' which anticipates the elimination of socialism from Eastern Europe.[29] They emphasise that commonality can only be based on the acknowledgement of difference, freedom of choice, and 'deep-going co-operation' between all the European nations, starting from an acceptance of the status quo.

In short, Gorbachev's conception of the 'common European home' appears to be of a piece with his conceptions of 'unity in variety' and of co-operation as 'creative co-development'. The fact that he and his advisers have resolutely refused to be more concise, is an optimistic sign that they are equally resolute in their wish not to lay down a 'party line' on the subject, but to initiate wide-ranging negotiations on the future shape of Europe in which all have an opportunity to participate.

Eastern Europe

Soviet policy towards Eastern Europe constitutes the acid test for many when it comes to evaluating Soviet intentions. Soviet expansion into Eastern Europe helped to originate the cold war and developments there have continued to be a major source of East–West tension ever since. There is no doubt that the tone and style of Soviet policy towards the countries of Eastern Europe has changed markedly under Gorbachev. However, there is as yet no agreement as to whether this also constitutes a change in substance.

Most commentators look to the explicit repudiation of the so-called 'Brezhnev doctrine' as the most reliable index of change. However, this is quite inadequate to the complexities of the question. Quite apart from the fact that the label 'Brezhnev doctrine' was never a Soviet term, reflecting rather the US obsession with 'doctrines', any overt attempt on Gorbachev's part to condemn the 1968 invasion of Czechoslovakia, which is what such a rejection seems to amount to in Western eyes, would constitute interference in the affairs of another country of the sort that Gorbachev is now explicitly rejecting, and which the very policy of *glasnost* itself rules out. Moreover, the situation within Eastern Europe is now so complex and volatile that the question of what constitutes an intervention is no longer obvious. After all, in certain circumstances non-intervention can be as disruptive as intervention.

That said, the accumulating evidence suggests not only that Gorbachev has repudiated the old neo-Stalinist approach to Eastern Europe, but that the East European countries are inevitably set on divergent paths, whatever the USSR might wish.

Thus far, Gorbachev has explicitly rejected every single plank of neo-Stalinist politics.

First, as remarked above, he has rejected the old Manichaean 'us versus them' scenario that has always constituted a central pillar of Soviet control within the socialist community.[30]

Secondly, he has rejected the Party's Stalinist pretensions to 'omniscience' both domestically and internationally, on the grounds that it results in the divorce of theory from practice, and the alienation of Party from people. As he remarked back in November 1987 in a speech to fraternal Communist Parties: the 'arrogance of omniscience is akin to fear of one's inability to deal with new problems. It testifies to the tenacious habit of rejecting other points of view out of hand. No dialogue, no productive discussion is possible. With the result that practice suffers.'[31] Moreover, during his visit to Czechoslovakia in April 1987 he insisted that 'No one party holds a monopoly on truth', adding that: 'No one has the right to claim a special position in the socialist world. The independence of each party, its responsibility to its people, the right to resolve questions of the country's development in a sovereign way ... these are indisputable principles.'[32] In the context, namely Prague, this statement even at the time did, in fact, constitute a considerable critique of previous Soviet behaviour, even if it was subsequently qualified by the ambiguous assertion that each Party had to take some account of 'the general interest' of the socialist commonwealth. By the end of the 1980s events had moved on considerably. The Soviet government newspaper *Izvestiya* published a critique of 1968, in time for the twenty-first anniversary of the invasion, as well as a profile of the Polish Prime Minister designate, Tadeusz Mazowiecki, a staunch Catholic and long-time Polish dissident. Moreover, this appointment was described as 'natural'.[33] A more official imprimatur one could not expect at such a delicate time.

Thirdly, Gorbachev has espoused the virtues of diversity and 'pluralism' in the socialist as well as the global context. Not only is 'socialist pluralism', or 'socialist democracy', now a central principle of domestic politics, it is also to be encouraged in the commonwealth generally.[34] Finally, Gorbachev has, on several occasions, explicitly rejected intervention or the use of force as a legitimate form of international behaviour. In his speech to the Council of Europe, he insisted that 'The philosophy of a common European home rules out the ... very possibility of the use or threat of force ... by an alliance against another alliance, inside alliances, or wherever it may be'.[35]

Taken *in toto*, therefore, the statements that Gorbachev has made to-date concerning the development of new relations within the socialist commonwealth, coupled with his recent emphasis on the central importance of the 'universal principle of free choice' constitute as complete a rejection of the 'Brezhnev doctrine' as Western critics can reasonably expect. Soviet imperturbability in response to events in Poland, where in 1989 a Solidarity-led government came to power, in Hungary, where the development of political pluralism was well under way, and the GDR, which opened its frontiers and undertook to hold free elections, confirms this to be so.

In any event, developments in Eastern Europe over the last forty years have demonstrated that the USSR can slow the pace of change but not prevent it. The diversification in the region is now such that only political expediency underpins the retention of a label which is supposed to encompass countries as utterly divergent as Hungary and Romania. Certainly, economic decline, political de-legitimation and cultural stagnation have been affecting all the East European countries, but the search for solutions will only increase their diversity, even in the case of those, notably the GDR, Czechoslovakia and Bulgaria, whose Parties held out for a while against reform. This does not mean that the USSR is likely to relinquish all its interests in the region, at least not while the old cold war structures remain in place. But it does mean that the definition of these interests is likely to change further.

Soviet–East European relationships will increasingly have to be based on the sorts of negotiation and compromise, the balancing of interests, that characterise relations among quasi-equals.

Conclusion

A popular approach in the Western literature has been to explain Soviet 'new thinking' as a response to the problems of managing decline.[36] It is argued that 'Gorbachevism' is a functional response to the USSR's military over-reach during the 1970s and to its incipient domestic economic and political collapse. According to this interpretation 'new thinking' represents a policy of retrenchment abroad and an imaginative means of gaining vital breathing space for the renovation of the Soviet system at home. It is not, therefore, about the profound reassessment of Soviet identity, rather it is about the management of change in order to make a more streamlined and efficient version of the *current* Soviet system globally competitive. It is for this reason on the whole, or some version of it, that Western leaders are generally reluctant to extend more than the most limited co-operation towards Gorbachev's administration.

The evidence suggests, however, that this is distinctly short-sighted. Even if Gorbachev began his tenure in office with this scenario in mind, the extent of the change which he has initiated, and the magnitude of the reforms required if an *efficient* and *productive* system is actually to be achieved in the USSR, will of necessity transform the identity of the system, whether the reformers wish it or not.

By the end of the 1980s it was no longer clear what the identity of the system should be. Gorbachev had certainly not rejected the label 'socialism'. But it was not obvious that he was certain what it meant, even if he had rejected Stalinism.[37] Moreover, the meaning of 'Leninism' had become obscure. Gorbachev castigated the dogmatic deformation of Lenin's work which occurred under Stalin and subsequently, but the furthest he had gone in indicating what 'true Leninism' involved was to suggest that it consisted in mastering 'the art of specific analysis of a specific situation'. In short, he appeared to be proposing such an open reading of the 'Leninist method' that it was bound to produce an increasing diversity of approach in both theory and practice which will inevitably move beyond the rather narrow confines of historical Leninism.[38] Further, it is distinctly noticeable that the term 'Marxism–Leninism' virtually disappeared from Gorbachev's vocabulary,[39] as did 'revisionism' and associated words.

While none of this confirms Gorbachev's ability to stay in power, nor the ability of the reformers to transform the system in any particular direction, it does suggest that the situation within the USSR, and within the socialist community generally, is now so fluid as to present the capitalist nations with a real opportunity to influence events. For the first time in its history, the USSR is extending an open-ended invitation to the capitalist nations to engage in the long-term renegotiation and harmonisation of interests. This may seem far-fetched, even Utopian, after forty years of cold war, but then who, six years ago, could have predicted the Gorbachev phenomenon?

Notes

1 See e.g. Igor Kondakov, 'Spiritual culture: old and new thinking', *Social Sciences*, Moscow, I, 1989, pp. 75–89.

2 Mikhail Gorbachev, *Perestroika, New Thinking for our Country and the World*, London, Collins, 1987, p. 144.

3 Seweryn Bialer, ' "New thinking" and Soviet foreign policy', *Survival*, July/August 1988, pp. 291–309.

4 Gorbachev, *Perestroika*, p. 17.

5 See e.g. ibid., pp. 21ff; *Pravda*, 28 January 1987.

6 Michael MccGwire, 'A mutual security regime for Europe?', *International Affairs*, LXIV, Summer 1988, p. 361.

7 See Gorbachev, *Perestroika*, p. 222; C. Jonsson, *Superpower. Comparing American and Soviet Foreign Policy*, London, Frances Pinter, 1984.

8 Bialer, 'New thinking', p. 293.

9 Stephen Shenfield, *The Nuclear Predicament. Explorations in Soviet Ideology*, Chatham House Paper 37, London, Routledge & Kegan Paul, 1987, ch. 8.

10 Gorbachev, *Perestroika*, p. 106, emphasis added.

11 Ibid., p. 146.

12 Gorbachev, *Pravda*, 29 June 1988.

13 A move which is still enormously controversial in the USSR itself, not to mention the rest of the socialist community.

14 Bialer, 'New thinking', p. 299.

15 Ibid., p. 300.

16 Gorbachev, *Perestroika*, p. 221. See also, e.g. Gorbachev, *Pravda*, 8 December 1988.

17 Gorbachev, *Pravda*, 8 December 1988, emphasis added.

18 Ibid.

19 Alexander Bovin, 'From the art of war to the art of negotiations', as quoted in Stephen Sestanovich, 'Gorbachev's foreign policy: a diplomacy of decline', *Problems of Communism*, January–February, 1988, p. 6, emphasis added by Sestanovich.

20 Sestanovich, 'Gorbachev's foreign policy', p. 6.

21 Bialer, 'New thinking', p. 302.

22 Ibid.

23 NATO of course is not willing until it has seen tangible results coming out of the conventional force reduction talks. See John Palmer, *Guardian*, 7 July 1989, p. 1.

24 MccGwire, 'A mutual security regime', p. 379.

25 See Hannes Adomeit, 'Gorbachev's policy towards the West', in R. F. Laird, ed., *Soviet Foreign Policy*, New York, APS, 1987, p. 95.

25 Gorbachev, *Pravda*, 7 July 1989.

27 Alexander Bovin as quoted in Adomeit, 'Gorbachev's policy toward the West', p. 98.

28 See V. Zagladin in *Moscow News*, 16 July 1989, p. 6.

29 Gorbachev, *Pravda*, 7 July 1989.

30 See also R. Walker, 'Marxism–Leninism as discourse', *British Journal of Political Science*, April 1989, pp. 161–89.

31 Gorbachev, *Pravda*, 5 November 1987.

32 Ibid., *Pravda*, 11 April 1987. See also T. M. Cynkin, 'Glasnost, perestroika and Eastern Europe', *Survival*, July–August 1988, pp. 310–31; D. S. Mason, 'Glasnost, perestroika and Eastern Europe', *International Affairs*, LXIV, Summer 1988, pp. 431–48.

33 Jonathan Steele, *Guardian*, 21 August 1989, p. 20.

34 Gorbachev, *Pravda*, 3 November 1987.

35 Ibid., *Pravda*, 7 July 1989.

36 See e.g. S. Sestanovich, 'Gorbachev's foreign policy'.

37 E.g. Gorbachev, *Pravda*, 11 May 1988.

38 See R. Walker, 'The relevance of ideology', in R. J. Hill and J. Zielonka, eds., *Restructuring Eastern Europe: Views from Western Europe*, Aldershot, Edward Elgar, forthcoming.

39 See Archie Brown, 'Ideology and political culture', in S. Bialer, ed., *Politics, Society and Nationality inside Gorbachev's Russia*, London, Westview, 1989.

Gorbachev and Soviet defence policy

The West has lived in the shadow of Soviet military power since the end of the Second World War. Despite the changes that have occurred in the Soviet armed forces their sheer size and capability have appeared as an unrelenting threat to NATO countries. Perception of a threat has been reinforced by the knowledge that the primacy of the offensive has long been the guiding principle at the heart of Soviet military thinking.

In addition to capability and military doctrine, a threat has been discerned from overall Soviet political intentions. It is the last of these which has given rise to widely varied interpretations about Soviet policy. But broadly speaking, there have been two schools of thought. One school, which includes Michael Howard and Michael MccGwire, suggests that political intent has been so moderated by pragmatic considerations that since at least the Cuban missile crisis the Soviet Union has not seriously entertained the notion of prevailing over the West in any meaningful way.[1] The other school, which had support in the Reagan Administration from luminaries such as Richard Perle, places greater emphasis on Marxist–Leninist ideology as the driving force of Soviet policy. According to this interpretation, the Gorbachev reforms are not a new departure, but are part of the continuing Soviet offensive with the ultimate design of a new world order in which the Soviet Union's adversaries will be significantly weakened.[2]

To a large extent the position which commentators adopt on political intentions influences their interpretation of Soviet defence policy. But what seems to be incontrovertible, and it provides the theme of this chapter, is that Gorbachev has sought to change fundamentally both the image and the underlying nature of Soviet defence policy as part of his wider reshaping of the country as a whole. The Soviet Union is still to remain a superpower in military terms but is to present a less threatening appearance to others. Prevention of war and a new defensive doctrine are to be the guiding themes. Security is to have much more of a political dimension than a military one.

Nevertheless Gorbachev cannot easily escape the Soviet military legacy of the past. The Soviet Union was created in revolution and war, and the early revolutionary armies had perforce to be moulded on those of former Tsars, for there was no other military talent on which to draw. The Soviet armed forces still very much rely on the distilled wisdom of Russian military experience from the past as well as that which they have gained on their own account, principally in the enormous and harrowing trial of strength against Hitler in the Great Patriotic War. What then are these influences from the past?

Fundamentals

Russian experience since the founding of the nation-state has been one of frequent invasion and subjection to attack. The Mongols under Batu Khan, a nephew of Genghis Khan, first occupied Russia in the thirteenth century and they stayed for two hundred years.[3] The Swedes, Poles, Tartars, Turks and a succession of countries invaded Russia before the nineteenth century. Napoleon captured Moscow in 1812. The Crimea was the scene of further invasion in the mid-nineteenth century. The present communist-ruled state was born in war in 1917 and survived through civil war when under siege from the interventionist countries and White Russians. The memory of the Second World War is seared into the Russian mind. The Soviet fear of attack based on historical experience has therefore been a genuine one.

The Soviet Union has, nevertheless, tended to overstress the external threats that it has had to face because in practice it has continually overcome its opponents and has steadily expanded its borders at their expense. In effect it largely pursued an expansionist policy to afford itself greater protection. Historically, Russian belligerence more than equalled that of its neighbours.

It was Napoleon who said that 'Geography is the fate of a nation'. This is certainly very true of the USSR. It is a country with few natural defensive boundaries. It is essentially one vast plain or steppe stretching from eastern Europe to Siberia, the Far East and the Pacific Ocean. The mountains all lie along the southern borders, through the Caucasus and Central Asia, and extend eastwards along the Sino-Soviet border.

The rivers, although long and wide, are slow-flowing and comparatively few in number. Geography therefore provided no defence against external attack but neither did it provide any obstacle to expansion. As Russia grew and became the largest of European nations in terms of population so it developed the urge to expand territorially as a 'natural right' and as a means to push outwards its defensive barriers.

Geographical and historical experience taught the Russians that the first priority of the state must be military power and the unquestioning fulfilment by the population of the country's military needs based on a considerable degree of over-insurance. The size of the country, the large population, its comparative economic and technological backwardness and vulnerable frontiers all served to convince Russian and Soviet leaders that superiority in men, and where possible weapons, was its greatest asset.

Gorbachev's inheritance

The Soviet military superpower of the mid-1980s was derived from this line of thinking and background. However, the strain which an inflated military establishment was imposing on the country became increasingly evident. Soviet strategic commitments were so diverse and its military power so overgrown that they drained the resources of the country on which they depended.

Defence spending to match the wealthier NATO members has been calculated by Western experts at somewhere between 15 and 17 per cent of Soviet GDP, increasing at a rate of 4 per cent or more a year from 1983. Some fifty-six army divisions and other arms were deployed in the Far Eastern Strategic Theatre, though not necessarily up to full strength. Afghanistan, whilst providing some military advantages was officially announced as costing $70 billion, with casualties estimated in the West at over 12,000 dead and over 35,000 wounded.[4] Naval construction was unrelenting as new aircraft carriers and a range of nuclear submarines entered service. The pattern was similar in all arms as modern armoured vehicles, aircraft and missile systems appeared in unabated succession. The strain on the economy was such that Brezhnev felt obliged to remind military leaders in October 1982 that whilst they would receive what was required for defence they would not necessarily get all that they wanted.[5]

Some challenges, such as that posed by the American SDI programme, were becoming beyond the Soviet capacity to meet. The situation as it appeared to this author writing in the autumn of 1984 was as follows:

Despite the enormously strong grip of the system the Soviet Union is, I believe, inherently unstable. A society that is virtually imprisoned, isolated and stagnating in its own country must, in the long term, be vulnerable to change as ideas and knowledge of achievements elsewhere in the world percolate through to the people. The portents are there: a restlessness in Eastern Europe; dissatisfaction with an ideology by some sections of Soviet youth; an ever increasing expansion of world communications and with it a greater penetration of the Soviet Union; a well established understanding that Western goods are generally much better than their Soviet counterparts; an increasing sluggishness and falling behind of the Soviet economy and finally a gradual passing of the generation which was steeped in the Revolution. Exactly when change will come or in what form is impossible to predict. It is a consolation to know that it must.[6]

Gorbachev became General Secretary six months later and the concept of *perestroika* was introduced.

Gorbachev's experience of defence matters was very limited before he entered the Politburo. His performance in rapidly dominating Soviet security policy is therefore all the more remarkable. In 1985 when Gorbachev became leader, President Reagan had not long before described the Soviet Union as an 'evil empire'. Pershing II missiles capable of striking targets inside the Soviet Union in a few minutes had recently been deployed in Europe. The degree of confrontation between East and West could hardly have been worse. It was this situation which had to be changed if the Soviet Union was to have the breathing space to revitalise its economy and adapt its political system.

It had long been recognised in the Soviet Union that nuclear war posed a double threat, to both the state and the Party. Nikita Khrushchev had shrewdly remarked that 'The nuclear weapon does not obey the laws of the class struggle'. Leonid Brezhnev, in an important speech in Tula in January 1977, confirmed that nuclear war held no promise of victory for either side.[7] War with the West, which held the threat of a nuclear outcome, was therefore to be avoided at all costs. If war arose, for whatever reason, its level of intensity was to be contained below the nuclear threshold and every effort was to be made to win or secure an advantageous position without resort to nuclear weapons.

This situation developed from the period in the late 1960s when NATO adopted the policy of flexible response and the superpowers began to approach nuclear parity, Soviet nuclear weapons provided an increasingly effective deterrent and NATO was no longer dependent on a nuclear trip-wire philosophy. In these circumstances the Soviet Union could begin to consider non-nuclear options in war and the possibility of making more effective use of its superior conventional strength.

As a consequence, the Soviet Union concentrated heavily on improving its conventional forces from the mid-1970s onwards but equally maintained its nuclear guard and did not deny the primacy of nuclear weapons as a last resort. Marshal N.V. Ogarkov, who was Chief of the General Staff until September 1984, advocated that nuclear weapons should be reduced in number and that more effort should be devoted to producing advanced conventional weapon systems based on emerging technology.[8] Such systems were regarded as being comparable to low-yield nuclear weapons. Gorbachev therefore inherited a situation in which the emphasis was on the development of powerful offensive forces and a military acceptance, by some at least, that the Soviet Union possessed more than sufficient nuclear weapons.

Gorbachev took advantage of this situation. A reduction in nuclear weapons would not only serve military ends but would also have a marked effect in improving East–West relations, thus allowing Gorbachev greater freedom of action for the economic and political changes which were his priorities. The achievement of a major foreign policy success would also enhance Gorbachev's own standing in the Party.

The result was a successful INF treaty and considerable progress with the START negotiations. The momentum was dramatically increased by Gorbachev's speech to the United Nations in December 1988 in which very substantial unilateral force reductions were promised. Although the reductions were probably driven principally by the need to achieve defence savings and to have them consolidated before the next five-year plan was due to begin (1991), they certainly also gave a strong impetus to the new negotiations on conventional armed forces in Europe (CFE). Large reductions in conventional forces, as CFE presupposes, would reflect a major shift away from the substantial forces required for surprise offensive operations. This brings us to consideration of Soviet military doctrine.

Military doctrine

First, it is important to appreciate that Soviet military doctrine is a philosophy of war. As with any philosophy it is both profound and pervasive. Yet it is much more than a casual collection of ideas about the nature of war. Soviet military doctine is a carefully constructed, coherent and unified system of views on the essence, aims and character of war, on preparing the country for it, and on the methods of fighting it. Doctrine therefore applies not only to war itself but also to the complete preparation of a country for war.

Doctrine has two major aspects: one that is socio-political and the other that is military−technical. As one might expect in the Soviet Union the socio-political aspect is the province of the Communist Party and therefore paramount. This involves the political aims of doctrine and the overall views on war, peace and neutrality as instruments of policy. The subordinate military−technical aspect is the concern of the military and is primarily related to the practice of war and how the armed forces are to be developed, trained and equipped for it. The military also determine the theory for the conduct of war at three levels − strategic, operational and tactical.

Gorbachev has had an impact on military doctrine in two significant ways. At the Warsaw Pact Political Consultative Committee in May 1987, Gorbachev and other Pact leaders announced that they were implementing a new defensive doctrine.[9] It is a theme which has since been developed and constantly reiterated. At the outset, the declaration, which clearly fell into the socio-political aspect of doctrine, seemed largely propagandistic. Doctrine under Brezhnev had for long been declared to be defensive, though it was all too apparent that Soviet and Warsaw Pact forces had been structured and equipped for high-speed offensive operations and not defence. Tank armies, of which the Soviet Union has developed a number, are the very essence of an offensive fighting force.

Early statements by military leaders on the new doctrine tended to be ambivalent. General D. T. Yazov, the Soviet Minister of Defence, stressed the defensive nature of the doctrine but at the same time made it equally clear that, following any defensive action to repulse aggression, Soviet forces had to be capable of conducting *decisive offensive operations* to destroy the enemy.[10] Marshal S. Akhromeyev, writing in 1987 when he was Chief of the General Staff, stated that 'defensive military action reflects weakness and failure'.[11]

These views were very much at odds with the portrayal of a new defensive doctrine.

Later pronouncements, however, made the picture somewhat clearer. In his Olof Palme Memorial Lecture in Stockholm in September 1988, Akhromeyev claimed that Soviet forces would in future be structured to reflect a non-offensive role. They would possess only a limited number of strike weapons. Force groupings and deployments would be changed to accord with defence missions. Arms production would be reduced. Nevertheless time would be needed to implement the changes.[12] In a further elaboration General M. A. Garayev declared at the Royal United Services Institute in October 1988 that the new doctrine would result in changes to operational planning, military regulations, training and instruction in all military schools.[13] The new defensive doctrine had also acquired an officially recognised legal status. It had been made mandatory throughout the armed forces by order of the Minister of Defence.

The foregoing statements imply a radical change in the composition, development and operational thinking in the Soviet armed forces from an offensive basis to a defensive one, and this is clearly what the Soviet Union intends should be construed from the new doctrine. However, it very much remains to be seen how the Soviet Union implements the new doctrine. The emerging shape of re-structured Soviet tank and motor rifle divisions leaves them as formidable combat formations fully capable of undertaking both defensive and offensive operations. Moreover, tank armies remain in the Soviet order of battle. The idea of a counter-offensive and the concept of victory are important aspects of the new doctrine. It is necessary therefore to evaluate the doctrine dispassionately as it develops rather than accept at face value the increasing volume of Soviet defensive rhetoric.

Reasonable sufficiency

The second point of impact that Gorbachev has had on military doctrine revolves around the concept of 'reasonable sufficiency' for defence. It is linked to Gorbachev's new ideas on the defensive nature of doctrine. The conceptual elements of 'reasonable sufficiency' appear to be:

■ Military forces should provide a capability for defence but not surprise attack or general offensive operations.

■ Strategic nuclear forces should have a capability for assured counter-strike but not first strike.

■ The overall military balance should be at progressively lower levels. Parity nevertheless remains a key principle.

■ Unilateral force reductions may be made where there are overriding reasons for them, such as economic necessity or a need to give impetus to arms control negotiations. But the preference is for multilateral reductions, particularly by the military.

■ Security is best achieved by political rather than military means.

In contrast, the military more often refer to 'reliable defence' or 'defensive sufficiency'. In their view such judgements about defence requirements are determined by the level and nature of the threat and not dictated by political or economic considerations. In other words it is for the military–technical sector to assess what is necessary for national defence. The implication is that the lure of 'temporary benefits' should not be allowed to lead to changes in the structure of the armed forces.

Gorbachev's 'reasonable sufficiency' and the military's 'reliable defence' are not the same creatures. The gap between these two concepts is considerable. Indeed, as Roy Allison indicates, there has been considerable resistance to the concept of defensive defence amongst the military, for offensive operational concepts are 'deeply ingrained in Soviet strategic culture'.[14] However, Gorbachev's increasing dominance over Soviet security matters, as evidenced by his announcement of major unilateral force reductions in December 1988, has largely overridden the military viewpoint and has served to underline the Party's renewed grip over the military. How has this been achieved?

Military leadership

The armed forces of the Soviet Union have always occupied a central and vital place in the history of the state. The military have afforded protection to the state and Party throughout the country's existence as the Soviet Union. They gained immense prestige from their success in the Second World War and subsequently from the military superpower status of the country. Their strength and authority, however, have always been jealously watched over by the Party.

In the last years of the Brezhnev era the military were run on a comparatively light rein. The political leadership was stagnating and the combination of Dimitri Ustinov as Minister of Defence and Ogarkov as Chief of the General Staff worked effectively as a strong team. The military had things very much their own way and received for the most part what they wanted. They must, however, have been aware that the economic base of the country, on which the armed forces depended, was becoming progressively weaker.

Gorbachev's first move was to address a gathering of very senior officers at Minsk in May 1985. Whilst it was not publicly known precisely what was said it seems reasonable to suppose that he gave an insight into his plans for the future and made it clear that the military and defence as a whole would play a central part in them. In any event it was not long before Gorbachev demonstrated by his actions that he intended to assume full responsibility for defence policy, military affairs and the development of the armed forces. Gorbachev's approach was typical of the communist method. He first overhauled the Party apparatus concerned with the military. In mid-1985 the ageing head of the Main Political Directorate of the armed forces was retired and a new much younger officer, General Alexei Lizichev, was appointed to the post. This was followed shortly by a major shake-up in the political administrations of almost all the important headquarters and commands. A Party spearhead was installed to supervise the subsequent changes.[15]

Gorbachev's next step was to begin to exert greater control over senior military appointments. General Yazov, who had been commander of the Far East Military District, and who seems to have impressed Gorbachev during his visit there in the summer of 1986, was moved to Moscow to become Deputy Minister of Defence for Cadres (Personnel). Age and ill health removed many senior officers between 1985 and 1987. The application of a general rule to retire at 70 also seems to have been implemented. This hastened the retirement process. Marshal V. I. Petrov, a First Deputy Minister of Defence, Marshal V. F. Tolubko, C-in-C of the Strategic Rocket Forces, Admiral S. G. Gorshkov, C-in-C of the Navy and General A. T. Altunin, the long-serving Head of Civil Defence and others all retired in this period paving the way for younger officers.

The most important leadership changes occurred, though, in the wake of the Matthias Rust affair (when a young West German pilot evaded interception and landed his light aircraft in Red Square). Marshal A. I. Koldunov, the C-in-C of the Air Defence Forces, was unceremoniously dismissed. But of much greater significance was the enforced retirement of Marshal Sergei Sokolov, the 75-year-old Minister of Defence. Sokolov was clearly an interim minister following Ustinov's death and had for some time appeared publicly isolated from other Politburo members. The Rust affair gave Gorbachev the opportunity to appoint Yazov as his new Minister of Defence over the heads of many more senior marshals, but he was only given a candidate seat in the Politburo, thus weakening the military's representation at the highest political level.

The last serving marshals were retired one by one in 1988 and the beginning of 1989. The first to go was Ogarkov from the post of C-in-C of the High Command of Forces in the Western Theatre of Military Operations. Akhromeyev followed, his retirement being announced, significantly, on the day Gorbachev revealed in the UN major cuts in Soviet forces. Finally Marshal V. G. Kulikov, a former Chief of the General Staff and C-in-C of the Warsaw Pact, was replaced in February 1989. At the same time changes in senior appointments were being made at Deputy Minister of Defence level and among Military District commanders. General B. V. Gromov, who had successfully conducted the withdrawal from Afghanistan, was given command of the important Kiev Military District which brought with it promotion to colonel-general. Together with General M. A. Moiseyev, the present CGS, he represents a new era of younger officers who will have to reshape the Soviet armed forces and who owe their preferment and allegiance to Gorbachev.

The situation has now been reached where the old guard has been swept away. Five marshals, no longer serving, were among the 'dead souls' who 'voluntarily' retired from the CPSU's Central Committee in April 1989. Younger officers now held the key posts, and with lower ranks than their predecessors. In fact, there was no serving officer with the rank of Marshal of the Soviet Union. The Minister of Defence was only a candidate member of the Politburo. Civilian defence specialists were increasingly putting forward views on security issues, much to the chagrin of the officer corps. Indeed, they were being officially encouraged to do so in order to break the monopoly of military advice. New centres for the study of defence matters were formed in the Soviet Ministry of Foreign Affairs and departments of the Central Committee.[16]

In July 1989 the military were subjected to a further level of control. A new Supreme Soviet Committee for Defence and State Security was established under the chairmanship of V. L. Lapygin. It was to have oversight over both the MoD and the KGB. The chairman described the purpose of the Committee as 'reliably ensuring the country's reasonable defence capability at optimum expenditure'.[17] To what extent the Committee has any teeth remains to be seen, but it gave Yazov a far from easy passage before confirming him as Minister of Defence. Its existence underlines the view that the authority of the military has undoubtedly been weakened and that of the Party strengthened in the defence field.

Perestroika **and the armed forces**

Restructuring was to involve the Soviet armed forces as much as it did the rest of the country. Not only would the new generals face purely military challenges, they were also charged with putting their own house in order in common with other sectors of the country. If anything they confronted a more difficult task because of the innate conservatism of the military establishment.

In the defence sphere *perestroika* was to be primarily concerned with improving the quality and efficiency of the armed forces and their readiness for war. This would be achieved by more practical training and by more realistic evaluations of fitness for war. It reflected a long-standing need to improve much that was repetitive and stultifying in the nature of Soviet military training. The term 'democratisation' has also been frequently coupled with military *perestroika*. It was to involve generating a greater sense of responsibility, awareness, and above all initiative in all ranks. General Yazov described 'democratisation' as the removal of all manifestations of formalism, stagnation, passiveness, red tape and complacency.[18] 'Democratisation' would contribute drive, initiative and efficiency to *perestroika*.

Apart from improvements in quality, *perestroika*, 'democratisation' and *glasnost* were aimed at eradicating the abuses of power by officers. There is some evidence that in the late 1980s greater openness occurred in the military press and that NCOs and enlisted men were allowed to engage in critical discussion.[19] But there was strong resistance, for the privileges and the advantages of rank as practised in the Soviet Union were not likely to be surrendered easily, particularly when many abuses were endemic. *Perestroika* was equally aimed at ensuring that regulations designed to counter racism and bullying would be enforced. This amounted to attempting to correct a régime which had been tolerated for years. Soviet officers provide the long-term career element in the armed forces, and are the only true military experts in a conscript force. As a result they bear heavy and time-consuming responsibilities. They have been naturally disposed to leave discipline to very young NCOs and even senior conscripts. Abuse in the form of bullying has been the result. When a senior rank strikes or abuses one who is his junior it is officially described by the Soviet military as being a 'Non-regulation mutual relationship'. This euphemistic phrase hides a most unsavoury face of Soviet militarism.

In these circumstances, and in view of the ingrained habits formed over many years, the implementation of military *perestroika* will be as hard as, if not harder than, its counterpart in the civilian sector of the Soviet Union.

Defence resources

In the past, the Soviet military long enjoyed priority for scarce materials and skilled labour. But it became increasingly clear that the ailing Soviet economy was less and less able to meet the military–technical challenges that lay ahead. Moreover, the military could not escape making their contribution to the succour of an economy which their requirements had so overloaded. There was little that could be done to change the defence content of the 1985–90 five-year plan and there was little evidence that defence procurement was in any way declining despite the claim in mid-1988 by General V.M. Shabanov, Deputy Minister of Defence for Armaments, that defence spending had been falling and would continue to fall.

However, in January 1989 Gorbachev announced that defence spending would be reduced overall by some 14.2 per cent and weapons procurement by 19.5 per cent. Savings will, of course, arise from the INF reductions, the withdrawal from Afghanistan, and the unilateral cuts to be made in force levels by the end of 1990, but it is clear that defence expenditure is to be curtailed well beyond these measures. In elaborating on the 1989 defence expenditure of 77.3 billion roubles, Nikolai Ryzhkov stated that the aim was to cut this amount by between a third and a half by 1995.[20] The next five-year plan should see substantial reductions, with a major contribution no doubt being anticipated from the CFE negotiations.

The expertise of the defence industries was called upon to support the weaker consumer sector. The defence industries have always contributed to the civil sector of the economy, but not with the same resources or the degree of quality control that has been devoted to their defence commitments. It remains to be seen how well the industries will adapt to a régime requiring them to meet both military and civil demands in the new 'self-accounting' environment. It seems likely that the strains will be considerable in an economy that is already weakened and struggling with reform.

The future

The declining state of the economy and the need for political change brought with them a growing realisation that overbearing military power has not been in the Soviet Union's best interests. Nevertheless the need for powerful military strength remains deeply ingrained both from historical experience and a requirement to defend a country covering one-sixth of the world's land mass. Soviet military policy is therefore being adapted so that strong high-quality forces are retained without presenting the threatening image that was so counter-productive in the past.

For the military this will be a painful process. Having been weaned on the vital importance of the offensive to achieve success in war, they cannot find it easy to accept changes in military doctrine imposed upon them. Their place in the Soviet state has also been weakened. They are clearly under much greater political control than hitherto. The long-serving and powerful marshals have been swept away and newer younger officers, owing their allegiance to Gorbachev, have been appointed to implement the new defensive doctrine and *perestroika* in the armed forces.

Changing the shape of the Soviet armed forces, however, is like trying to alter the course of a supertanker. It takes time and distance to realise any significant change of direction. The massive size of the armed forces gives them an in-built resistance to change. Moreover, the Soviet military in the form of the General Staff exercise immediate control over the forces and dominate the formulation of military strategy. Within the framework of the new defensive military doctrine they maintain that offence and defence are interlinked concepts. They see no contradiction between a proclaimed defensive doctrine and a combination of offensive and defensive operations to defeat an enemy, a task from which the General Staff is not absolved in the event of war. Whilst the Soviet political leadership will continue to stress the defensive nature of the armed forces the Soviet military will no doubt strive to ensure that they retain a strong offensive element in an all-round capability. The armed forces are therefore in for a difficult period. Their final shape and structure will be subject to differing political and military emphases and the uncertain outcome of arms control agreements yet to be concluded.

The economic situation is inescapable. Although the military almost certainly believe in their hearts that their needs should continue to be met they must at the same time appreciate the parlous state of the economy. Their problem is that economic recovery will take a long time. This inevitably means that the weapons programme will be cut, but it may be some time before the effects of such cuts become apparent and the military have to square up to this reality.

Gorbachev has put aside, at least temporarily, the ideological struggle with the capitalist world and at the same time has redefined Soviet security policy. This is causing a major upheaval in the Soviet military establishment when other areas in the Soviet Union are also being subjected to a similar pattern of turmoil. Associated ethnic and social unrest may yet make Gorbachev more dependent on, and thus more beholden to, the Army if the law-and-order situation deteriorates further towards widespread civil disobedience. The one certainty is that change in the defence sphere will continue if only for economic reasons. Meanwhile the military–technical aspects of doctrine and the structure of the armed forces will remain in a state of flux for some time to come.

Notes

1 See e.g., Michael Howard, 'The future of deterrence', *RUSI Journal*, June 1986, pp. 3–10; Michael MccGwire, 'Deterrence: the problem – not the solution', *International Affairs*, LXII, Winter 1985/6, pp. 55–70.

2 James Sherr, 'Strategy, economics and the new technologies – the Soviet response', in Christopher Coker, ed., *Drifting Apart? The Superpowers and their European Allies*, London, Brassey's, 1989, p. 129.

3 C. N. Donnelly, *Red Banner; the Soviet System in Peace and War*, London, Jane's, 1988, p. 17.

4 S. de Banzie, 'Afghanistan: coming home to roost?', in *RUSI Defence Yearbook*, London, Brassey's, 1989, p. 105; IISS, *The Military Balance*, London, 1987, p. 31.

5 'Meeting of military leaders in the Kremlin', *Pravda*, 28 October 1982.

6 R. C. Plummer, 'Service as a diplomat in Moscow', *Royal Engineers Journal*, September 1985, p. 168.

7 L. I. Brezhnev, 'Speech in Tula', *Pravda* and *Krasnaya Zvezda*, 19 January 1977.

8 Marshal N. V. Ogarkov, 'The defence of socialism: the experience of history and the contemporary period', *Krasnaya Zvezda*, 9 May 1984, p. 3.

9 'Concerning military doctrine', *Krasnaya Zvezda*, 30 May 1987.

10 Army General D. T. Yazov, *On Guard over Peace and Socialism*, Moscow, Voyenizdat, 1987, p. 34.

11 *Krasnaya Zvezda*, 9 May 1987.

12 Marshal S. F. Akhromeyev, 'Arms control and arms reduction – the agenda ahead', Olof Palme Memorial Lecture, 29 September 1988, SIPRI, Stockholm.

13 Colonel General M. A. Gareyev, 'Soviet military doctrine: current and future developments', *RUSI Journal*, Winter 1988, pp. 5–10.

14 Roy Allison, 'New thinking about defence in the Soviet Union', paper for the British International Studies Association and International Studies Association Convention, London, 18 March–1 April 1989.

15 M. Mackintosh, CMG, 'Changes in the Soviet High Command under Gorbachev', *RUSI Journal*, Spring 1988, pp. 49–56.

16 Edward L. Warner III, 'New thinking and old realities in Soviet defence policy', *Survival*, January/February 1989, p. 19.

17 V. L. Lapygin, 'Interview with the Chairman of the Supreme Soviet Committee for Defence and State Security', *BBC Summary of World Broadcasts, Soviet Union*, 1 July 1989, SU/0497 C/3.

18 Army General D. T. Yazov, 'Democratisation in the Soviet Armed Forces', *BBC Summary of World Broadcasts, Soviet Union*, 22 November 1988, SU/0315 C/9.

19 Natalie Gross, '*Glasnost* and the Soviet military', in *RUSI Defence Yearbook*, London, Brassey's, 1989, pp. 159–73.

20 N. I. Ryzhkov on the economy and defence spending, *BBC Summary of World Broadcasts, Soviet Union*, 9 June 1989, SU/0478/i.

11 *Michael C. Pugh*

Prospects for international order

The previous chapters have examined the politics of each superpower functioning within the constraints of relative decline. As the super-powers are in transition, so the world is in *structural* transformation. The way in which states are constrained by the ordering and functioning of the international system is changing. Two questions about the structure of international politics will be addressed in this concluding chapter. First, what kind of order is likely to emerge as a consequence of relative superpower decline and international systemic change? Second, will the new order produce greater stability than the post-war bipolar system?

What kind of order?

Analysts agree that for international relations the chief consequence of the Second World War was the shift from a multipolar system of dispersed power to bipolarity. Several general observations about the aftermath of this upheaval are worthy of note. First, the system did not completely function along a bipolar axis; some areas, such as the Middle East proved impossible for the superpowers to control. Today, indeed, the majority of the world's states claim to be non-aligned, though a great many have strong orientation towards, or dependency upon, one or other superpower. Second, from the 1960s a *polycentric* situation arose. States such as China and India, and entities like the European Community, though hardly matching the power of the United States and Soviet Union, could create alternative centres of decision making. Third, as the superpowers found their global interests increasingly difficult to sustain, so smaller powers and regional subsystems become more significant, giving rise to greater *pluralism*.

Thus Australia, although an ally of the United States and by no means a great power, functions as an independent centre in the South Pacific. Fourth, it can be argued that relative superpower decline and the diminishing relevance of military strength to many post-industrial states, means that the current 'bipolarity with polycentrism' is in the process of transforming into multipolarity with several, relatively equal, power sources. Finally, global *interdependence* is a key feature of the late twentieth century. In economic life regional integration, the high mobility of capital, and the activities of international institutions and multinational corporations (some of them wealthier than individual states), have reinforced transnationalism. In security terms it is commonly argued that the superpower 'poles', too, are interdependent not merely for war-avoidance but for mutual reassurance.

To examine the trend away from the bipolar system I have chosen to concentrate on two areas where its erosion has seemed particularly important: Europe and the Asia–Pacific region.

Europe undivided

The chief factors in maintaining the cold war alliance system in Europe have been high levels of threat perception and alliance discipline under superpower hegemony. Threat analysis has often been based on 'worst case' assessments – that each adversary was plotting the subordination or ultimate elimination of the other. For political leaders, soldiers and officials it was a relatively simple matter of portraying a malevolent adversary, against which only a strong, alert alliance could offer a deterrent. But as threat perceptions changed once more in the 1980s, and as a consequence of reform in the GDR and demolition of the Berlin Wall, the problems of maintaining discrete camps will become more acute in the 1990s.

Bloc discipline had never been watertight, especially away from the central front. The Warsaw Treaty Organisation failed to incorporate Yugoslavia or retain Albania. The most obstreperous member, Romania, negotiated the withdrawal of Soviet forces in 1958 and thence refused to concede transit rights. In Western Europe, leaders encouraged US dominance to strengthen the fundamental tenet of NATO security provision – Atlantic coupling. However, member states varied in their enthusiasm for hegemony and integration. France left NATO's command structure in 1966 and Norway, among others, imposed conditions on military co-operation. Nevertheless, the superpowers used various means, from argument to coercion and, in the Warsaw Pact, naked force, to uphold vital security interests and maintain discipline. When the Hungarian leader, Imre Nagy, told Khrushchev in 1956 that he wanted Hungary to become neutral, it undoubtedly contributed to the Soviet Union's violent reaction. When the Danish Folketing voted in 1988 to strengthen Denmark's policy against nuclear weapons on visiting warships, the United States (and the UK) threatened to withhold security cover. But what happens when superpower potency is eroded? What are the implications when a leader of resistance to hegemony is virtually canonised, as Nagy was in 1989?

In the past the mutually exclusive security system in Europe was simple to comprehend. Merely because the security dilemma led to an open-ended arms race did not justify abandoning it. According to strategic fundamentalists, the consequences of doing so would have been worse than exploring common security with the adversary. However, the 1980s witnessed not only a change in the Soviet security outlook, but also a dramatic shift in West European threat perception – in spite, or perhaps because, of acrimonious East–West relations between 1979 and 1985. Judging by opinion poll responses to the question: 'Which superpower poses the greater threat to Europe?' (e.g. in *The Times*, 13 December 1985), West Europeans reduced the United States under President Reagan to a 'moral equivalence' with the Soviet Union. Such pressure on the United States should not be underestimated. Indeed new *détente* after 1985 was not simply a product of the Soviet Union surrendering to domestic economic pressures or US technological and military prowess. The defence sector in the United States was always potentially more vulnerable to the depredations of public scrutiny than that in the Soviet Union. The political effects of the Irangate scandal and the demise of ideology in Reagan's second administration also reinforced US willingness to proceed to CSBMs and disarmament.

The new picture of the other side was not always clear. NATO leaders depicted the Soviet system as ramshackle and beleaguered, though still sufficiently powerful to warrant a strong Western deterrent posture. But the situation had switched from the certain, if latent, threat to a more speculative, uncertain one. Uncertainty remains because Mikhail Gorbachev might fall. His reforming zeal might be replaced by a recrudescent isolationism or 'two-campism'. Alternatively, the Soviet empire and the Warsaw Pact might disintegrate into anarchy and pose unforeseeable threats to Western prosperity. Yet on both sides in Europe each adversary was permitted, even encouraged, to penetrate the other's domain and appeal to public opinion. In the 'revolutionary summer and autumn of 1989' the exchange of visits by General Secretary Gorbachev, President George Bush and Prime Minister Margaret Thatcher were replete with ironies. Gorbachev was more popular with Ruhr steel-workers than with striking Siberian coal-miners. Thatcher gave succour to the Solidarity campaign for workers' rights whilst being accused of 'union bashing' at home. Nevertheless, the politics of penetration increased the problems of bloc discipline. It lacked credibility for NATO politicians to argue that Gorbachev's peace offensive was aimed at public opinion to the detriment of Western unity when these same politicians presented him with opportunities to score points on home territory. Ironically, as the prospect of a close relationship, if not unity, between the two Germanys loomed in November 1989, Thatcher's voice was among those calling for an understanding of the USSR's security fears. Thus the Warsaw Pact came to be considered by its ideological foes as a force for stability!

If the Soviet threat had legitimised NATO's cohesion, then changed threat perceptions were bound to exacerbate long-standing internal strains about burden-sharing, economic protectionism and force modernisation. In the months preceding the NATO summit of May 1989, a dispute erupted over modernising the short-range nuclear system, Lance. The Federal Republic of Germany, backed by a majority of other members, insisted on SNF negotiations with the Soviet Union to lower the nuclear threat to Germany. The United States and Britain opposed this as undermining the NATO strategy of flexible response whilst the Warsaw pact remained superior in conventional forces. Portrayed in the Western media as the most serious split in the Alliance since the US bombing of Libya in 1986, Bush confounded the Cassandras by forging a compromise which postponed a follow-on-to-Lance decision until 1992. But the dispute revealed the limited room for US manoeuvre. In effect the Bush Administration recognised this and backed the West German Chancellor, Helmut Kohl, and Foreign Minister, Hans-Dietrich Genscher, rather than Thatcher. The 'Iron Lady', had become a rusting asset in European affairs. It was eventually obvious in Washington that West Germany was prepared to fail this particular nuclear loyalty test.

Radical critics argue that superpower hegemony has been maintained since the 1950s by a kind of 'nuclear imperialism'. Certainly, the Reagan Administration's nuclear ideology led it to define the

Western Alliance as a seamless web of nuclear deterrence.[1] But the credibility of extended deterrence had eroded as a consequence of Soviet strategic parity. Further, the declared goals of SDI in 1983, the Reagan–Gorbachev proposals at the Reykjavik summit in October 1986, the 1987 INF agreement, and the *unilateral* naval nuclear disarmament of 1989 lent respectability to the notion of denuclearisation or at least gave credence to concepts of minimal deterrence. Kohl's wish for SNF negotiations largely reflected his need to court electoral popularity. However, Genscher, who was popular, no doubt sensed that the US commitment to Europe was diminishing and considered that the policy was a logical outcome of the decision in principle at Reykjavik to accept a zero INF treaty, for the Germans were now exposed to short-range systems.

Yet there was no doubt that the Federal Republic remained firmly committed to NATO. If allies are confronted with nuclear loyalty tests, it suggests that deployment of a particular weapon system to support a military strategy is more important than political goals. An alliance is not simply about military strategy, and Genscher saw a historic opportunity to scrap the cold war pattern in Europe. Indeed the dispute illuminated the paucity of coherent political thinking in NATO, suggesting perhaps that it was an unsatisfactory vehicle for responding to Gorbachev's initiatives. As NATO's Secretary General, Manfred Woerner, noted, the Alliance lacked an articulated political strategy for promoting peaceful change in the 1990s.[2]

Disarray in the 1980s and the prospect of a new order in central Europe generated *angst* about NATO's survivability. Challenges to US hegemony had already resulted in the end of SEATO in 1977 and the disaggregation of ANZUS in 1985, both far less integrated than NATO. However, in the late 1980s there seemed a danger of NATO withering from lack of communism (or even from exposure to academic and journalistic diagnosis). Long before the Berlin Wall came down, commentators agreed that the structure devised for the 1950s was outdated and an inordinate burden on the United States. To mention just one assessment, David Calleo wrote that trans-Atlantic quarrels have traditionally been self-limiting, but that an 'essentially American protectorate for Europe' was no longer viable.[3]

However, for a highly integrated, élitist organisation to either unravel or reform, there have to be alternative attractions as well as dissatisfactions, and it is not clear what the alternatives to NATO might be. The most appropriate direction might be a reversion to the sort of European arrangement, though with close integration of forces, which existed before NATO became part of US global containment. Several observers, including former US Secretary of State, Henry Kissinger, have called for a stronger European role including a European SACEUR, European responsibility for ground forces, and European prominence in regional arms control. In fact there exist well-established bilateral and multilateral European activities, notably in arms procurement.

But if the direction is clear, the structure is not. As John Palmer points out, Atlanticism has deep political roots – a reality acknowledged by Gorbachev in sketching trans-European security.[4] European governments have been traditionally as much agitated about signs of US–Soviet collusion as they have about sabre-rattling. Thinking about restructuring would be like encouraging the United States to abandon Europe. Thus, although schemes were proposed for accrediting the European Community with competence in the realm of defence, EC governments excluded military security from the reform process which culminated in the 1986 Single European Act. Quite apart from compromising Ireland's neutrality, the idea of defence debates in the European Parliament was no doubt anathema to those anxious to retain NATO's primacy and US involvement.

A possible basis for increased West European defence integration is the Western European Union, founded in 1948, remodelled in 1954 with German and Italian participation, and reactivated in 1984. The WEU is both smaller and greater than NATO. It is smaller in membership; but greater in having a constitutional assembly, a tighter security commitment and more extensive geographical range (as evidenced by its co-ordination of naval intervention in the Persian Gulf in 1987). Enthusiasts see an expanded role for the WEU but one strictly limited by subordination to NATO goals.[5] It is an obvious instrument for co-ordinating European policy within NATO but in time it might develop greater autonomy in dealings with Eastern Europe.

By the late 1980s the Warsaw Pact was in considerable disarray, its façade of unity crumbling under democratic and nationalist pressures. The Soviet Politburo offered greater encouragement to pluralism than at first the Czech or East German leaderships could stomach. But a Soviet condition for pluralism in the GDR and Poland was continued fulfilment of Warsaw Pact duties. The Polish Coalition Government reassured Moscow in this respect. Continued acquiescence in Soviet hegemonic security demands, at a time of *détente* and falling defence expenditure was an affordable price for domestic liberties. The Brezhnev doctrine ended in Poland in 1981, when *internal* repression substituted for invasion; its valedictory (or so one hopes) was spoken by Gorbachev in Strasbourg in 1989.

Although Gorbachev argued that military confrontation in Europe was anachronistic, he also expressed a keen awareness of the stabilising function of the alliance system. The reunification and neutralisation of Germany are unlikely to make progress except in the context of new stabilising measures such as security guarantees, legal recognition of the existing frontiers of Europe, and considerable reduction in military confrontation. In some respects both superpowers are content with the traditional lines of demarcation, for as poet Robert Frost put it: 'good fences make good neighbors'. The precipitate demolition of the Berlin Wall created problems for both sides. Also, the Soviet Union does not necessarily seek to decouple the United States and Western Europe. A West European defence community, perhaps with its own nuclear weapons, might be destabilising. Gorbachev's concept of a European home was not so much designed to dismantle existing structures as to stake a claim for Eastern bloc inclusion in the political and economic future of Europe. In spite of the grand rhetoric, Gorbachev's policy has been essentially minimalist, expecting the East Europeans to sort out their own problems while the Soviet leadership is preoccupied with nationalist unrest in the Republics.

A wider structural problem than bloc defence is how to devise an appropriate forum for conducting inter-bloc political relations, and whether there should be a pan-European political order. As long as it is subservient to NATO, the WEU cannot pretend to an independent role in common security. The Conference on Security and Co-operation in Europe (CSCE) is probably too large and cumbersome. The two institutions which reformers in the Eastern bloc consider relevant to *their* interests are the Council of Europe and the EC. The former is an embryonic pan-European forum of twenty-three members including neutrals. It has no enforceable authority but provides a useful role in discussion of legal, cultural and environmental questions. The eventual accession to full membership of some East European states is conceivable. The EC is even more essential in weakening the European divide. Indeed Bonn's place in a revived *Mitteleuropa* is most likely to meet with the approval of neighbouring states in the context of accelerated social and monetary integration. The Eastern states will grow more dependent on the EC for investment, trade and general economic salvation.

The blocs are less likely to fragment completely than change their character. This does not mean that neutrality will spread. Perhaps neutral states have acquired international credibility, as peace-keepers through the UN and as mediators in common security debates. For example, in the Conference on Security and Co-operation in Europe, the Neutral and Non-aligned Group (mainly Austria, Finland, Sweden, Switzerland and Yugoslavia) contributed to the proposal for CSBMs. But in a period of transition, neutrality is unlikely to gain *new* adherents unless the superpowers revert to confrontation. Ironically, whilst opinion in some neutrals is concerned about neutrality being marginalised in a more integrated EC, the UK government quibbled about accelerated Austrian membership apparently because another neutral would weaken the EC's already imperfect subservience to the cold war system. For its part the Soviet Union dropped its objection that Austria could not join without violating its neutral status. The British fear is probably unfounded, and Efraim Karsh's research suggests a decreasing divergence between neutrality and alliance security.[6] Austria's accession, and the association of Hungary and the GDR would strengthen the West's glacis in central Europe, already partly constructed by trade and investment between the two Germanys.

More likely than neutrality is the extension of qualified or semi-alignment, especially on nuclear deployment issues. In other words, a greater pluralism would ensure that the blocs are changed from *within* rather than dismantled, a process defined by Richard Falk and Mary Kaldor as 'dealignment'.[7] In so far as the ability of the superpowers to determine the future shape of Europe will be limited, they will have to accept that allied states will be more hard-headed about marrying their interests with collective security requirements. Nevertheless, the task of managing change may be easier in Europe than in Asia and the Pacific.

Pluralism in the Asia—Pacific rvgion

The potential for pluralism was greater in Asia and the Pacific because of the non-alignment of China and India — though they have used bipolar competition to exact concessions from the superpowers. Nor in the prevailing conditions did either superpower establish integrated blocs comparable to NATO or the Warsaw Pact. The US was more successful than the USSR in creating an alliance network. Apart from SEATO and ANZUS this was based essentially on bilateral ties. In the view of Americans who envisaged a Pacific rather than European post-war destiny, bilateral treaties had the advantage of simplifying consultation with allies. But the ties between one or other of the superpowers and Japan, Taiwan, the Koreas, the Philippines and the Vietnams were increasingly matched by suspicion of superpower hegemony among less committed states. For example, in the 1970s and 1980s ASEAN and South Pacific Forum countries, though firmly in the capitalist camp, frequently took independent stances on such issues as nuclear-free zones. Gorbachev's Vladivostok speech in 1986, which called for a CSCE-style régime in Asia, not only drew negative responses from the United States and Japan, but some states, such as India, were suspicious of a Eurocentric model dominated by the superpowers.[8]

Of the leading regional powers, Japan has gained force projection capabilities and its substantial navy has protected sea lines of communication out to a distance of 1000 nautical miles. However, there remains considerable reluctance by the population to accept a military role in place of the United States. Japan may not be an alternative hegemon, but its economic strategy was extraordinarily successful in gaining control of large slices of the world's markets, in acquiring foreign assets, and in developing high-technology manufacturing. Whether Japan will undermine the free-trade system from which it has been such a major beneficiary will depend on its assumption of political responsibilities for regional and world order. But the problems of Japan's exerting constructive influence are manifold, including its cultural insularity.[9]

In foreign relations Japan has followed the kind of internationalism normally associated with small states: prominent support to the UN, offers to finance peacekeeping in Cambodia, and protecting energy sources by remaining friendly with both sides in the Gulf War. Nevertheless in the mid-1980s, Prime Minister Yasuhiro Nakasone undertook diplomatic initiatives around the world, and by the end of the decade foreign aid, mainly to Pacific and Indian Ocean countries, came second in total (greater in percentage of GNP) to US aid, as did the number of its voluntary workers abroad. As Takashi Inoguchi points out, public opinion polls in Japan indicated the general acceptability of under-writing international economic stability. But Inoguchi also detects anxiety about the future direction of society: 'The almost blind belief in loyalty to big business firms has lost its appeal'.[10]

The People's Republic of China is an even greater imponderable, though there is no obvious reason why it should abandon non-alignment. China increased its diplomatic and aid efforts in the Pacific, but whether it can play a wider and more positive role seems doubtful in view of the unattractiveness of its political régime and its continued support for the Khmer Rouge which delays any settlement in Cambodia. The extent to which China honours its guarantees to Hong Kong after the transfer of sovereignty in 1997 will be a test of Beijing's respect for international order. China's economic potential was increasingly realised with external assistance in the 1980s, and some experts predict that by 2020 its economy will be larger than Japan's. Such growth was stalled by a reduction in external co-operation after the political repression of the popular democracy movement in 1989. But, as Gerald Segal remarks, in view of its historical ambition to unite Chinese territory and its potential prosperity China is unlikely to be a status quo power.[11]

Elsewhere, security concerns are primarily domestic and economic. The pressures for political liberalisation and economic pragmatism have been strong, even in ideologically tough régimes such as Vietnam, South Korea and Taiwan (where martial law was lifted in 1987). With some exceptions, the East Asian economies will remain buoyant. Taiwan, for example, has one of the highest trade surpluses in the world and will become increasingly important in regional aid provision. Whether economic dynamism will push Japan, Taiwan and the United States closer together or make them competitors is one of the great conundrums in forecasting for the region. It will depend partly on the attitudes of other states.

There is likely to be more economic co-operation. But two basic problems arise regarding integration: who promotes it, and who participates. The Pacific Community concept emanating from Japan after 1976, was suspected by other states of being the Second World War Co-prosperity Sphere in disguise, this time with American support. An Australian initiative of 1989 for an Asia–Pacific free-trade organisation tried to exclude the United States, causing annoyance in Tokyo and Washington. The incorporation of socialist economies might be problematic, yet to ignore China and the USSR would be imprudent and provocative. By the end of the century, the most probable outcome is various loose associations similar to ASEAN.

Multipolarity and diversity of interests in the Asia–Pacific region mean that any future realignments are unlikely to be formalised in treaties of the kind which the US signed to contain the Soviet Union and China. In security matters there is a distant prospect of institutionalising discussion of arms control and confidence and security building measures, but it would have to appeal to all four major military powers. Not surprisingly, Gorbachev's proposal of September 1988 to give up Vietnam bases in exchange for the US renouncing bases in the Philippines made little headway in view of American reliance on maritime power. Reagan and Nakasone also rejected subsequent appeals for negotiations on CSBMs at sea. The Bush Administration may prove to be more flexible, but the most likely route to progress is through reciprocal unilateralism. As part of its improvement in relations with China, the Soviet Union reduced its forces on the Sino-Soviet borders and in Mongolia. In the late 1980s the Red Navy cut its naval combatant strength in the Pacific by 10–20 per cent and restricted its naval deployments in Japanese as well as more distant waters.[12] For its part, the United States abandoned plans to modernise some of its tactical and short-range nuclear naval systems, and the Pentagon investigated reducing its forces in Korea.

To conclude this part of the discussion we should note that several new constellations in Europe and the Asia–Pacific region have been predicted:

- an 'Amerippon' integration of the US and Japanese economies to secure US preferential access to Japanese technology and sustain what former US Ambassador to Tokyo, Mike Mansfield, regards as 'the most important bilateral relationship in the world today';[13]
- a combination of Asian 'tigers' led by Japan, with the US and China in a rival constellation;
- a Third-World link-up between India, ASEAN, and Pacific Forum states with a commitment to containing nuclearism and securing better deals for primary producers;
- a US–USSR consortium to counter Asian and Western European challenges;
- a European–Soviet bloc to rival the US and Asia.

The permutations are intriguing. But the argument here has been that the continuing challenge to bipolarity from an undivided Europe and a pluralist Asia–Pacific will occur in ways which grow naturally from historical circumstance. Globally significant shifts will probably not be manifested in dramatic realignments. If this is not merely wishful thinking, then the prospects for stability seem fair.

Prospects for stability

The future 'stability' of the international order is a vital issue in a book on superpower politics because it is arguable that the uneven growth of states accounts for great wars and that great powers in decline are a source of destabilisation.[14] In a system akin to Milton's fallen man, 'Created sicke, commanded to be sound', a definition of stability should allow for an element of dynamism, friction and crisis. But at the very least a stable order would be one in which cataclysmic war and widespread famine were absent, in which the important states recognised the legitimacy of the system, and in which no single actor dominated and no independent powers were eliminated. But we should also recognise that states purporting to uphold 'stability' may be perpetuating a flawed system which happens to suit their particular interests rather well.

From the vast literature and the long-standing debate on the relationship between international structures and stability there is space here to note only two conceptual lineages, both dating from the 1960s. The first, formulated by Kenneth Waltz, contends that bipolarity is more stable than multipolarity, partly because it fosters crisis control and inter-bloc interests in maintaining a balance of power. Further, the superpowers restrain others, including allies, from going to war. This suggests that if extended deterrence weakens so will restraint on allies. However, we should note that just as there have been numerous conflicts involving military force or the threat of it between socialist states, so there have been numerous instances of US allies becoming involved in militarised disputes.[15]

A contrary hypothesis considers that a multipolar system caters for a greater plurality of interests; there are more opportunities for trade-offs and reaching agreement. Although there is a greater chance of some maverick state behaving recklessly in a multipolar system, bipolarity is inherently unstable because it causes friction with allies by over-centralising disputes and fostering hazardous relations between two alliances.[16]

In addition to such theories and their variants, several data-based projects have attempted to resolve the issue through correlation analysis. For example, the International Crisis Behavior project (ICB) investigated the frequency and severity of crises in the period 1930–80. The ICB defined international crises as breakpoints in relations between states and other international actors in which there is a high probability of military hostilities. Many variables, including economic decline, alliance formation, and quality of life, have been correlated with conflictual behaviour by states. However, preliminary ICB findings, sensibly hedged with caution, on the relationship between crises and the international system, suggest that bipolarity is the most stable, multipolarity less stable, and polycentrism the least stable structure. Venturing beyond correlation and into *causal* explanation, the ICB inquirers resort to abstract logic no different in principle from that employed by Waltz. They argue that polycentrism and multi-polarity involve a larger number of potentially adversarial relationships. Also, with more decision centres, agreements take longer to reach and then supervise. The drawback in a bipolar system, they say, is that fewer states are represented in decision making and thus decisions are more likely to be contested.[17]

However, even the ICB's correlations may be defective in certain respects. The project emphasises military power as the arbiter of polarity. Like Stalin's quip, 'How many divisions has the Pope?', this discounts the ability of powers to influence, cajole, or defy through a range of non-military capabilities. Even so, an assessment of war, the least stable outcome of a crisis, suggests some modification of the theory. In the multipolar period of 1906–46, there were fifteen wars, including the two world wars. In the period dominated by superpower confrontation, 1946–84, there were over seventy.[18] Indeed, the frequency, if not severity, of war since the advent of bipolarity indicates a need to qualify the notions that there has been a 'long peace', or that global interdependence has a pacifying effect.

In the main, Western concepts of international stability are based on inter-state crisis and conflict. But the majority of post-1945 military disputes have been anti-régime conflicts in Asia, the Middle East and Africa. Some of them can be said to have damaged the international system. In so far as the Vietnam conflict originated as a 'civil war', it can be seen as a turning point in US hegemony. Other civil wars have been sustained by arms supplies from external powers, often in furtherance of bipolar competition. Indeed a weakness of post-war bipolarism has been its irrelevance for the interests of Third World states, whose chief vulnerabilities are to natural disasters, weak social and political integration, and world markets. In broader terms, too, an international structure based on the military power of sovereign states may perpetuate the causes of Third World instability. Repressive régimes are accorded international legitimacy and lack incentives to 'mobilise people for social development and state formation'.[19] From such a perspective, only the OECD states benefit from bipolarity and economic interdependence.

This leads us to consider the nature of economic dominance and the 'hegemonic stability theory'. Its original proponent, Charles Kindleberger, argued that a single dominating economic power engenders stability and free trading, though he specifically allowed for the possibility of an international institution taking the role of hegemon.[20] Research in the 1980s supported the theory by correlating economic dominance with world economic performance (as measured by trade and investment). It was found that the United States had remained economically dominant and that international growth remained vigorous. This did not mean, however, that stronger pluralism would have had a different result, though undoubtedly it would have complicated exchange rate management.[21]

More jaundiced views of economic dominance stress its exploitive aspects. A theory which equates US hegemony with stability might be viewed as merely justifying US employment of trade and aid to sustain its own interests rather than the health of the international system. The Reagan Administration's refusal to sign the UN Convention on the Law of the Sea indicated, for example, the limit of US interest in a global regulatory régime. Whilst the United States is a relatively open economy, food producers in Europe, South-East Asia and Australasia complain that the United States heavily subsidises agriculture, restricts food imports and depresses prices by dumping rice, wheat and sugar on the world market. According to some observers, the 1987 US Trade Bill, directed largely at Japan and other Asian dynamos, was bound to increase political corrosion between the United States and its allies.[22]

The problems of the North–South divide have hardly changed since addressed by the 1980 Report of the Independent Commission on International Development Issues (chaired by the former West German Chancellor, Willi Brandt). The Brandt Report called for considerable transfer of resources from North to South because the world economy was functioning so badly it was damaging the interests of all nations. The OECD states and the rich Group of Seven have been generous in aid but still failed to match the Brandt Report's recommendations. Aid dependence is no doubt pernicious, but much depends on the development strategies which aid supports. Detailed regression analysis of direct US aid in the Reagan and Carter Administrations suggests that military inducements and economic penetration lay behind assistance to developing countries.[23]

Aid offered by the World Bank and International Monetary Fund has conditions attached which exacerbate social instability and increase the vulnerability of states to international markets. These agencies, nominally part of the UN, are controlled by the contributing states; the United States has a veto under the IMF's articles of agreement. President Reagan stressed that foreign aid was dependent upon the domestic economic policies of the donor nations and, with congressional support, cut the American contribution to IMF development aid. Similarly, the burden of debt, bloated by high interest rates, affected development in Africa and Latin America, and led indirectly to riots in Venezuela in February 1989. Proposals put forward by US Treasury Secretary, Nicholas Brady, may go part-way to writing off Southern debt. But without a bolder plan underwritten by Japan, and greater flexibility on the part of IMF officials, chaos in the international financial system, as well as further political instability in debtor countries may result. Whilst it is true that the world economy cannot do without the US dollar, no less can it do without the yen, the Eurodollar and the petrodollar. From the point of view of Third World states the structure of the international economy is manifestly unjust, and arguably their dissent from the value of US economic control contributes to disorder in the system.[24]

From the above arguments about stability it is tempting to conclude that the nature of the international system is not a key variable. This does not mean that the international system is neutral. Bipolarity, polycentrism and multipolarity affect stability in different ways. Multipolarity makes organisation difficult. But in Asia reduced bipolarity also correlates with economic growth and increased stability. In South America, inter-state relations have become more stable, according to Walter Little, as the US loses its ability to manipulate the East–West issues. By contrast, Central America remains prey to interference.[25]

It should also be clear from the foregoing that in addition to contentions about polarity and stability, there are arguments about the extent to which *policies* rather than system structure are important factors in the equation. Rather than structures and forces which are beyond any state or group of states to control, Susan Strange argues that the key cause of economic instability has been decisions affecting the financial system. Decision makers in the capitalist centres have mismanaged credit, interest rates, international debt and exchange rates in the quest for speculative gains.[26]

But within the limits of their influence have the superpowers behaved responsibly to make bipolarity stable? One school of thought marries public good with self-interest. United States policies in particular had rebuilt the West European and Asian economies, promoted decolonisation, mediated to good effect from the Middle East to Southern Africa, and reinforced structural stability by establishing a system of nuclear deterrence with commonly understood rules.[27]

Sceptics would reply that the 'peace' has been partial, blighted by irresponsible brinkmanship, missed political opportunities and appalling waste of resources. The superpowers, it might seem, have fostered a distorted view of world politics as a Manichaean struggle between incompatible systems; in furtherance of this they have used force, putting foreign civilians at risk, but not their own. Only with a belated appreciation of the limits of their power, and at some cost in casualties in Vietnam and Afghanistan, did they behave with greater responsibility.

As for nuclear deterrence and its rules, obviously we cannot ignore the fact that there has not been a nuclear or conventional war between the superpowers. But strategists have tended to perceive and present the link between nuclearism and stability as causal rather than casual. The slogan 'nuclear deterrence works' is a simple one. Yet it takes no sophisticated intellectual leap to appreciate that, quite apart from arguments about morality or political opportunity costs, the slogan is based on an assumption that, in the absence of nuclear weapons, either superpower would have been tempted to employ military force against the vital interests of the other. There is no firm evidence that Stalin would have turned the pressure on Berlin in 1948 into a *casus belli* if the United States had not been an atomic power, or that the United States would have tried to roll back the Soviet troops from Czechoslovakia in 1968 if the Soviet Union had been nuclear free. Furthermore, the evidence for effective American nuclear threats, against China in Korea for example, is at best ambiguous. Perhaps, as Richard Lebow remarks, the truth is that nuclear weapons have induced greater caution in statesmen, but also allowed confrontationists to push that caution to greater limits.[28]

To a large extent the debate about behaviour versus structure is an artificial one. The two factors are entangled because policy makers are informed and ill-informed by their world views and judgements about the international system. Nor are they able to act as free agents. Systemic change also opens up opportunities for changing policy.

In the trend to multipolarity it would be unwise to overlook such potentially destabilising developments as unrest in Eastern Europe or the proliferation of ballistic missile technology which extends the range of weapons systems. Nuclear weapons proliferation is also a worrying prospect, even though disarmament by the superpowers will in theory reduce the 'nuclear imperialism' which some threshold states offer as the reason for keeping their options open.

But the advent of multipolarity holds out the prospect of releasing states from the security dilemma, from constraints on the pursuit of common security and from an ideological distortion of the needs of Third World states. It also opens up greater opportunities for the United Nations to exert influence. Having suffered a US-induced budgetary crisis in 1985, the Secretary General's tasks were facilitated in the second half of the decade by improved relations with the Security Council. Gorbachev reformed the Soviet attitude, and in 1987 announced payment of contributions in arrears. Soviet officials not only promised to support peacekeeping, they proposed revival of the Military Staff Committee, a permanent UN reserve force and training system, and extension of US operations to the sea.[29] Partly as a consequence of the decline of bipolar confrontation, the UN was called upon to mediate a ceasefire in the Gulf War, arrange terms for the Soviet withdrawal from Afghanistan, and play a role in bringing peace to Angola and Cambodia.

The UN and other international agencies will also be called upon to help address new global concerns such as environmental pollution. Environmental problems cannot be treated simply through unilateral efforts; and in 1987 over thirty governments were willing to tackle the causes of ozone depletion on a global basis by signing a Protocol to the 1985 Vienna Convention for ozone protection. Nor can environmental issues be tackled without transferring resources from industrialised states to developing states. The industrialised world has been responsible for the vast majority of pollutants, and Third World countries cannot improve their standard of living if their development is curtailed by anti-pollution measures. Such problems would have arisen with or without cold war bipolarity, and will inevitably produce tensions and perhaps conflict. But the decline of bipolarity will at least ensure that such issues gain a higher placing on the international agenda of states than cold war concerns.

Common security and crisis prevention

How then will the superpowers manage their predicaments? There is no model of international security upon which they can reasonably rely in a more polycentric and perhaps multipolar world. Views about the new situation are diverse. Is the cold war a thing of the past, as Gorbachev insisted in his Council of Europe speech in July 1989? Or does it continue as Brent Scowcroft argued shortly after being appointed Bush's National Security Adviser? Even as the Bush Administration assessed the Gorbachev initiatives, Secretary of State James Baker spoke in terms of the US having 'won' the cold war, as if Reagan's trebling of the US debt was a plan for squeezing the Soviet Union.[30] Whilst some in the West argued that to encourage Gorbachev would enable the Soviet Union to regenerate a strong threat, others such as the US Committee for National Security (including Paul Warnke, Carter's principal SALT negotiator, and the former CIA Director William Colby) pressed the need to take advantage of what might be a limited opportunity to redefine the security problem and reach arms control agreements with the Soviet Union.[31] Indeed, any Western effort to seek military superiority or undermine the Soviet system is likely to be fruitless and destabilising.

There is a strong possibility, reflected at the Bush–Gorbachev summit in December 1989, that both superpowers will seek common cause as their controlling interests diminish. But in view of the risks each side would take in dealing with the new circumstances, it is absolutely essential to institutionalise negotiation and monitoring for crisis avoidance. This would recognise that peace is something more than an absence of war, and more than just provision for management during a crisis. An agreement on the Prevention of Dangerous Military Activities signed by the Soviet and US Chiefs of Staff in June 1989 had a limited application but signified a willingness to engage in tension reduction. In Europe, revision of military strategy imposed by free access between the Germanys, demographic constraints and arms control agreements might take each side towards concepts such as 'non-provocative defence'. But confidence in the process would certainly be enhanced by the creation of risk-reduction centres and planning for graduated and reciprocal tension reduction on the lines proposed by Charles Osgood as long ago as 1962.[32]

Stability will depend partly on the willingness of superpower politicians to seek opportunities for association in the shifting distribution of power. If they move towards common security they will no longer need to maximise military power. If they accept, as many of their allies have done, that resort to armed force seldom benefits a modern state, then this should promote stability. Perhaps the Soviet populace has one slim psychological advantage over US citizens – an inured sense of embattlement since 1917. In the United States, in spite of the 1930s Depression and the Vietnam experience, confidence in an expansive future based on technology and the power of the market-place remained largely undimmed. Managing affairs in the context of diminished bipolarity, however, may be an uncomfortable experience, placing a premium on cautious responses to challenges to hegemony.

The arguments of Senator Eugene McCarthy, a renegade who failed in his attempts to gain the US presidency in 1968 and 1976, may yet triumph. His scholarly realism could serve to guide the citizens of both superpowers:

We must ... attempt to assay our real power as compared with our assumed responsibilities. We must reassess our obligations, formal and informal, legal and extra-legal. We must establish, if we can, standards for selection of responses, both as to place and degree. We must set priorities and continue to seek with other nations, a broader and more realistic distribution of responsibility for this world.[33]

The shrinking relevance of bipolar preoccupations will require such wisdom for the preservation of stability. Happily, in making assessments of superpower politics for this book the authors have uncovered signs which encourage a sense of optimism.

Notes

1 Michael C. Pugh, *The Anzus Crisis, Nuclear Visiting and Deterrence*, Cambridge, Cambridge University Press, 1989, pp. 9–10, 136; Peter Hayes, 'American nuclear hegemony in Korea', *Journal of Peace Research*, XXIV, December 1988, pp. 351–3.

2 Manfred Woerner in the *Guardian*, 26 April 1989, p. 1.

3 David P. Calleo, *Beyond American Hegemony, the Future of the Western Alliance*, Wheatsheaf International Security Series, Brighton, Wheatsheaf, 1987, p. 3. See also Stanley R. Sloan, *NATO's Future, Towards a New Transatlantic Bargain*, Basingstoke, Macmillan, 1986, p. 189; Walter Goldstein, ed., *Fighting Allies. Tensions within the Atlantic Alliance*, London, Brassey's, 1986, pp. 3–4; François Heisbourg, 'Can the Atlantic alliance last out the century?', *International Affairs*, LXIII, Summer 1987, pp. 413–42.

4 John Palmer, *Europe without America? The Crisis in Atlantic Relations*, Oxford, Oxford University Press, 1987, pp. 29, 156.

5 Alfred J. Cahen, 'The Western European Union and the European dimension of common security', *RUSI Defence Yearbook, 1989*, London, Brassey's, 1989, p. 29.

6 See Efraim Karsh, *Neutrality and Small States: the European Experience in World War II and Beyond*, London, Routledge, 1988; Harto Hakovirta, *East–West Conflict and European Neutrality*, Oxford, Clarendon, 1988.

7 Mary Kaldor and Richard Falk, eds., *Dealignment – a New Foreign Policy Perspective*, Oxford, United Nations University and Basil Blackwell, 1987, pp. 14–16.

8 Mikhail Gorbachev and Rajiv Gandhi, 'Joint Press Conference', New Delhi, 28 November 1986; Kevin P. Clements, 'Common security in the Asia–Pacific region: problems and prospects', *Alternatives*, XIV, January 1989, pp. 52–3.

9 Marvin S. Soroos, 'Global interdependence and responsibilities of states: learning from the Japanese experience', *Journal of Peace Research*, XXV, March 1988, pp. 17–29.

10 Takashi Inoguchi, 'Four Japanese scenarios for the future', *International Affairs*, LXV, Winter 1988/9, p. 15.

11 Gerald Segal, 'As China grows strong', *International Affairs*, LXIV, Spring 1988, p. 231.

12 Segal, 'Pacific arms control: new Soviet initiatives', *Council for Arms Control Bulletin*, 44, June 1989, p. 5.

13 Mike Mansfield, 'The US and Japan: sharing our destinies', *Foreign Affairs*, LXVIII, Spring 1989, pp. 3–15.

14 Robert Gilpin, *War and Change in World Politics*, Cambridge, Cambridge University Press, 1981, p. 239.

15 Kenneth N. Waltz, 'The stability of a bipolar world', *Daedalus*, 93, Spring 1964, pp. 881–909; Erich Weede, 'Extended deterrence, superpower control and militarized interstate disputes, 1962–76', *Journal of Peace Research*, XXVI, February 1989, p. 15.

16 K. Deutsch and J. D. Singer, 'Multipolar systems and international stability', *World Politics*, XVI, April 1964, pp. 390–406; Gilpin, *War and Change*, p. 89; Phil Williams, 'US–Soviet relations: beyond the Cold War?', *International Affairs*, LXIV, Spring 1989, pp. 274–6.

17 Michael Brecher, Jonathan Wilkenfeld and Sheila Moser, *Crises in the Twentieth Century*, I, *Handbook of International Crises*, II, *Handbook of Foreign Policy Crises*, Oxford, Pergamon, 1988; Brecher and Wilkenfeld, 'Crises in world politics', *World Politics*, XXXIV, April 1982, pp. 380–417; Patrick James and Michael Brecher, 'Stability and polarity: new paths for inquiry', *Journal of Peace Research*, XXV, March 1988, pp. 33–41.

18 See Ernst B. Haas, 'War, interdependence and functionalism', in Raimo Väyrynen, ed., *The Quest for Peace*, London, International Social Science Council and Sage, 1987, p. 116.

19 Caroline Thomas, 'New directions in thinking about security in the third world', in Ken Booth, ed., *New Directions in Strategy and Security*, London, Unwin Hyman, 1990, ch. 11.

20 Charles Kindleberger *The World in Depression*, Berkeley, University of California Press, 1973, p. 308

21 Michael C. Webb and Stephen D. Krasner, 'Hegemonic stability theory: an empirical assessment', *Review of International Studies*, XV, April 1989, pp. 183–98.

22 Bernard K. Gordon, *Politics and Protectionism in the Pacific*, Adelphi Paper 228, Spring 1988, pp. 52–5.

23 James H. Lebovic, 'National interests and US foreign aid: the Carter and Reagan years', *Journal of Peace Research*, XXIV, June 1988, pp. 126–9.

24 A weak hegemon may be more conciliatory. See Duncan Snidal, 'The limits of hegemonic stability theory', *International Organization*, XXXIX, Autumn 1985, pp. 588, 612.

25 Walter Little, 'International conflict in Latin America', *International Affairs*, LXIII, Autumn, pp. 590, 601.

26 Susan Strange, *Casino Capitalism*, Oxford, Blackwell, 1986, p. 23.

27 J. L. Gaddis, *The Long Peace: Inquiries into the History of the Cold War*, Oxford, Oxford University Press, 1988; Samuel P. Huntington, 'The US – decline or renewal?', *Foreign Affairs*, LXVII, Winter 1988/9, pp. 90–3.

28 Richard Ned Lebow, 'Deterrence reconsidered: the challenge of recent research', in *Survival*, XXVII, Jan.–Feb. 1985, pp. 26–7; Adam Roberts, 'The critique of nuclear deterrence', in *Defence and Consensus: the Domestic Aspects of Western Security*, Adelphi Paper 183, London, 1983, pp. 11, 16; McGeorge Bundy, 'The unimpressive record of atomic diplomacy', in Gwyn Prins, ed., *The Choice: Nuclear Weapons Versus Security*, London, Chatto & Windus, 1984, pp. 42–54.

29 Vladimir F. Petrovsky, 'New Soviet view of peace-keeping', speech at UN seminar, Salzburg, 4 August 1989, Austrian Foreign Ministry text. See also Antonio Donini, 'Resilience and reform: some thoughts on the process of change in the United Nations', *International Relations*, IX, November 1988, pp. 289–315.

30 J. L. Gaddis, 'The evolution of US policy goals towards the USSR in the postwar era', in S. Bialer and M. Mandelbaum, eds., *Gorbachev's Russia and American Foreign Policy*, Boulder, Colo., Westview, 1988, p. 324.

31 Committee for National Security, *New Opportunities for US Arms Control Initiatives*, Washington DC, 1989.

32 Charles E. Osgood, *An Alternative to War or Surrender*, Urbana, Ill., University of Illinois Press, 1962.

33 Eugene McCarthy, *The Limits of Power: America's Role in the World*, New York, Holt, Rinehart & Winston, 1967, p. 7.

Further reading

1 Introduction – the debate on decline

Clark, Ian, *The Hierarchy of States. Reform and Resistance in the International Order*, Cambridge, Cambridge University Press, 1989.

Dibb, Paul, *The Soviet Union. The Incomplete Superpower*, 2nd edn, Macmillan and IISS, 1988.

Kennedy, Paul, *The Rise and Fall of the Great Powers. Economic Change and Military Conflict from 1500 to 2000*, New York and London, Random House and Unwin Hyman, 1988.

Nye, Joseph, 'Understanding US strength', *Foreign Policy*, LXXII, Fall 1988, pp. 105–29.

2 Sparring partners – the record of superpower relations

Garthoff, R. L., *Détente and Confrontation – American–Soviet Relations from Nixon to Reagan*, Washington DC, Brookings Institution, 1985.

Grosser, A., *The Western Alliance – European–American Relations since 1945*, New York, Continuum, 1980.

Halliday, F., *The Making of the Second Cold War*, London, Verso, 1983.

Moreton, E. and Segal, G. (eds), *Soviet Strategy towards Western Europe*, London, Allen & Unwin, 1984.

Spanier, J., *American Foreign Policy since World War II*, New York, Holt, Rinehart & Winston, 1985.

Yergin, D., *Shattered Peace: the Origins of the Cold War and the National Security State*, Boston, Houghton Mifflin, 1977.

3 From Reagan to Bush – political change in the United States

Abernathy, M. Glenn, Hill, Dilys M. and Williams, Phil (eds), *The Carter Years: the President and Policy Making*, London, Pinter, 1984.

Brauer, Carl M., *Presidential Transitions: Eisenhower through Reagan*, New York, Oxford University Press, 1986.

Buchanan, James M., *et al.*, *Reaganomics and After*, London, Institute of Economic Affairs, 1989.

Crawford, Alan, *Thunder on the Right: the 'New Right' and the Politics of Resentment*, New York, Pantheon, 1980.

Dougherty, James E. and Pfaltzgraff, Robert L., *American Foreign Policy: FDR to Reagan*, New York, Harper & Row, 1986.

4 The legacy of Reaganomics

Bluestone, Barry and Harrison, Bennett, *The Great U-Turn: Corporate Restructuring and the Polarization of America*, New York, Basic Books, 1988.

Kymlicka, B. B. and Matthews, Jean V. (eds), *The Reagan Revolution?*, Chicago, Dorsey Press, 1988.

Palmer, John L. and Sawhill, Isabel V. (eds), *The Reagan Record. An Assessment of America's Changing Priorities*, Cambridge, Mass., Ballinger, 1984.

Salamon, Lester M. and Lund, Michael S. (eds), *The Reagan Presidency and the Governing of America*, Washington DC, Urban Institute, 1984.

Stein, Herbert, *Presidential Economics. The Making of Economic Policy from Roosevelt to Reagan and Beyond*, New York, Simon & Schuster, 1984.

5 US defence: the Reagan legacy and the Bush predicament

Adams, Gordon and Cain, Stephen Alexis, 'Defense dilemmas in the 1990s', *International Security*, XIII, 4, 1989, pp. 5–15.

Bulkeley, Rip and Spinardi, Graham, *Space Weapons*, Cambridge, Polity Press, 1986.

Diebel, Terry, 'Reagan's mixed legacy', *Foreign Policy*, Summer 1989, pp. 34–55.

Sagan, Scott, *Moving Targets: National Strategy and National Security*, Princeton, NJ, Princeton University Press, 1989.

Talbott, Strobe, *The Master of the Game: Paul Nitze and the Nuclear Peace*, New York, Alfred Knopf, 1988.

6 The Bush Administration's foreign policy review

Williams, Phil, 'The Reagan defence policy', in Hill, D., Moore, R. and Williams, P., eds, *The Reagan Presidency: an Incomplete Revolution*, Basingstoke, Macmillan, 1989.

Williams, Phil, 'US–Soviet relations: beyond the Cold War?', *International Affairs*, LXIV, Spring 1989, pp. 273–88.

7 *Glasnost* and Soviet political reform under Gorbachev

Bialer, S. (ed.), *Politics, Society and Nationality inside Gorbachev's Russia*, London, Westview, 1989.

Hill, R. J. and Frank, P., *The Soviet Communist Party*, London, Allen & Unwin, 1986.

Kelly, D. R., *Soviet Politics from Brezhnev to Gorbachev*, New York, Praeger, 1987.

Miller, R. F., Miller, J. H. and Rigby, T. H., *Gorbachev at the Helm*, London, Croom Helm, 1987.

8 The politics of *perestroika* and the Soviet economy

Bergson, Abram, *Productivity and the Social System – the USSR and the West*, Cambridge, Mass., Harvard University Press, 1978.

Hewett, Ed A., *Reforming the Soviet Economy: Equality vs. Efficiency*, Washington DC, Brookings Institution, 1988.

Matosich, Andrew J. and Matosich, Bonnie K., 'Machine building: *perestroika*'s sputtering engine', *Soviet Economy*, IV, 1988, pp. 144–76.

Nove, Alec, *The Soviet Economic System*, 3rd edn, Boston, Allen & Unwin, 1986.

Yasin, E., 'Positions on restructuring and the price of competence', *Soviet Review*, XXX, July–August 1989, pp. 30–53.

9 'New thinking' and Soviet foreign policy

Dawisha, Karen, *Eastern Europe, Gorbachev and Reform. The Great Challenge*, Cambridge, Cambridge University Press, 1988.

Gorbachev, Mikhail, *Perestroika. New Thinking for our Country and the World*, London, Collins, 1987.

Laird, Robbin (ed.), *Soviet Foreign Policy*, New York, APS, 1987.

Mandel, Ernest, *Beyond Perestroika. The Future of Gorbachev's USSR*, London, Verso, 1989.

Shenfield, Stephen, *The Nuclear Predicament. Explorations in Soviet Ideology*, Chatham House Papers, 37, London, Routledge & Kegan Paul, 1987.

10 Gorbachev and Soviet defence policy

Donnelly, C. N., *Red Banner; the Soviet System in Peace and War*, London, Jane's, 1988.

Gareyev, Colonel General M. A., 'Soviet military doctrine: current and future developments', *RUSI Journal*, Winter 1988, pp. 5–10.

Gross, Natalie, '*Glasnost* and the Soviet military', in *RUSI Defence Yearbook*, London, RUSI, 1989, pp. 159–73.

MccGwire, Michael, *Military Objectives in Soviet Foreign Policy*, Washington DC, Brookings Institution, 1987.

Warner III, Edward L. 'New thinking and old realities in Soviet defence policy', *Survival*, January/February 1989.

11 Prospects for international order

Booth, Ken (ed.), *New Directions in Strategy and Security*, London, Unwin Hyman, 1990.

Calleo, David P., *Beyond American Hegemony. The Future of the Western Alliance*, Wheatsheaf International Security Series, Brighton, Wheatsheaf, 1987.

Gilpin, Robert, *War and Change in World Politics*, Cambridge, Cambridge University Press, 1981.

James, Patrick and Brecher, Michael, 'Stability and polarity: new paths for inquiry', *Journal of Peace Research*, XXV, March 1988, pp. 31–42.

Webb, Michael C. and Krasner, Stephen D., 'Hegemonic stability theory: an empirical assessment', *Review of International Studies*, XIV, April 1989, pp. 183–98.

Index